So far from Home

The remarkable diaries of Eric Evans, an
Australian soldier during World War I

So far
from Home

Edited by Patrick Wilson

Kangaroo Press

SO FAR FROM HOME
First published in Australia in 2002 by Kangaroo Press
An imprint of Simon & Schuster (Australia) Pty Limited
20 Barcoo Street, East Roseville NSW 2069

A Viacom Company
Sydney New York London

© Fraser Gregg 2002

All rights reserved. No part of this publication may be reproduced, sorted in a
retrieval system, or transmitted, in any form or by any means, electronic, mechanical,
photocopying, recording or otherwise, without the prior permission of the publisher
in writing.

Cataloguing-in-Publication data:

So far from home : the remarkable diaries of Eric Evans, an
Australian soldier during World War 1.

ISBN 0 7318 1068 6.

1. Evans, Eric S., 1897-1985 - Diaries. 2. World War,
1914-1918 - Personal narratives, Australian. 3. Soldiers - Australia - Diaries. I.
Wilson, Patrick. II. Title.

940.48194

Cover and internal design by Gayna Murphy, Greendot Design
Typeset in Bembo 12pt
Printed in Australia by McPherson's Printing Group on 79 gsm Bulky Paperback

10 9 8 7 6 5 4 3 2 1

In loving memory of Ralph Hahn
(1937–1996)

FOREWORD

Eric Evans, my grandfather, was eighty-eight when he passed away in 1985. Eleven years later, my grandmother died and I made a most remarkable discovery. I was clearing up my grandparents' home in Johannesburg, South Africa, where they had lived for many years, when I chanced upon a small military kit-bag tucked away under my grandfather's bed which had remained untouched since his death. To my great surprise it contained various medals, scrolls and certificates, along with fourteen small weather-beaten booklets, neatly tied together with a red ribbon. On further inspection, it became clear these were diaries. Little did I know that they would turn out to be one of the most significant records to survive the Great War of 1914–18. On glancing through them, though, the vastness of the story before me became clear.

I, together with my partner Jenny Hahn, pursued the idea of exploring the potential of Eric's wonderful diaries. To this end Jenny spent three months transcribing the delicate pages of the diaries into a format which could be presented to publishers and historians.

The inital support of the Australian High Commission in Cape Town reinforced mine and Jenny's determination to share this enthralling story and was the start of a voyage which has taken us around the world, thrice.

The overwhelming world-wide interest in the diaries from various parties, including government officials and the international media, culminated in securing a publishing contract with Simon and Schuster, who shares our enthusiasm for these unique diaries.

We now live in Ireland, where we are in the early stages of turning these diaries into a film.

Fraser Gregg, Ireland, January 2002

CONTENTS

Foreword vi
Acknowledgments viii
Introduction 1

THE DIARIES
CHAPTER 1 ∽ The voyage over 11
CHAPTER 2 ∽ Preparations in England 40
CHAPTER 3 ∽ The bullring 60
CHAPTER 4 ∽ The reunion 72
CHAPTER 5 ∽ Ypres 96
CHAPTER 6 ∽ In hospital 103
CHAPTER 7 ∽ Back in action 116
CHAPTER 8 ∽ Blighty 131
CHAPTER 9 ∽ On the mend 158
CHAPTER 10 ∽ Fighting again 187
CHAPTER 11 ∽ Victory! 212
CHAPTER 12 ∽ Waiting for an 'Aussie' 231
CHAPTER 13 ∽ Homeward bound 244
CHAPTER 14 ∽ Dot 256
Epilogue ∽ 261
Glossary ∽ 263
About the editor ∽ 268

ACKNOWLEDGMENTS

Thanks to Stephanie Gregg and Louise Hahn, our mums, whose love, support and encouragement while we pursued our dream has been steadfast and invaluable – at times we were sure you wondered what on earth we were doing! Stephanie, for your words of wisdom – never taken lightly. Louise, for the many hours spent proofreading the manuscript.

To our extended family – Alison and Ian, Mark and Andrew – thanks for always being there.

To Simon & Schuster, our publishers, especially Angelo Loukakis, Brigitta Doyle, Julia Collingwood and Jacquie Brown – who have shared our dream and encouraged our input in producing this magnificent book.

To Rose Creswell, of Cameron Creswell, our agent, who opened the door to our relationship with Simon & Schuster and whose encouragement has continued to motivate us.

To Patrick Wilson, who dedicated his time to editing these wonderful diaries into the format we have today – thanks for his input and ongoing contributions.

To Brigadier Henry Wilson, a vital link, whose encouragement and belief in the project has spurred us on.

To Matt Anderson and Lee Cooper of the Australian High Commission (in Cape Town and London, respectively) whose encouragement and support were inspirational.

The international media, including CNN International (Eileen O'Connor), Tim Butcher (*Daily Telegraph*, London), Rodney Bennett (*Manly Daily*, Sydney), Andrew Unsworth (*Sunday Times*, South Africa), John Robbie (702 talk radio, South Africa), Tanya Mullholland and Martin Jordison (567 talk radio, South Africa), Robbie Stammers (Inyati Publishers), Ian Cook and Amanda Palmer (Channel 7, Australia), John Clarke (ABC Radio, Australia) and Jeremy Lovell (Reuters).

To Dave George, for your interest and input.

To James Earl Jones, for half an hour of inspiration never to be forgotten.

And all those not mentioned and those connected to the motion picture – thank you, too!

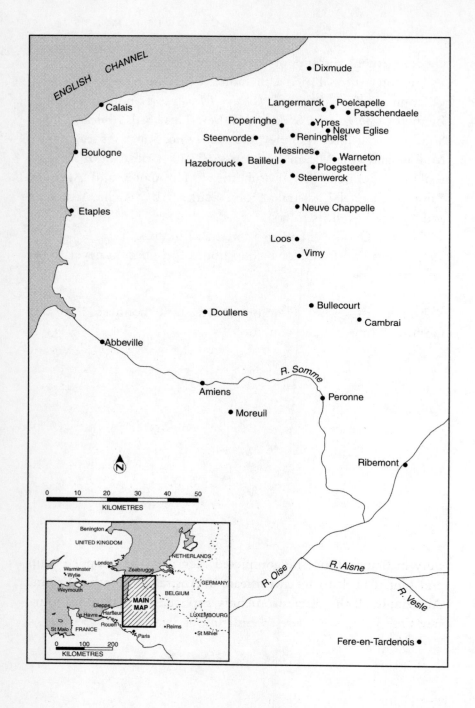

INTRODUCTION

THESE REMARKABLE DIARIES are not only a comprehensive record of a young man's experiences during World War I, but also an insight into the heart of a man in love. They tell the story of Eric Evans's love for his girlfriend back home in Australia, and how throughout the horrors of war he clings to the hope that he will return to find comfort in the arms of the woman he loves.

Diaries were banned on the Western Front for security reasons. Despite this a number were written, but Eric Evans's are extraordinary. Beginning with his voyage from Australia and ending with his reunion with his family in 1919, the diaries provide a fascinating and complete picture of the life of a young man on a tour of duty in France. Once he completed each diary, he wrapped it up and sent it back to his sweetheart in Australia, Dorothy Wright. Amazingly, all the diaries somehow survived the hazardous journey. One volume was even found among baggage rescued from a steamship sunk by a submarine in the Atlantic!

It was primarily for Dorothy that the diaries were written. They tell of a young soldier and his emotions as he fights to come to terms with life away from home, and with the glory, futility, horrors and evils of war. His relationship with Dot, as he called her, also provides an integral part of this remarkable story.

Eric was nineteen years old at the beginning of these diaries —
which, with his mature prose style and comic turn of phrase, is
easy to forget. It is also important to remember that despite his
youth he was a sergeant and therefore responsible for a number of
men, many of whom were his senior in years.

Eric Evans was born in Sydney in 1896 and grew up in a typical
middle-class family in the seaside suburb of Manly, on Sydney's
north shore. Although his parents, Sydney and Alice Evans, were
separated, he retained close relationships with them both. He and
his sister Elsie and brothers Harold (known as 'Rastus', King of the
Surf, by his peers) and Raymond lived with their mother in
Berkley Road, Manly, until his departure for the war. A keen
sportsman and a sound, if not overly dedicated, student, Eric's love
was the beach, and his childhood was spent surfing and swimming.
The latter enabled him to become a lifeguard in the holidays — a
job that in an age before pop stars and cult sportsmen, by all
accounts, afforded him considerable status among his peers and
not inconsiderable attention from members of the opposite sex.

'It will all be over by Christmas' was a sentiment expressed by the
majority of soldiers from all sides as they left for the front. Such confidence, partly the result of the vast increases in the size of armies
and armaments production in the years preceding August 1914,
soon proved misguided. While waiting for the midnight deadline,
the British foreign secretary, Sir Edward Grey, wrote: 'The lamps are
going out all over Europe. We shall not see them lit again in our lifetime.' [1] Yet he was among the few who envisaged the potential
implications of a modern war. Indeed, from the outset a wave of war
fever swept through Europe and it was not long before countries
outside the immediate European theatre were to reveal their alle-
giances.

Britain's dominions rallied to the call. On every road and track
throughout Australia, men of all classes, trades and religions
moved towards their capitals. Like so many other young
Australian men, Eric Evans had no hesitation in signing up for
what promised to be an adventure of a lifetime, and hurried to

enlist at Victoria Barracks, Sydney. Indeed, his army number, 847, shows he was among the first. After tampering with his birth certificate to prove to the military authorities that he was above the legal age of seventeen, he joined up. The New South Wales quota of volunteers was called the 13th Battalion and was to form part of the 4th Brigade, commanded by Colonel John Monash. In fact, so great was the rush of volunteers to join, many were turned away after medical examinations. Only the healthiest passed the stringent test: the physique of these men was such that the 13th was often referred to as 'the battalion of big men'. At over 6 foot and with a rugby player's build, Eric fitted in easily.

The metamorphosis from civilian to soldier took these volunteers less than two months. Building a new battalion was, of course, haphazard at times. Sergeant Laserron recalls one case in which a newly formed company in the 13th was asked: 'Is there anyone here who wants to be a sergeant?' [2]

By 23 December the battalion, now ready for action, embarked on the liner *Ulysses*. Destination: Alexandria, Egypt.

No breakthrough had been achieved by any of the powers as 1914 came to a close. With their initial war plans shattered, a new phenomenon in war emerged – stalemate. Horses and lines of advancing infantry men proved no match for the defensive strength of trenches and machine guns backed up by heavy artillery. While the fighting on the Eastern Front between the Russians and the Central Powers (Germany and Austria–Hungary) was more fluid, in the West early German advances were halted at the Marne, and soon both sides became bogged down in the mud of Flanders.

A war of attrition followed, with both sides, particularly the Allies, attempting to wear down the other using all means at their disposal. The result was massive casualties with few gains. The names 'Champagne', 'Neuve Chapelle', 'Ypres', 'Vimy' and 'Loos' became synonymous with appalling losses of men for the gain of sometimes miles, sometimes metres, of shell-ridden soil.

Faced with deadlock on the Western Front, Churchill began a search for other battlefronts. With Turkey having joined the Central

Powers, it was envisaged that a victory there would open up the Dardanelles strait to supply ships that could provide much-needed weapons and food to Russia. The most optimistic 'Easterners', as they were known, also hoped that not only would Turkey be knocked out of the war, but that neutral countries such as Bulgaria and Greece would then join the Allies and help force Austria–Hungary out of the war. Winston Churchill, first lord of the Admiralty, was certain that a naval force was all that was needed, but that plan was aboted following a disasterous large-scale operation in March 1915, in which a third of the battle fleet was put of action. It was decided instead that troops should be landed on the Gallipoli Peninsula.

The invading armies, led by General Sir Ian Hamilton, included ANZAC (Australian and New Zealand Army Corps) troops. Among them were the men of the 13th Battalion, who had arrived in Alexandria on 31 January 1915. Here, they and the rest of the expeditionary force were subjected to further heavy training. A month and a half later, the battalion was taken to Lemnos in Greece. A Special Force Order from General Hamilton left them in no doubt as to the importance of their objective:

> 'Before us lies an adventure unprecedented in modern war. Together with our comrades of our Fleet we are about to force a landing upon an open beach in face of positions which have been vaunted by our enemies as impregnable. The landing will be made good by the help of God and the Navy; the position will be stormed and the war will be brought one step closer to a glorious end.' [3]

Eric landed on the Peninsula on 25 April, in what was to go down as one of the worst-planned campaigns of the war. The Turks were waiting for the troops, thousands of which were killed or wounded attempting to take the enemy's excellent defensive positions. Stalemate soon followed, with the Anzac soldiers forced to dig in on the slopes overlooking the beaches. A day later, Eric was badly wounded when he attempted to break through the Turkish defences. One bullet passed through his thigh, another smashed his right heel. He was evacuated and taken to Alexandria from where, once his condition was stabilised, he embarked on HMS *Glengorm* and was transported to the 1st Australian Auxiliary Hospital in Middlesex, in England. The 13th Battalion's landing strength on 25 April had been twenty-five officers and 934 other ranks; its strength by the beginning of May was nine officers and 500 other ranks.[4]

In November 1915, Eric was declared 'unfit for service' and he returned to Australia. It seemed as if the war was over for him. Meanwhile, through Allied incompetence and stout Turkish defence, further attempts to break out of the beachhead proved disastrous. With the casualty list mounting to a quarter of a million, it was decided to pull out. By 9 January 1916 all 135 000 remaining troops had been successfully evacuated without a single loss of life. It was a brilliant end to a miserable campaign.

While Eric was recovering in Australia, the war raged on. The year 1916 was to witness some of the most bloody battles of the war. First, the Germans launched an offensive against the French forces at Verdun. General Eric von Falkenhayn, realising the symbolic importance of this old fortress town, declared that his aim was to 'bleed the French white'. He nearly succeeded, but under the determined and inspirational leadership of General Pétain, who famously vowed '*Ils ne passeront pas*' ('They shall not pass'), the French held out. An estimated 650 000 men died in the fighting.

Meanwhile, the British were massing troops for an all-out assault in the Somme region. The offensive began with a six-day bombardment, during which over a one-and-a-half million shells were fired along a 50-kilometre front. Douglas Haig, the British commander, confidently predicted that by the time the troops crossed no-man's-land 'not even a rat' would be alive. Yet the first day, 1 July, proved a failure of catastrophic magnitude with over 57 000 casualties. By the time the battle ended, with a gain of some 11 square kilometres, the number of British dead had risen to a staggering 420 000.

The 13th Battalion, although not involved in the early stages of the fighting, arrived soon after to reinforce this 'big push'. The recorded history of the 13th Battalion recalls the sight of the soldiers they had come to relieve: '... pitifully weak. Their bronzed faces clearly reflected great strain.' The battalion, facing crack German troops, once again acquitted themselves with distinction and fully lived up to their new name, 'the Fighting Thirteenth'. The battalion's official history recalls how in bayonet attacks the men, who had been taught to yell when charging, screamed 'like maniacs anything that came to their heads – 'Ho, ho! I-yah! Halloo! Eat them alive! Imshi toute-suite! Wagga Wagga! Run, Fritz!' German troops soon had the highest regard for the fighting qualities of their Australian counterparts. Some 600 men in the 13th, which had been reinforced since the Gallipoli campaign, became casualties during the Somme offensive and, compared with some of the other battalions involved in the fighting, this number was considered light. Of the 1100 'originals' who had set sail on the *Ullysses*, only 144 were left with the battalion by the end of 1916.

After the slaughter of so many thousands of young men, war weariness was taking a grip, not just in Britain, but among belligerents all over the world. Enthusiasm among volunteers was fading. In 1916 Britain introduced conscription. Although Eric volunteered to return to the fighting late that year, the fact remained that recruiting figures from Australia had dropped dramatically. Indeed, by 1917 the number of Australians enlisting was little more than a third of the June 1915 figure.

Eric made a remarkable recovery from his injuries and was determined to return to the fighting and do his bit. As he set sail to England in February 1917, there seemed little reason for optimism. Nationalist aspirations arguably provided the Allies with most hope. In Arabia, the Arab revolt against their Turkish foes was gaining momentum, aided by British officers such as T.E. Lawrence. They were not alone. Jewish groups were also striving to rid Palestine of the Turks. Meanwhile, it was hoped that Czechs, Slovaks and Poles would pursue their national goals at the expense of Austria–Hungary.

The great hope was for the United States to declare war on Germany. This seemed highly unlikely. Despite considerable losses of ships and civilians to German submarine warfare, the United

States was determined to pursue its policy of neutrality. 'There will be no war. It would be a crime against civilisation for us to go in,' President Wilson assured his people on 4 January 1917.[5] To make matters worse, a number of Allied countries were looking frail. Both Belgium and Serbia were clinging on to a tiny fragment of their soil, while the Italians were suffering major retreats against Austria. Most serious of all, it was apparent that, internally, Russia was becoming increasingly unstable.

Tsar Nicholas I, who had appointed himself as commander-in-chief in February 1916, was now being personally blamed for the military retreats on the Eastern Front. Even General Brusilov's brilliant drive into Austria failed to raise the population's morale. Hunger and growing disillusionment at the millions of deaths were endemic, as were rumours that the tsar's German-born wife, who had been left in control of government while her husband was at the front, was involved in an affair with the sinister monk Rasputin. Rasputin was assassinated, but after an unusually severe winter and an outbreak of strikes, the Western allies had every reason to fear that Germany might soon only need to fight on one front alone. Britain also was suffering. German U-boat activity was hitting the country hard and there were real fears that it could eventually starve Britain into submission.

It was at this time that Eric set sail again, this time for Britain. This section of his diaries begins on Wednesday, 17 February 1917.

Patrick Wilson, Reading, England, 2001

---

1 As quoted in R. Jenkins *Gallery of Twentieth Century Portraits*, David & Charles, London, 1988, p. 101.
2 As quoted in T.A. White, *The Fighting Thirteenth*, Tyrrells, Sydney, 1924, p. 16.
3 As quoted in *ibid*., p. 26.
4 *ibid*., p. 27.
5 As quoted in M. Gilbert, *The First World War*, Weidenfeld & Nicolson, London, 1994, p. 306.

This Diary is the
property of

847 Sgt. Evans E.S.

13th Bn.

A.I.F.

to whom will the
finder please return.

In the event of
my death please
forward same to
my mother : —

A.E. Evans,
88, Berkley Rd.,
Manly
N.S.W
Australia

To my comrade 26 / 8 / 1918

Dearest comrade — Dorothy

I end my happiest memories. Dorothy, you moulded my character, you made me a better man. You gave me what my soul craved for — love and friendship …

Now I can but wish you the happiest. I am satisfied to think that you, as well as I, have spent many beautiful and happy days. You've been to me a great and potent force and if my love has caused you joy, I'm glad, and sorry I can carry it no further. But now it is over and I charge you to forget me except only as a pleasant memory. May you meet the man of your choice and, being married, live happily with your husband and your children.

Should my diary be returned, I have asked Father to give it to you unread. It is my soul, and as you think fit, so will you let your friends — my friends — read it.

Mother will give you any little keepsake you would like. I haven't specified anything because my heart is too full.

Now God bless and keep you, Dorothy, my love.

Eric

CHAPTER 1

THE VOYAGE OVER
~⊃⊂~

Time of journey: 63 days

Wednesday 7th February 1917

Dorothy didn't come down to Woolloomooloo Wharf.

Having said goodbye to all at home, midnight found Father and I on the Manly boat. I asked the others not to join us as emotions were running high enough as it was. We met Lieutenant Brierly, another returned 13th man, and Sammy Knox, in the Railway Unit, on the wharf and made our way to the Hotel Carlton until the time came to return to the showgrounds. From there, we marched down Oxford Street to Woolloomooloo Wharf, where I said a final good-bye to Father and mustered the men.

A piercing whistle broke off a difficult farewell and it was a relief to board ship.

At 7 am all was completed and the crowd waiting outside was allowed on the wharf. To the tune of the Liverpool band the mob hungrily rushed to the edge of the wharf, some hysterical, some laughing, some crying, shouting, singing and calling 'Good luck' and other such well wishes. Paper ribbon streamers were eagerly bought from men on the wharf and soon myriads of coloured streamers were connected from friends on the wharf to boys on the transport. It was a pretty sight to see, but a terribly depressing one also. To see the frantic calls and signals of the broken-hearted mothers, sweethearts and sisters, some unable to withhold their feelings and crying openly, others painfully endeavouring to conceal the fact that the lump in their throats was almost too big to bear, but others again were bright and happy, throwing kisses and cheering up their own particular friends with kind messages.

The troops themselves were beginning to show signs of being affected by this show of feeling, and I must admit a lump was in my throat – I had thought that this particular feeling was for evermore a stranger – as I looked down on the crowd. At 7.15 am we slowly drew away from the wharf. People shouted and waved and the paper ribbons tightened. One by one the ribbons broke and they were eagerly pulled ashore and devoured by the crowds as souvenirs. At last, but two remained – a green and a white. The green parted – almost immediately the white followed and we had severed our connection with the shore.

On the far end of the wharf I spotted Father waving a handkerchief. I waved back and felt sure I saw him wiping his eyes. I do hope not. Slowly the boat drew away amid the shouts and gestures of our friends. Their voices gradually became indistinct and an eerie quiet descended among us. This didn't last long as within minutes some launches filled with people began sailing round and round the ship in a bid to catch a last glimpse of their loved ones. From one came the shouts of 'Three cheers for Sergeant Edgar – Three cheers for Sergeant Nolan – Three cheers for Sergeant Evans.' After about quarter of an hour a Manly boat whistled 'cock-a-doodle-doo' and all ships in the vicinity took the cue. The searchlights then played on us as we went out. It was a beautiful sight.

After such a send-off there was little anyone could say and we all just stood looking toward the fading glow of Sydney. I feel no regrets and have no doubts that I am doing the right thing. This is the beginning of a great adventure and an opportunity that few could ignore. However, as Sydney disappears from sight, I can't help but think of Dorothy and the wonderful thirteen months we have spent in each other's company. I will miss her. As is engraved on the watch she gave me yesterday – *Quis separabit?*

Friday 9th February 1917

Letters were handed out after breakfast yesterday. Two were for me
– from Dot and Elsie, giving me last greetings. Dot's one was particularly lovely:

> *I have never been good at saying goodbyes, as you know, and this one*
> *was so terribly hard. Please understand, but I knew that I would feel*
> *too heartbroken for words if I came to the wharf to bid you farewell.*
> *Anyway, this isn't goodbye for I know that you will be back here safe-*
> *ly in no time at all. Thank you for a wonderful time. I want you to*
> *know that I have never been so happy as I have been with you. I will*
> *miss not talking to you about everything and anything, not having*
> *you beside me as I play my piano, not going to the beach with you and*
> *laughing at you showing off on your board, not going to the Steyne*
> *Hotel for tea followed by those long walks. I'll even miss your singing!*
> *We can get through this and that will mean we can get through any-*
> *thing. I will write as much as possible and will think of you a lot —*
> *maybe too much. Come back soon, Eric. I am so proud of you.*
>
> *Your loving girl and eternal comrade, Dot.*

What a letter! I have read it again and again, and it has filled me
with happiness.

Things are going fine and there are comparatively few cases of
seasickness. Thankfully the Wiltshire is a good boat. It is carrying
about 1630 men at present but may pick up some more along the
way. We passed Wilson's Promontory at 7.30 am and are veering to
the south a bit. The coast of Victoria is becoming dim.

The atmosphere is a little strange on the boat at the moment –
a mixture of excitement tinged with apprehension. I, for one, am
under no illusions of the task that faces us. No longer is there a
sense that the war will be over this year, or even the next. If that
is the case then we will be part of a good deal of scraps. Let's just
hope that we can make a difference. A number of the lads have

never been abroad before. 'What's France like, Sarge?' I was asked by one of the boys. The truth is that I don't really know. We are all entering into an unknown world. On the whole though, the lads are in good heart and keen to make a good show of themselves.

This morning's parade was followed by some physical training, O'Grady drill and lecturettes. It serves to pass the time away. I have just arranged for a concert from my troopdeck. We have several professionals, so the concerts on the boat should be good. I'll miss not listening to Dot playing to me. How spoilt I have been over the past months.

I've a fair lot of men. They're already calling me 'the baby-faced sergeant'. It is important that they don't find out I am nineteen or I fear they will have problems taking orders from me. If only I could grow a proper moustache.

Saturday 10th February 1917

There was a bit of a rumpus this morning with two stowaways reported. They were home service birds who wanted to do their bit in France. It seems they had got on board with all their gear a day before sailing on the plea that they were baggage guards or something. The orderly officer discovered them sleeping in one of the lifeboats. Good luck to them. The war would be won a lot faster if everyone showed such spirit. They have been taken on strength and posted to one of our south-western battalions.

Unfortunately thieving has already made an appearance. It is appalling to think a man will steal from a comrade. It's not even petty thieving, either, for some have lost considerable sums of money, Gillette razors, etc. We will have to get a hit inspection.

The boys did me the honour of electing me their sports representative on the journey. There is about £90 in cash prizes for the sports, given by the Garrison Institute for presentation, so we have something to look forward to. Men have already begun training for the boxing. There have already been a few friendly scraps and this morning a man was knocked clean out. It was very prettily done and amazingly the recipient of the blow didn't even get angry on regaining consciousness. Some of my boys are a pretty tough breed and, although their discipline is a little wayward, I feel confident they'll give a good account of themselves in battle.

The weather is getting colder and some of the sergeants are complaining like mad. We are in the Bight and it's getting rough. All beds in the hospital are filled – mostly chronic seasickness and other minor complaints, but two were admitted today with more serious ailments; one with pneumonia and a silly little fool with VD. The latter is in isolation. It's certainly not going to be the last case if the men put their intentions into action. Most of the sergeants' talk today has been centred around pretty French ladies. Even the married ones don't seem to be deterred from entering into the subject. When Edgar mentioned this to Walsh, he just joked, 'Look mate, it's only right that we should confirm Franco–Australian relations.' Some men have no shame.

Had to crime someone for smoking between decks, but it looks as though young Lucas, our 'pet madman', has somehow managed to get away with telling the OMS to 'go to hell' today. He meant it, too. I admire him for his youthful spirit. He is clearly underage and I should know, but it seems that his only aim is to get over to France and take on the German Army single-handedly. I hope the realities of warfare don't give him too much of a shock. Anyway, I have decided that I must try and guide him if he is to avoid getting into further trouble. There is at least hope for Lucas. Private Munday, on the other hand, is quite simply a bad egg. He is going to have to be watched. I don't trust him. He has already started a few rows among the lads and is a poor influence altogether.

I should sleep well as I've just been issued with a mattress and pillow. One or two of the sergeants have yet to be issued with them and there was a certain amount of foul-mouthed envy, particularly from Sergeant Walsh, on seeing me walk into the mess quarters. Knowing Walsh, he will probably try and take them, but he won't get very far.

Sunday 11th February 1917

Church parade today. The chaplain, who does not meet with my approval, speaks with a haughty air and is too affected and unnatural.

His sermon, based on David and Goliath, prompted Friedman to walk away, saying: 'Hope he wasn't inferring that we're David. Goliath didn't have a bloody machine gun.' We find the Roman Catholic padre missed the boat and all wonder if it was intentional.

Today we were treated to our best dinner of the journey so far – poultry, plum pudding and fruit included. Chatted to Paddy Nolan. It's good to have an old mate on board. He might be four years older and married but, like me, he is ambitious and very just with the chaps. Rather too fond of swearing, and I tell him so. He is certainly my best friend on the ship and, as we both have seen action before and were wounded at around the same time, we share a certain bond.

Of the other 13th Battalion sergeants on board the most I can say is that they vary. Nolan is undoubtedly very good but I knew that anyway. I have also been impressed with Sergeant Friedman – an Afrikander, single, aged twnety-four, talks a lot and is a good instructor. He commands respect and is well liked. While he is well read and humorous, he can sometimes be immoral in his talk in the mess and shows little respect for women. When he laughs, his eyes disappear and he looks like a purring cat. Is a Jew but not religious. He makes a strong NCO.

Sergeant Walsh – a professional grader, a bombastic character and a boaster of the worst grade. Married, but you wouldn't know it. Is not always honest and tries to make us believe he is a 'big' man. I am not deceived. He is not liked, not least because he bullies his men. Has been in camp two years or thereabouts and seems to get on with the heads. You cannot insult him directly for he takes what you say as a joke and has hide enough for a dozen. I wish he were in another unit.

Lastly, there is Sergeant Edgar – a schoolteacher, single, aged twenty-five. He is a chap innocent of the world and is ashamed of it. Fond of girls, works hard, has a kind heart and a good manner, and is ambitious but is unmistakably a schoolteacher. Rather too lax as a rule but is fairly well up in his work. As he has always dealt with children, he seems to have no understanding of men's natures and this painfully evident lack of knowledge on the vices of this world does not make him a good soldier. He is our weakest link, excepting for Walsh perhaps. Having said all of this, I like him and I'm glad he's with us. He has the metal to mould.

I am about to have a game of 500. I must stop gambling soon, although I'm doing rather well at the moment. It's hard to avoid and the men are prepared to stake anything, be it cigarettes, watches, pens and probably even their sisters if they get half a chance!

Monday 12th February 1917

Lost on our game of cards last night. Damn it. When I awoke today it was quite rough and cold, raining like the devil. Some of us sergeants were still in bed when I heard a voice say: 'You lot should be out of bed. It's 7 am, all you men should be up. There's a bloody war on, you know.' Thinking it was a sergeant jesting, I retorted rudely. 'Eh! What?' said the voice. I looked round – it was Major Hanis. I subsided, looked silly and apologised. He was not best pleased and his eyes could have killed.

The truth is that I am not sorry at all. I don't like him. I suppose I should speak up for officers in the 13th Battalion but I can't with Hanis. He is surly and of a sullen disposition, cruel I think, very peremptory and does not inspire confidence. His wife has a very harsh face, by the way. He treats his NCOs with no respect and doesn't trust any of them. He can be quite pleasant but is too changeable to rely upon. He takes little, if any, interest in the men of his command, their comfort, etc. and the men do not like him. His knowledge is book knowledge I fancy, and while one is lecturing he interjects with theories of his own. He expects everything to be referred to him sometimes and at others he allows me to carry on with the company. He is quite unsatisfactory – to me, at any rate.

The sea is rough and just as two of our sergeants were finishing breakfast, a particularly large wave came through the porthole and entirely drenched the two. There was a scatter, and we all roared at the sight of these two half-drowned rats wiping the water from their faces and clothes.

Had to take boat drill today, which involved informing the men of our evacuation procedure in case of accident, etc. 'There's only enough boat room for twenty-five men and, as we have double that in our unit, it seems only right that married men with families should have first opportunity to get off.' Amid the laughter and groans, one man plaintively asked whether he could be admitted to a boat if he married in Durban. I pointed out that it was impossible for him to produce the necessary two children in the time allowed. Sergeant Friedman actually managed to sell his place to one fool. Once the allocation had been completed we informed the remainder that they shouldn't worry as the boats usually overturn in the panic and that one is far better off on the rafts provided!

The boat drill was followed by a blindfolded boxing contest, which was productive of much mirth, especially when one man accidentally mistook one of the crowd for his opposition and landed a weighty left hook on Edgar. What idiots men must be to enter these kind of games. I think I'll just watch!

I've been reading a little, the first book for many, many months and I cannot settle to it. Strange – my mind has been persistently on the topic of women, women, women. Their influence is remarkable. I've been grading those I know and their influence on me. I haven't decided if it is good or bad, but I hope the former. Does platonic friendship really exist? I think not, but still arguments galore have been running through my head. These are but snatches of what is passing in my mind. I do wish they'd leave me alone. I think I'll go on deck and walk or exercise it off.

Tuesday 13th February 1917

Land sighted at 3.30 pm – just discernible with the naked eye. Betting as to whether it was land was freely indulged in – it was. Talking of betting, I've laid three to one we don't call at Fremantle. I hope I'm right as I'd miss the money, but if I lose at least I'd be able to post letters home.

Tonight I was playing cards with some of the sergeants and the subject of women came up. The boys noticed I was keeping conspicuously quiet. 'What about you, Evans? You're always writing letters. You must have a tabby among them.' 'Well, there is one girl

– Dorothy,' I replied. And then, I don't know what possessed me – perhaps it was Nolan's rum shots – I began: 'Yeah, Dorothy. Fat Babe's the best.' 'Fat Babe!' they exclaimed in unison, seemingly finding my nickname for Dot a source of great hilarity. 'No,' I interjected, annoyed at their laughter, 'she's beautiful.' 'How old is she?' Friedman blurted out. 'Seventeen,' I replied, only to be met with yet more laughter. 'Seventeen! Well, I hope you got a right and proper send-off.' That was the final straw. I'm afraid, and I'm not proud of it, that I threw my cards on the deck. I was angry with myself for talking about her and upset that her name should be brought up in the lurid conversation of a bunch of sergeants with nothing but disgusting thoughts in their heads. They don't understand and I don't want them to. Anyway, it has taught me a lesson that I should have learnt before. At least Nolan did come and apologise. He's a good mate and I know he meant it.

Thursday 15th February 1917

I won my bet, as we are now well away from Fremantle, heading west-northwest. Spent most of the morning learning 'singlesticks' from an ex-naval man.

I've had a complaint from my company about the filthiness of two men in the company. I lined them all up today and told them we would have a washing parade tomorrow. Warm water in tubs, 2 pounds of soft soap and six scrubbing brushes were brought out. 'Right, boys. Word has come to me that one or two of you didn't pay heed to your hygiene classes. Tomorrow I need six volunteer workers to clean the dirty offenders publicly, in all their nakedness.' The boys expect some fun but I'm afraid they are to be disappointed, for as I passed the showers today, Scrooge, for that is one of the culprit's nickname, and his mate were at it hammer and tongs, scrubbing themselves!

A rather funny thing is happening at the moment. Lucas has entered tomorrow's boxing tournament and is being touted as the battalion's secret weapon. The boys are training him as I write. I hope it is not going to end in tears. I have warned him against it but to no avail.

At present, a fierce debate is raging on deck as to why we've enlisted to fight. Edgar is insistent that the only reason he joined up was to save and uphold the Motherland and the Empire. It is a brave line to take with some of these men. Walsh, who is all talk, got quite hot-headed: 'You're talking rubbish, Bill. Everyone is here because they fancy a bloody good scrap. I just want a fight and it is a hell of a lot more interesting than going to some local bar. We're here to show those Huns that we are the best bloody fighters around.' Edgar was finding it hard to compose himself, as other sergeants started to round on him. 'You're traitors, bloody traitors, if you haven't got loyalties to the Empire. Like it or not, most of our ancestors came from Britain. Anyway to be the best fighters in the world, you've got to have discipline – something that we can hardly boast about. Let's face it half the men on board haven't saluted an officer in their life.' Nolan was smirking away as the others leapt to defend the AIF. Friedman was first: 'Since when have you needed to salute to the enemy or to march in perfect order towards their guns? Let the Poms do that if they want an early grave.' And so it goes on.

Friday 16th February 1917

The fight I spoke of yesterday came off and Lucas knocked out his opponent. It was mighty impressive and he is rapidly becoming our regimental mascot. I fear that he has, however, got rather carried away with it all. 'I'll take on anyone who dares,' he shouted victoriously as the lads held him aloft. I fear it was a rash pledge which has, as a result, led to him being matched to fight the Railway Unit champion.

There is a concert up on deck but the crowd is so dense that one cannot get near the place. The sky is beautiful tonight. I've never seen anything like it in Australia.

I've been thinking of home rather too much lately and I think I'm a tiny bit homesick. I wonder what Fat Babe is doing?

Saturday 17th February 1917

A school of perhaps fifty to 100 dolphins were gambolling around our boat today, leaping out of the water and creating great excitement on board. Sadly, Lucas provided us with a rather faster form of amusement as his much-hyped fight lasted less than a minute. It was not a pretty sight.

Monday 19th February 1917

Yesterday, I went to the Church of England service, which wasn't bad, although I was terribly sleepy throughout. I left my watch in the sun during the service and came away without it. When I returned a minute or two later, it was gone. To say I was upset would be an understatement, but this feeling soon turned to anger as I wouldn't have lost that watch for anything. It represented to me the memory of my happiest days — those wonderful thirteen months with Dorothy. Thankfully, I found it that afternoon, after rooting around the corporals' mess quarters. I feel much better now, thank you.

Later, I went on deck and got into conversation with some of the men. To my amazement, I found myself spinning my story of Gallipoli. It came as a shock to me as I simply hadn't even mentioned the word during my time in Australia, and I had to stop.

Just reached 'the danger zone'. We now have all portholes closed and deadlights over them. A submarine guard is being picked and armed in case of accident. All men with active service are being pressed into service and three gun crews have been detailed. The men, of course, have hardly noticed but I, for one, intend to sleep snug-close to my life belt — I've no wish to provide food for the fishes.

I think I'll begin to write letters ready for Durban. I am missing Dot.

Wednesday 21st February 1917

Last night was awfully rough and everyone was ordered below at 8 pm. It did not trouble me at all and I dreamt that I was talking to Dorothy at the Steyne Hotel. I awoke to find myself awash — I sleep on the floor of course — but was too lazy to move, so I just got a thorough wetting.

The storm is still raging as I write. The waves are crashing against our portholes, which have been screwed over with iron guards, with quite a disquieting force. Tins and dishes dash from one side to the other and water is freely pouring down our companionway. The mess orderlies are a source of great hilarity, slipping and falling with the tucker in all directions. Seasickness is rife. All lights are to be extinguished at 6 pm in future for fear of a 'raider' supposed to be in the vicinity.

The sergeants have been telling dirty yarns all day – some of them most disgusting, too. I wish I were able to get away from this atmosphere because it's jarring on me somehow tonight.

Sunday 25th February 1917

Mail closes at 12 noon Monday so we are not too far from Durban and my fifteen letters are now safely posted for the censor's approval.

Wrote over twelve pages to Dot. Reminded her of my vow not to forget the wonderful moments we shared. It seems such a long time since we first set eyes on each other in the hospital in Sydney. It was, as I wrote in the letter, love at first sight as I watched this brown-haired girl with big blue eyes walk in. I was intrigued by her beauty – so innocent and yet assured, and as she began to play on the piano in the corner of the recreation room, her charms further multiplied. It wasn't long before she had a sizable audience and yet it was to me that she seemed to occasionally glance at with a sweet, dimpled smile. At the end she approached me: 'You're Eric, aren't you?' I remember being taken aback. She said, 'My mother knows yours and you fit her description perfectly.' It wasn't long before she was coming every day and the lads in the ward increasingly began to tease me after seeing her arrive one afternoon with chocolates. The truth was that I had met a soulmate and a beautiful one at that. We could talk for hours sometimes and share silences at others. I knew then as I know now that I had met someone very special.

Monday 26th February 1917

A chap has just brought down wireless news to the effect that the Germans have been bombarding coastal towns and have actually penetrated the Thames mouth. Is it true, I wonder?

For the last few days we have been steering very erratically. It seems we've been sailing in circles today. Various conjectures are rife as usual and we have informed our friend Lucas that we are returning to Australia as the war is over. He is quite perturbed. What he doesn't know is that we expect to arrive in Durban sometime on Wednesday.

Payday today, with every man receiving £1. Fortunately, I have made a few pounds through gambling, which will make leave all the more enjoyable. In the mess tonight, we sergeants agreed to enter a rickshaw race when we arrive at Durban on Wednesday. There's a 5/- sweepstake on the outcome and it should produce some fun.

I was, as a result of a conspiracy, made to sing at the concert tonight on the troopdeck. The men clapped the efforts of the sergeant major but my showing was quite poor, I'm afraid!

By the way, the major told me that he censored my letters and that I had more girls than anyone on the ship. I only wrote about fifteen. He remarked that he didn't read them, which was jolly decent of him and just as well given the sentimental one I wrote to Dot.

Wednesday 28th February 1917

At around 8 pm last night we spotted the beam of what was taken to be a lighthouse, and at 6 am land was seen through a misty air and no-one would leave the deck, even to get breakfast. An hour or so later, we paraded in full service dress. We were tied up at The Bluff for coaling and it wasn't long before the 'coolies' were on the scene, selling bananas, etc. Soon after, we were transported across to the town in a suction dredge. Fell in and headed by the buglers, we marched in column up as far as the post office, where we were dismissed until 10.30 pm that night.

Durban! The city of rickshaws and cleanliness! I went straight to the municipal baths and had a good swim and clean-up. Then, with Sergeant Nolan, I went up the main street and had a good look around the town and sampled its refreshment rooms. The town is clean and open, the shops not big and usually one or two storeys. Incidentally, I think there are special prices for Australian soldiers.

The trams are excellent, municipal-owned and free to soldiers, but it seems so incongruous to see picturesque rickshaws along-side modern trams. Everywhere one looks there are huge Zulus with fantastic horns, head decorations and painted legs, carrying their human freight at a fast trot. They charge about 6d per mile but can sometimes fleece strangers if they are not careful, as Edgar discovered to his cost. Rickshaws are company-owned and the Zulus hire them for 2/6 per day. In front of the strangers they put on a show with wind noises, showing off and endeavouring to entice you to enter their 'shaw. The ride is pleasant and the men jog at a good pace, except when going up-hill.

We took a rickshaw to the beach. It is simply marvellous to see what has been done since I was last here. An enclosed surf, swimming baths 100 yards long, fantastic promenades and beautifully designed refreshment rooms make me wonder if the Manly alder-men are alive. Why cannot we take a leaf out of Durban's book? The surf, I'm afraid, would not suit most of the Manly folk and surely not Dorothy! Managed to hire a board and some onlookers were quite impressed, I think.

There is a Tommy regiment leaving for India tomorrow and the town is full of soldiers. Some of the Australians tease them merci-lessly with exaggerated salutes. Such behaviour only highlights our own indiscipline. Talking of which, the Miners Corps mucked up so much when they were here that the hotels are closed to soldiers and we are treated very charily. I've heard some terrible stories about their treatment of the local girls. Can they really be true? Fortunately, the last two batches have made a good impression.

Tonight we had our rickshaw race, with three men in each carriage, but it rapidly turned into a farce. Great fun. There was a gross weight of about 36 stone in our 'shaw and our man weighed about 8 stone. It was remarkable and marvellous to see. At one point we leant back, rais-ing the man in the air – where he was left kicking for some ten sec-onds. This is not to be recommended, as sometimes the passenger is pitched out. Sergeant Edgar was damn near concussed as a result.

Thursday 1st March 1917

We were not allowed ashore until after dinner, although the Catholics went to church and a town piquet was sent out. I regret to say three of our men were caught and one was so drunk he had to be carried on board. I fear that will be the end of his leave.

In the afternoon, Nolan and I went and had another surf. I bought some sandshoes, pyjamas and got my photos. Later, we made a car trip into the hills. The view is magnificent and I got some photos. The streets are good and lined with trees. Fences are supplanted by low hedges and shade trees are plentiful. Houses are open and large, with verandahs, usually white and apparently reinforced concrete. Nowhere in Australia have I seen such a pretty suburb. Most houses have large grounds and plenty of trees, and in one I noticed a placard saying: 'Soldiers and Sailors in uniform are allowed to use this garden'. A Red Cross convalescent home is up this way and is absolutely ideally positioned.

This was followed by a good dinner at the Hotel Royal. Nolan rather led me astray with the local liquor and, on meeting up with Sergeant Edgar and a couple of Queenslanders, it was agreed we should explore the 'drum' area known as Fountain Lane. Rickshaws were duly requisitioned and on reaching it, I'm sorry to say the place was heaving with Australians. Most of the houses were so full up that we could not gain admittance. At last we got into one house where there were two girls. Sergeant Edgar, for whom such a visit was an education, was amazed at the scenes and kept repeating the words 'I don't believe it.' He had never seen such a place before and it wasn't long before he got sick of it. The two Queenslanders, on the other hand, were sorely tempted but it took all Edgar's schoolmasterly skills to persuade them otherwise.

Friday 2nd March 1917

The early-morning muster revealed I had three absentees. We are better off without them as they are all shanghais. They will probably be caught and shipped aboard the next transport. At 7 am we slowly drew clear of the wharf.

The Durban feeling will take some shaking off, as will my

headache. The place will hold some very pleasant recollections in my mind for all times. What a time I've had! How I wish Fat Babe had been with me to 'do' the sights – except, of course, Fountain Lane.

Sunday 4th March 1917

I hear we are due in Cape Town at about 8 pm and we may not be allowed ashore. Land, very rugged and inspiring, can be seen from the starboard bow.

Gambling is rife on the boat and there are some high stakes in the chess, euchre and draughts tournament. I soon backed down and did some photo fixing as I would like to send some back to Dot.

Oh, I forgot to mention yesterday that a transport struck a mine near the Cape – eight lives lost and the troops, the Middlesex Regiment, were sent back to Durban in a boat which arrived as we left. I took a photo. I think they were the Tommies we saw on the first day. Seeing the state they arrived back in made quite an impact on the boys, having seen them leave in such immaculate style a day before.

Monday 5th March 1917

A most disturbing thing happened to me last night as we were approaching the Cape. It was a calm evening. A concert was going on, but it was too crowded and I decided to make my way to the upper deck. The one thing about being on a boat with nearly 2000 other troops is that one doesn't get any time to be on your own. It was a beautiful night. Only the stars and the distant lights of the Cape illuminated the pitch-darkness. The view from the bow was spectacular. Dulcet tones and sporadic applause could faintly be heard in the distance, but my eyes kept transfixed on the shimmering glow of the port in front of me.

And then it happened. Without consciously realising my action, I began to grip the rail – tighter and tighter. There I stood, rigid, just staring into the headland. My thoughts turned to Gallipoli and I felt myself sweating as I remembered those terrible minutes we spent being rowed toward the mainland. It all came back to me – the flames, the rattle of gunfire, the random screams of shells and the splashes of water as they crashed around us. I could almost taste the spray of the salt water. All those details that I'd hoped I had lost forever came back. Even the faces of those men with me – some whimpering, others feigning smiles, some just with their eyes closed. All gripping their rifles tighter and tighter.

Thankfully my thoughts were disturbed by Major Hanis. 'What the hell are you doing, Evans? Didn't you hear me calling you? This is a restricted zone for officers only. What the hell's wrong with you? You look in a right state. Go back to your men on the middle deck. The concert's over.' I apologised, but any remorse could not disguise an obvious relief at being interrupted. 'News is that we are stopping off at Cape Town tomorrow,' Major Hanis said. 'Oh, that's good news, sir. The boys will be happy about that,' I uttered. 'You look tired, Sergeant.' 'I'm all right, sir,' I replied.

The truth was that the whole experience has given me quite a jolt. I had tried to blank out any thoughts of Gallipoli for thirteen months. Just never even talked about it. I'd even found myself join-ing in the bonhomie of the lads as we set off, but this brief lapse has had quite an impact. I can't help thinking about it. It was as if the Lord was just helping to prepare me for feelings that I had blocked off for over a year. I think it has done me good, really.

I awoke early this morning and came on deck at 6 am. It was still quite dark and cold, with a stiff wind blowing. Table Mountain is very rugged and inspiring, and its top is covered in clouds. There are several boats anchored in midstream and at 11 am we began to move in. We passed the *Ayrshire* and shouted greetings.

We have just moored alongside the pier and are all very excit-ed, as it looks like we are going to be allowed ashore. Table Mountain is a most wonderful sight with its rough granite sides and flat top, and at present the top is still covered in a snow-white cloud. Paddy Nolan and I are determined to climb it.

Later: We paraded at 4 pm and were all marched down the wharf, headed by the buglers. With the 13th Battalion leading with its flag, we moved off down the town. We marched about a mile and then up the main street, through a beautiful garden lined with large trees. As soon as we were dismissed, Paddy and myself were taken down to the pier by Sergeant Friedman. A most beautiful place on concrete with an open-air concert pavilion in the centre – just what we want at Manly. This is free to the troops but 2d is charged to civilians on the pier and swimming is indulged with dressing sheds under the pier. The view from a tower at the end of the pier is beautiful (110 steps to the top).

Cape Town is not very lively at present. Australian troops are given the cold-shoulder by the white residents, chiefly on account of the fools the miners made of themselves. They say it was dangerous for any girl to be about after dark while they were here. As at Durban, the tales of their doings are too disgusting to mention.

There are roughly three classes, or even four. The whites (English descent), the Dutch, the Capes and black races. The Capes are half-breeds of all description and our troops get on well with them. I'm afraid the result will land a good number of our men in isolation with all sorts of diseases. The first two classes are not mixing to any great extent with us, and of course the fourth are left alone. We are allowed all over the town except No. 6 district – the native quarters with many drums, etc. Life is cheap there. It is said some of our men were killed, sandbagged, a few months ago over there. Such events won't deter these boys, though.

Tuesday 6th March 1917

Took the lads for a short route march this morning and halted at Sea Point, where we were agreeably surprised to find the lady of one house offering tea, soft drinks and cigarettes. Had quite a jolly time and talked to a number of residents. They think the Australian troops are the finest in the world and make great fighters. There is trouble with recruiting here and they point to Australia as a good example to follow!

We were granted leave and marched in the face of a stiff wind, which tore at our flag and nearly swept our bearer away altogether. Later, Sergeants Friedman, Nolan and Edgar and I caught the train to Rondebosch and walked to Groote Schuur of Cecil Rhodes fame. We saw the estate and his house but could not get inside, as Botha was at home. Another train ride took us to

Muizenberg, a further 15 miles. The seaside resort has good surf and the place is very fine, reminding me a lot of Scarborough. The granite hills come almost to the water.

On arrival back in town, Sergeant Nolan flirted most abominably with the Dutch waitresses in a tearoom. To give him credit they seemed to fall for his charms! 'You're so different to the men over here,' one of them said as we left. 'You boys can come back any time,' the other girl giggled as we left to return to the boat. Oh, I have a confession: I have been smoking – about ten cigarettes in two days – but have resolved to chuck it.

Thursday 8th March 1917

Lord Buxton reviewed us yesterday on the wharf. Following that I had a good rest and am feeling fully refreshed. Later, I went to the baths at Sea Point with Nolan, Edgar and Friedman. The water is lukewarm and awfully nice. I stayed in for almost an hour and partook of the hospitality of the free soldiers' pagoda. We then went into town and visited the old market square, had a light lunch, then took a tram to Camp's Bay, 11 miles return, over the mountain side. Sergeants Nolan and Friedman are some lads with the ladies and I get a great deal of amusement listening to them talking. It is good to see Paddy on such good form after all he has been through this past year.

Friday 9th March 1917

Last night we discovered that a trip up Table Mountain had been arranged for today. Nolan and I decided to join the party. We left the ship early in the morning with rucksacks and waterbottles filled, feeling very excited about our imminent adventure.

We had one officer and fifty others, including NCOs and privates, and we set off to meet our guide, a Mr Haywood, up in town. He is a white-haired man of about sixty-five and takes a great interest in climbing. In fact, it is through the Mountain Club that we got the invitation to go on the trip, and the ladies of the town provided our lunch of sandwiches, cakes and pears. We took the tram to Kloof Nek (700 feet) and then skirted the mountain until we came to Stinkwater Ravine. We began our ascent and it proved hardgoing for some. Due to the size of the group, things were going slowly and Paddy somehow managed to persuade Mr Haywood to allow us to go ahead. Probably on account of his persuasive skills, I was of the opinion that Nolan had some climbing experience, but, as we talked and climbed, it became clear that he knew as little about mountaineering as I did.

Our only guide was an old map given to us by one of the residents we had tea with on Tuesday. The summit at this point was covered by cloud. Undaunted by what, with the benefit of hindsight, was utter foolishness on our part, we began climbing. Climbing, good Lord! Upwards we went, sometimes slipping, sometimes crawling, but determined to reach our goal. Many a laugh was had as we clawed toward our destination.

The fact that we were totally out of condition didn't help and we were compelled to take many rests in order to both catch our breath as well as to tend to our cuts and grazes. Native flowers were abundant and very pretty, and I took a number of pictures of the scenery.

By midday the sun had burnt out any remaining cloud and began beating down on us remorselessly. Our water bottles were beginning to get low and so we started to ration ourselves. Thankfully, we did at least manage to find some rough tracks and we climbed for about 2400 feet on narrow paths and ledges. By 3 o'clock we had reached the summit – some 3456 feet higher than we had been at the beginning of the day. Paddy and I had made it and, intoxicated by the beauty of the panorama and our sense of achievement, we embraced.

Paddy shouted out, 'We're back!' and I joined him. Less than a year and a half ago, we were being shipped back to Australia, wounded. And now we were on what felt like the top of the world. It was a wonderful moment and one that I will remember for the rest of my life. For an hour we sat and admired the view sometimes talking, sometimes needing to say nothing.

The ascent took four hours and another four hours were taken going around the top of the mountain. It is fairly flat and good walking. We then made our way down to the alpine hut by the reservoir, where an old gentleman, after his initial surprise at both the state of us and the fact that we had no guide, filled up our water bottles. The reservoir is practically the only water supply for Cape Town and is at a very low ebb. As a result the water is cut off daily at 2 pm in the town.

We entered our name in the book provided for those who complete the ascent and then wished him well. We commenced our downward path and hurried forward. Our downward path didn't take long – about an hour – although we were lucky we didn't crack our necks, as we slid nearly all the way. The trip was wonderful but awfully tiring – equal to a 25-mile march, I'm told. The view is unsurpassed by anything I have ever seen and it was well worth the trip.

Sunday 11th March 1917

Spent yesterday surfing. Woke up today still feeling very tired and sore in the thighs. Parade at 6.30 am revealed one absentee, Private Munday. Surprise, surprise! I'd always suspected he would be a shanghai. As anticipated, my three men lost at Durban came aboard. We moved out from the wharf at 7.30 am and anchored in the bay.

An hour or so later, my absentee came aboard in a pitiful plight. He had been two days in a drum with a native woman, drinking and abusing himself. In the process, she had doped him, taken his money and even his teeth. He was just able to crawl aboard and collapsed. He has been taken to isolation and given a wash-out. Poor Munday. He's a bully and a waster, but I can't help feeling sorry for him.

Tuesday 13th March 1917

Today I had four men crimed – the four absentees. Three forfeited nine days' pay, the other was given two days' detention. VD, as a result of Cape Town, is beginning to appear. We are to call in at Sierra Leone. There is a shortage of water and, while we have enough to drink, washing is only permitted at stated periods.

Won in high jump today. Less satisfactory was the squad drill competition and I feel inclined to hide my head in mortification following my lads' performance. 'Don't worry, Sergeant,' one of them said, 'we'll make up for it in the field.' I hope so.

The sergeants are still teasing Lucas, our pet madman, who today asked what was done with a man whom we couldn't make into a soldier. Sergeant Friedman told him that such men were carefully placed on fatigue in a place where shells fell thickly in order to give him a proper taste of soldiering like. He was suitably impressed!

Saturday 17th March 1917

St Patrick's Day today, and a half-holiday on the strength of it.

To go between decks is like walking through a Turkish bath. The heat is awful and water is scarce. Heaven help the mess orderlies. Had to borrow eight men today for duties as I have so many men sick or in hospital – measles. Two more cases of gonorrhoea to report as well.

Daydreamed of home in the sun all day. I am beginning to believe I am both sentimental and romantic. What an awful complaint to have in war!

Tuesday 20th March 1917

At dusk last night, there was a movement among the convoy and we deployed, steadied down and put on speed, steering all over the place. Possible threat of U-boats?

I have developed a severe sore throat. The lime juice Father gave me is proving a great boon in the tropics in spite of the fact that some unprincipled beggar has been helping himself. Nothing is safe on board.

Sergeant Walsh is an unmitigated boaster. While we were playing cards he tried to persuade us that he had had his way with two women during our stay on the Cape. Unless he sneaked off to the drum area, which he vehemently denies, he is surely telling a lie.

The war news is very good at present. Reports of an advance of 10 miles on a 45-mile front and rumours of cavalry activity give a most favourable outlook.

Wednesday 21st March 1917

Today the submarine guard had rifle practice at a target – a log of wood with a red flag attached, towed behind the *Kent* at various ranges. We all had a good laugh as we watched the bullets splash harmlessly on the sea some distance away from the log, but it hardly provides us with much confidence! The truth is that the guard as a whole is an awful concern. It is composed of sixty Railway Unit men and thirty from 19th Battalion. They mount from daylight to dark, armed with rifles, but no ammunition! They are posted all around the boat deck and in the bows and stern. If they sight a submarine, their orders are to inform the OC, file down to the magazine and get cartridges. The senselessness of it all! The whole business is a farce. They might as well just be ordered to halt the approaching submarine when at hailing distance, and enquire as to its business. If it fails to stop – then throw rifles and bayonets at it and report to the OC. Such is the wisdom of our 'heads' in this matter.

Walsh has sworn an oath that no-one will dare to try to duck him on Neptune's Day and has absolutely defied me to try myself. I intend to cool his ardour.

Tonight I had a fine talk with several chaps – Winn, Brown, Purcell, McLeod and Maitland. They are different from the hard-drinking and womanising sergeants in the mess. Purcell, our French teacher, is also a fine philosopher; Winn is extremely interesting; Brown a university graduate and a master of All Saints, Bathurst; McLeod a bachelor friend of Winn's; and Maitland, an inexperienced chap of about nineteen. Winn and Brown are married, the latter only five months ago.

We commenced on the subject of heredity and the power of will to eliminate these hereditary traits and characteristics. It led to other matters, including platonic friendship, and we discussed freely, giving personal cases. I was guilty of discussing Dorothy and myself with little things left out, of course, and I don't think she would have minded. They said it was either love or the prelude to it! I laughed and asked them if they would like me to confess.

All in all, it was a good evening and I enjoyed talking about something beyond gambling, beer and women. I'm no prude, but the language in the sergeants' mess is obscene and filthy all the time, and many of the jokes are lewd. It does have its humorous side, though, and I am sometimes forced to laugh against my will. 'Bastard' is included in virtually every sentence.

Saturday 24th March 1917

It is Neptune's Day, when lots of people wear fancy dress and a large amount of officers and men get condemned and are given a good soaking. I wonder if I will be a victim by the end of the day! There is certainly an excited feeling around the ship as people sort out their clothes. Yesterday, I even let a man off parade to finish his costume.

Later: Immediately after dinner, crowds began to collect on and around the deck set apart for the tank, and by 1.30 pm there was not one available position. The tank was a sail hung with about 3 foot of water in it.

There was a procession led by a hideous band and we had Neptune and his wife, two mermaids, a rickshaw man, a Zulu, two Bacchuses, a muse, two Aborigines, a dancer, the Kaiser, the Crown Prince and others, including a clown, etc. The costumes were excellent considering the material at hand – rope, tins, tops of bottles and sundry rags. Neptune's wife was easily the best.

The whole proceedings were uproariously funny and wet – water everywhere with the bosun every now and then turning the full force of the hose upon the crowds. Officers, NCOs and men were tried and condemned, and Lieutenant Bauman provided much fun in constructing the cases. Some of the charges laid down were distinctly humorous: washing his neck with a collar on; demanding meat in his stew; bathing in a dixie; drinking his bathwater; eating his soap and cleaning his teeth, etc.

Let me give a rough outline of a case: Lieutenant Buchanan, about 17 stone, Railway Unit, charged with causing a permanent list to port, pleaded not guilty and was loudly condemned by the prosecutor. Neptune expressed amazement at such a puny and diminutive man causing such a thing and condemned him to a shave and two duckings. He was lathered with a paintbrush and flour and water, then shaved most artistically by a barber with a sawlike-edged wooden razor, and then ducked after a severe fight in which several others got a ducking. The crowd roared and at the critical moment the bosun turned on the hose and we retired with mouths full of salt water.

Major Hanis and Lieutenant Brierly were both dipped and we all wailed with laughter when the sergeant major was a victim – his crime being that too much food was wasted on his moustache. The adjutant also went in, as did the Presbyterian padre, which led to a great dust-up. My highlight was, however, the moment when Walsh, who had defied a number of us to dunk him, was seized and carried down struggling to the tank, where he all but fainted. The doctor excused him, much against the wishes of the crowd. He swears vengeance on the men who carried him down – poor fool! I confess to being one of them!

We disposed of about forty people and things got very lively. I was expecting to be crimed but wasn't. After helping drag Walsh, I watched proceedings from the saloon deck. At the end all the officers of Neptune's court were well ducked and by 4.30 pm the thing was finished with. It was good sport but I was dashed tired and glad to see the last. A water fight then took place and it took a good hour before order was restored. We all enjoyed ourselves, I think, and I shall certainly remember the event.

Monday 26th March 1917

I have just been informed that the USA declared war on Germany at 10 am this morning. I wonder!? The troops are all celebrating the news but it might be speculation. Surely the Huns will get the message that they can't win? They're a stubborn lot, though. As Nolan said: 'You've got to give them some respect. They think they can take on the world and win, and they're doing quite a good job of it.'

Sighted land yesterday afternoon. By 5 pm today we were abreast of Freetown and entered the channel, which is by all accounts heavily mined. There is another convoy here and numerous men-o'-war. We understand there is no shore leave and the lads are disappointed. Bumboats are alongside as usual, charging exorbitantly, and the men are paying cheerfully.

We took in water all night. This morning we got rid of £1 million sterling in bullion, which we didn't even suspect the existence of! It has been transferred to a man-o'-war. There are rumours we may stay here some time.

Tuesday 27th March 1917

Moved off this morning. I'm glad to be on the way again and we are told to expect to be in England on the 10th, approx. Rumours about the USA entering the war have proved unfounded.

Sunday 1st April 1917

It's April Fools' Day! Thankfully I was not caught, although jokes abounded and many of our NCOs were victims of pranks.

We were all badly caught by a wag's attempt, on the wireless notice board, to inform us that the result of the NSW elections was Nationalists 38, Labor 32, and Liberals 18. It also declared that Mr Holman was beaten for the Cootamundra seat by a narrow majority, and that Mr Meagher would lead the Nationalist Party. Nearly all the ship was taken in.

This afternoon we had a fine, though sticky, time, running off the bun-and-treacle fight – it was a scream. I crowned the winner with a sticky hand much to the amusement of the crowd. Other sports included potato and wheelbarrow races and a high-jump competition. Still not exactly feeling A1 yet, but I gave the lads a few rifle exercises. My old friend Lucas is giving a good deal of trouble. He is a dashed nuisance but has plenty of spirit.

Thursday 5th April 1917

Orders have been published that from Sunday onward, life belts are to be worn continuously, no sleeping on deck, no noise or smoking after dark, portholes permanently closed and deadlights lowered as we will be in an extremely dangerous area.

Sergeant Friedman has gone to hospital and is in a bad way – temperature 105. I am awfully sorry for the poor chap as he is awfully good-hearted. Must write a few letters before bed.

Sunday 8th April 1917

I had a pretty rotten night and felt very bad indeed. 'Dog disease' has still got a grip of me – my tonsils are swollen, eyes burning, temples aching. My joints are leaden, too. Temperature 104.2 this evening but no beds available in the hospital. Bill Edgar got me some eucalyptus and I dosed myself.

It's just my luck to get this at the end of the voyage. Preparations are being made for disembarking at 8 pm Wednesday. We are to get our kit bags tomorrow. It is rumoured that two destroyers were seen on the horizon this morning. We are steering a zigzag course and change direction every twenty minutes. I hope our convoy gets in A1. Rumour has it that U-boats are causing serious amounts of trouble in these waters.

The Railway Unit have been making themselves obnoxious. They're rotters! All night their rows, catcalls, and obscene and rotten behaviour keep everyone awake. We're all getting tired of them and a scrap is imminent.

The *Wiltshire* is a thing of the past – the trip is complete. New friends have been made and in years to come I shall remember the happy times (excluding the last week) I have spent on board on the journey over. Goodbye *Wiltshire*!

Monday 9th April 1917

I was very bad today – I wouldn't have cared for one moment if we had been torpedoed. Getting ready for disembarkation. I had a good deal of muck to throw out. Our bags came up from the hold and all the men are sorting out and getting ready. Everyone is walking about with pleased grins, and doubtless thinking of the time to come in London. I, poor fool, feel more like the frozen rabbit we had for dinner.

At dusk nine dark patches appeared on the horizon and soon a bunch of destroyers was among us, sweeping around, dodging in and out in a truly pretty way. It is certainly reassuring to see them around. Should be in Devonport on Wednesday morning. We all have a more comfortable feeling about our chances of survival against a submarine attack.

Wednesday 11th April 1917

We were up at 5 am by the new time – clocks put on an hour for the new daylight saving. I was shivering madly but came up on deck to watch us slide through a crowd of little minesweepers. Plymouth Sound was infested with little boats and destroyers of all sorts and sizes. We lay off for about half an hour, and then proceeded down to the Devonport naval docks. Rain, sleet and snow. Welcome to England! My voice has practically gone which made organising the train embarkation difficult. After a little chaos, everyone boarded.

Stopped at Exeter and were provided with free hot buns and tea by the Exeter Ladies' Committee, as I had been before when I came through wounded, though this time not so lavishly. Finally arrived in Codford at 6 pm where we detrained and lined up for a 3-mile march to our camp. Codford is 14 miles southwest of Salisbury and is included in the term 'Salisbury Plain'. Halfway on our journey I was deadbeat – so much so that Nolan helped to carry my bag. A bagpipe band gave us music to march to and enlivened us considerably. In fact, I feel certain that I would have dropped out had it not been for them.

When we arrived I was feeling on death's door but my morale was instantly lifted on seeing my old 13th Battalion friends, Sergeants Jack and Hall. I don't know whether they or I were the most taken aback. Some of my old mates have been chaffing me about 'swinging the lead' for so long in Australia and others are calling me a fool for coming over again. You can't win! They insisted on taking me to the staff sergeants' quarters, where they made my bed and gave me a brandy. The latter did me the world of good and gave me the strength to go and see my men.

My heart has gladdened at seeing my old mates, and Nolan and I were told all the gossip and news of the old battalion. By all accounts they have been performing heroically in France. Hall tells me that the attack on a place called Stormy Trench in February was among the hardest fighting our battalion has had to face in the war. Enemy counterattacks were repulsed again and again despite great loss of life – around 230 killed or wounded in the action.

We managed to capture a good deal of Huns, who have since stated that they thought the troops were specially trained storm troops, given the speed and efficiency of our attack. Captain Murray,

'Mad Harry' as he is affectionately known, was awarded the VC for his part. He is quite some soldier. From being a lance corporal at Gallipoli he must have been promoted faster than anyone in the Allied army, and his list of decorations goes on forever. By all accounts Murray led the hand-to-hand fighting, and carried three wounded diggers to safety while besieged by incessant shelling. He and his men then succeeded in repelling wave after wave of German attacks (one consisted of no less than five separate bombing attacks). His company's fighting strength dwindled from 140 to forty and it looked as if they were going to be forced to give ground, but he rallied his men and, revolver in hand, shot three Germans and captured three others in the process. Some dog!

CHAPTER 2

PREPARATIONS IN ENGLAND

Friday 13th April 1917

My throat is better. A day of dental inspections, kit inspections and route marches. Four were absent because they had contracted VD. The dilly coots! Two were old stagers: one was a discharged cured man and the other a concealment.

Sunday 15th April 1917

Yesterday, we were to be inspected by General Sir Newton Moore but he did not turn up. Another guy did the inspection and took the salute at the march past. I suppose it was too cold for 'Salutin' Moore', as he is called. Talking of parades, the most noticeable thing since our arrival has been the saluting by all Tommy soldiers. We have since learnt it is a most important point and is insisted upon. It was an agreeable surprise to me, I can tell you. The boys have generally been put through their paces.

One of the Tommy sergeant majors, by the name of Jabson, gave us a right drill-bashing yesterday. He is some guy – an old Imperial soldier and looks it, roars like a bull and is a typical British warrant officer. He can give orders on parade as only an Imperial can, but he is a real decent chap off parade. Never heard a voice like it. 'You may not like the man with the pip, but you WILL salute him. You are not saluting him. You are saluting Her Majesty, the Empire and the commission. Any man who doesn't will be crimed. Are you moving in the ranks?' At this point he singled out Munday. 'Private, are you proud of your country?'

'Yes, Sergeant Major,' Munday retorted.

'Well, are you proud of your regiment?' Munday again replied he was. I was beginning to enjoy seeing my troublemaker being put through his paces.

'Well, why are your boots so dirty?' He screamed. At this point, Munday's ego could take it no longer and he whispered his contempt for Jabson, to which there was an almighty roar of 'CRIME THAT MAN!' and Munday was summarily marched off the parade ground. The response to this was a load of sheepish glances at their poorly polished boots. He then went on to talk about the rifles we were holding: 'Keep your rifle clean at all times. You'll learn soon enough if you don't. Treat it like a woman. Never let it leave your side. Take care of it and it will take care of you. In the trenches it is muddy, very muddy, and if you get dirt in the barrel then you may as well stand out in no-man's-land and shout "Shoot me" for all the use you'll be.'

On returning from the parade, my unit was removed to isolation on account of those meningitis cases on the boat. It's a darn nuisance! We have little option now but to play cards in the sun, which inevitably means gambling. I managed some photo printing and developing before our throat inspection. There is to be a big 17-mile march tomorrow with full packs.

Monday 16th April 1917

After breakfast at 6.30 am, the whole of the camp, with the exception of the latest reinforcements, marched out with a dinner ration of two thin slices of bread and jam to Sutton Veny Hospital. Sergeants Hall and Jack managed to entertain Nolan and myself the whole way with tales from the front and the latest in soldiers' songs. At the hospital, a swab of cotton wool was put down our throat and the saliva was taken away for a meningitis test.

Wednesday 18th April 1917

Hurrah! Got three letters tonight, including one from Dot, and I read and enjoyed all. But Dot's letter (numbered three – I haven't had the second yet) was a pleasure and a great reviver:

Eric – I'll wait for you no matter how long it takes. You're my most treasured possession in the world. Of course I know you'll be busy and it won't always be easy for you to write, but please just send me a note every time you get a chance so that I may be assured of your good health. The days go by very slowly with the thought that you are putting yourself in danger. I used to think I was busy but now seem to find too much time to think about what perils you may be facing. I know you want to be an officer but don't be silly and put your life in unnecessary danger to prove yourself. I, for one, need no further proof of your qualities and I just wait for your return.

My, but it was good. Oh Dot, how lucky I am. Of course I will write to you at every given opportunity.

The doctor advised me to stay out of the route march and I had a pleasurable day relaxing and writing to Dot and home.

When the lads came back from Lark Hill, I was expecting to hear about what a hard day it was. Instead they were utterly overexcited and spent the next few hours recounting their unexpected inspection by the King. I feel terribly jealous and am cursing my illness for preventing me from going. Dash it! Lucas is ecstatic about his encounter with royalty, as is Sergeant Edgar. I can hardly listen to them. At least there was an exceptional supply of tucker for tea on their return.

Sunday 22nd April 1917

Things have been lively in France. The 13th Battalion has been badly cut up at Bullecourt, with 400 prisoners taken. Twenty-one of our officers out of thirty killed, missing or wounded and other casualties are equally heavy. By all accounts the attack was a farce and our troops had no chance. It makes me sick to hear about it. How on earth did the generals think that we could break through one of the most heavily defended parts of the German front line with no artillery to support us and only a few unreliable tanks? It doesn't take a military strategist to realise that half a division isn't going to stand much of a chance smashing the Hindenburg Line, after crossing the widest belts of the cruellest wire. The 4th Brigade losses that day were horrifying – over 2300 casualties.

Had I been in France now I'd have got my star. My luck again! But anyhow, we'll soon go now and I'm volunteering for the next draft. The officer said today we'd be off pretty soon. The weather is beautiful now, warm and sunny and I'm enjoying it immensely.

I wonder how all are doing in Australia. I've been reading my letters again – they do make one awfully sentimental and that's no good for a soldier.

On visiting the mess today, I found the sergeants in the bar drinking madly. It was awful and I am sorry to say Sergeants Hall, Jack, Friedman and Walsh were paralytic drunk by 11 am. I am disgusted with the display.

Tonight, practically the whole of the reinforcement has followed their example and got drunk. The sight was something abominable to see. Our chaps were mad drunk and kicking up an awful row. At one point an almighty fistfight took place. Tables and chairs flew in all directions. Even Nolan got involved, as did Edgar. Can you believe it? If only his pupils had seen him! Rumour has it that Walsh, the dilly, started the brawl. He is without tact and has been making a lot of enemies. There is bound to be some trouble in the morning.

I got letters from Mrs Wood and Mrs Jones, both giving invitations to come and stay in London. I must send a cable home to Dot tomorrow wishing her happy returns.

Monday 23rd April 1917

We have a big sick parade this morning. It is hardly surprising after last night's excesses, and I wonder how many are genuine cases and how many are just suffering from overindulgence. Sergeant Walsh has gone to hospital. He sustained a very bad gash to the eye. Needless to say he couldn't remember anything about last night.

I have just had news that a draft of 115 is to be prepared for

Friday but I don't think they will allow any of my reinforcement to go, although a number have expressed their willingness to go without leave! I think much more of these men now. There is a genuine feeling of excitement that we might be allowed to join it. Young Lucas, of course, was the first to put his name on the list.

Received seven letters including two from home and one from Dot. It's been wonderful reading them. Hep, an old friend of Dot's, made a particularly interesting remark: 'Dot misses her glorious cavalier to a very great extent. Her own actions seem to denote she is lonely as she has asked me to come and stay at Manly. She must be in the last stages of boredom to extend such an invitation.'

Dot's piano recital at the Exhibition Concert received thunderous applause. Good on her! I am greatly pleased but hardly surprised. I've yet to hear any musician rival her since leaving Australia. It is good to know that Mrs Wright misses me.

The isolation, alas, that I called a farce has been tightened because Private Munday was caught out of bounds at 10 pm at night. It landed all the NCOs in trouble and a few of the sergeants took him aside to teach him a lesson.

I have written seven letters today.

Wednesday 25th April 1917
Anzac Day!

This morning I took the reinforcement on a little route march through Steeple Langford, Hanging Langford, Little Langford and Wylye, a small and very interesting village, and back to camp, a distance of about 6 miles.

This afternoon was a half holiday and Anzac sports day, open to 4th, 13th, and 12th training battalions. The prize, the Anzac Cup, is given to the battalion with the greatest number of wins. There was a great turnout. The New Zealanders performed their war cry and dance. I won the long jump right out, as well as my heat in the 75 yards championship, but jiggered myself for the high jump and couldn't even do 4 feet. My ankle is in agony, but it has been a good day and I have received lots of congratulations from the lads in the battalion. Even Major Hanis made a pleasant comment, and that is praise indeed!

I'm sorry to say our sergeants in this camp are setting an awful example in the way of drinking. At the sports they were absolutely awful, staggering all over the place. One of the privates who was drunk rolled a full barrel of beer from under the counter while the attendants were not looking and away down the hill. I didn't hear what happened, but he is certain to be crimed.

Had a good talk about marriage with Bill Edgar tonight. It made me wish that I had a little girl too – Dot.

Thursday 26th April 1917

The second anniversary of my wound! I spent the morning writing a letter to Dot and it gave me a great amount of pleasure. I'm afraid I'll have to crime four or five lads for unclean huts.

By the way, Walsh tells me I'm developing into an imperialist. It's not true although I find it a compliment, as I am proud to be a serving soldier of the British Empire and feel that the Poms do get things right when it comes to military matters, especially discipline.

Friday 27th April 1917

This morning a whole crowd of 24th Reinf. 14th Battalion arrived in camp, having been torpedoed on the *Ballerat*. None of them had anything except what they stood up in. Some were covered by just blankets. Many were cold and in a pretty bad state. It was a pitiful sight. They had obviously been through hell, but most seemed quite optimistic.

I have been told by one of the chaps that a submarine was sighted at 10 am on the 25th but was then lost. Unfortunately the SS *Ballerat* only did 10 knots and that afternoon, as Anzac Day celebrations were beginning to get swinging, the submarine came up from the rear on the port side and discharged a torpedo. It struck well aft and broke the shaft.

By all accounts, there was a fair amount of confusion. Thankfully, a destroyer came to the *Ballerat*'s side and the men slid down the ropes onto the destroyers' decks in whatever they had on. The whole operation worked remarkably well and very few lives were lost. The submarine was caught and blown to smithereens three hours later. Everything has been made as comfortable as possible for them. I took some photos of them reading letters and standing around telling their experiences.

Sunday 29th April 1917

I forgot to mention that Ned Hancock, in the Railway Unit, has got meningitis, but is recovering. The 16th Battalion had a fatal case and the funeral is tomorrow. I do hope this will be the end of the awful disease.

Private Munday returned here today under escort, having been caught in Salisbury. He is a total liability. The chaps are gambling a lot. Walsh is the worst and he is losing steadily. Bill Edgar is caught in the swim, too, and bids fair to become a confirmed gambler. Paddy Nolan, like me, is getting awfully frustrated with this inactivity and is trying to get on the next draft. I'm getting awfully sick of this place. We've been in isolation eighteen days now.

Federal election voting for soldiers takes place on Tuesday. I wonder what the result will be.

Tuesday 1st May 1917

May Day! I wonder what is happening in Germany on their great 'labour' day?

The forces voted today and the lack of intelligence displayed by the men, even when the ballot paper was clearly and concisely explained, was astounding. A number even boasted they didn't know who to vote for and so voted for the same as the man in front of him. These men are given a vote because they are twenty-one and I, who am in every way their superior in thought and education, am denied the privilege on account of my age. It brings home to one the unfairness of the position and the folly of giving the franchise to some dopes.

I had a bit of trouble in covering up the fact that I wasn't yet twenty-one. It would have been fatal to my authority if I had been found out. I managed it rather skilfully, notwithstanding the fact that Brown and Richmond were polling clerks. I don't think they even suspected that I wasn't entitled to vote.

We have formed a 'baby' guard. All lads under nineteen are in it and they have been transferred to my hut for me to keep my paternal eye on them and to teach them discipline. Among them are Private Winn, an exceptional young man who will make a fine soldier, and, of course, young Lucas. Overall, they are not a bad lot, but I foresee a little bit of trouble if Private Munday is given an inch. I'll put my foot down from the jump.

Wednesday 2nd May 1917

The first draft was due to go tonight, but meningitis has appeared among some of the group and the whole lot are to be isolated. The outbreak of this disease is becoming alarming. I do hope it keeps away from this unit. I think the sooner I get away from here the better. The disease is causing considerable fright in camp.

Another worry is the rumour that a German submarine has sunk an Australian mailboat just off Plymouth. Alas for my mail, I'll miss the letters from home and from Dot. But it's all in the game, I suppose.

9.45 pm – Hurrah!! Out of isolation! We are free! Free! I can see leave for Friday.

Friday 4th May 1917

Went up the hill locally known as the Pimple yesterday and did so much bayonet fighting and physical training that my ankle is still throbbing like mad. It has never been right since the Anzac sports day.

I am in the guardroom tonight. Our job is to ensure that the prisoners do not cause any trouble, and certainly don't attempt to break out. Most of the soldiers who are locked up are those who have committed petty crimes, or disobeyed orders, etc. There are, however, some very desperate characters to mind. Some are confirmed rogues who have been caught stealing, fighting, or worse. Eight are in confinement on bread and water, having been discovered attempting to escape yesterday. They had cut a hole in the

floor and placed a blanket over it while the earth was dug away
to allow men to creep through and under the guardroom. Here
they met with a difficulty which was to prove their downfall.
Galvanised iron is placed around the piles holding the building
where the ground falls away from the level and in it are cut air
holes about 6 feet by 6 feet.

They got as far as one of the holes and commenced to cut it
open with an entrenching tool, but made such a row as to alarm
the guard and they were captured just in time. An extra sentry was
posted and the eight men were handcuffed and placed in cells. The
ringleader is notorious and has twice before escaped from detention. He is a bad-looking brute, too.

I intend to keep awake all night. I've given strict instructions to
the sentries to keep alert, as I don't intend that the job will cost
me a court martial and the probable loss of my stripes.

Oh yes, last night a most awfully cowardly thing happened. A
chap was paid, along with the rest of the reinforcement. While he
was talking to two of my shanghais, it is alleged that these two
knocked the other down, brutally kicked him in the head, splitting
it in the process, before stealing his pay – a matter of 25/-. Not
content, the two then endeavoured to rob our pet, Lucas, but he
was too fly and informed me.

I investigated and the result is the two are now lodged in the
detention room with six charges against each. I am certainly not
vindictive, but I hope they get six months' hard. They, too, have
already attempted to escape but I caught them A1. They got quite
aggressive and punches were thrown. To my amazement, I floored
one of them. I pretended that I wasn't surprised and I think that
the lads were rather impressed!

Mumps has broken out in hut 12 and they are isolated. Poor
chaps, they'll miss their leave I'm afraid.

I have had, of late, a most restless feeling. I'm out of sorts. I can't
set my mind on my work. My thoughts wander constantly. I day-
dream, am irritable, impatient and altogether a break-up. I know
what it is. It's love. Dorothy is constantly on my mind and I can't do
anything about it. One thing will fix me, at least temporarily, and

that is a quick draft to France. I simply must do something pretty quickly. This stagnation, in my present state, will drive me mad.

Tuesday 8th May 1917

My Dot is a great little comrade. She has written eight letters up to 18th March. Two a week! It gives me such an amount of pleasure to read the letters, but I must say she can be awfully childish in her ways sometimes. I do wish she wouldn't, as I dislike it awfully. Perhaps I am just getting more serious. I hope not, although I suppose when you are training to kill people it's hard not to. War does age, but I hope I won't lose my sense of humour when writing to my babe.

A draft of ten men, including Paddy Nolan, is leaving tonight. I wished him luck and told him I would be out there as soon as possible. I'll miss his friendship. How he persuaded the adjutant he was fit to go, when none of the others who came across on the *Wiltshire* have been selected yet, I will never know! Before he left I gave him a photo that I took of Table Mountain. I am hoping to be in the next draft, so it won't be long before I see him again. Before leaving, he said: 'Cheer up, Evans. You'll still get your commission and no doubt see a fight or two. The way things are going, we'll be generals by the time the war's over!'

Gambled at American Banker and lost 17/7d in five minutes, so I called off. Edgar is making a fool of himself against the professionals and is still playing ... and losing! He is also acquiring a taste for the bottle. It's amazing how a camp like this can corrupt!

I am told our leave is not to be until Monday week. Dash it!

Wednesday 9th May 1917

Today there was a little trouble over my action involving the attempted break-out of the two prisoners and the scuffle that ensued. I was sent over to see the adjutant, as they claim that I initiated it. The whole thing made me particularly wild.

Major Hanis seems to make everything as hard as possible for his NCOs – awfully sarcastic, too, with a smile always on his face. 'Right, Evans. What's this I hear about you giving those two men in the guardroom a private lesson in punching? You are meant to be setting an example.' Before I'd had time to explain that we had acted in self-defence, he dismissed us with the words 'If I hear it happening again, you won't just be guarding the prisoners, you'll be one of them.' I dislike him more and more.

In the afternoon I wrote a pretty rough letter to Flip's father, which I hope he does not take offence at. I felt I had to do it after the way I treated Flippy about enlisting. I have had time to think about what I said and I was wrong, as is his father. It must really hurt the lad to be deemed a shirker, especially among people he knows. I do hope my letter will have the effect of stopping his father bullying him into joining up. The truth is that he, above all others, should know that Flip is utterly unsuited to army life.

I'm still feeling lonely and would love to have Dot in my arms.

Sunday 13th May 1917

Given a lecture on the evil of going with women in London. The lads, of course, laugh at the advice and I must admit the lecturer, a doctor, was hardly likely to inspire confidence. He had a putrid way of talking, with a squeaky voice — like a girl. Certainly, the precautions taken by the military to prevent VD are good and extremely necessary. Each man is given a card of instruction and warning, a Nargol outfit, known by the boys as a 'dreadnought', for prevention of syphilis and gonorrhoea. French letters are force-fully advocated and cost 2/- per dozen.

One reading this would probably be surprised, even offended, but it is true and absolutely necessary among a certain class of people. I don't hold truck with it, perhaps, but I recognise that it is necessary to force a man to protect himself. Men who are perhaps to be killed in a very short space of time are hardly to be expect-ed to control any sexual desires.

The unit has jumped from the second to fifth week of training. It seems that they are hard-pressed for reinforcements on the other side of the Channel.

A concert by a London party was given tonight. Fair and even good in parts, but one old maid, of perhaps forty or fifty summers, sang and everyone burst into hysterics. She sounded like a Ford car needing a new inside – her voice had evidently worn out. We gave her a standing ovation and she sang an encore! Spirits are high, as leave begins tomorrow.

Monday 14th May 1917

Parade at 6 am and then marched to Codford train station. On arrival at Paddington, the crowd fell in, and I managed to duck away to the tube. Sent a telegram to Mrs Wood to advise of my arrival and later bought some good souvenir badges for Dot.

Buses are on strike so I was compelled to taxi everywhere I wished to go. In the afternoon I visited St Paul's Cathedral, a wonderful place, especially the Whispering Gallery. By the end of the day I was dashed tired and glad to get to Manor Park, where I was warmly welcomed by Captain and Mrs Wood and their youngest daughter, Laura.

After tea, Laura and I walked over to Ilford to see two of the married sisters. They were kind and enquiring, but got on my nerves attempting to get me to talk about my wartime experiences. I didn't feel it was appropriate and if I had told them what I had seen then they would have probably wished they hadn't asked. Diverted the conversation and had great fun allowing them to guess my age – the attempts ranging from eighteen to thirty-five! I didn't correct them.

Arrived home at about 10.30 pm and was shown to the guest-room soon after, where I am writing this. Captain and Mrs Wood have been awfully good to me. All the family (including Frances, who I met late in the night – she goes nursing after her work until 9 pm – jolly bully of her – she is a sport and I like her immensely) have remarked on my great likeness to their family. I am glad I came here.

Tuesday 15th May 1917

Slept like a top. Laura went to work at 8.30 am and Frances rang up and got the day off to take me around. Awfully kind of her and I fully appreciate it.

We went to the West End together, mucked around, bought an

album and did other shopping. Sent Mrs Jones, one of my mother's old friends from years ago, a telegram that I was in London. In
the afternoon went to *Zig Zag*, a revue in which George Robey
figures. It was a scream and I laughed all the time. Returned home
and played cards till about 11 pm. What a splendid day and all
thanks to Frances.

The Woods all had the opinion I was shy when they first met me,
but now have changed their minds. Frances says I am very self-con-
fident, dictatorial, conceited and even egotistical! Alas for that last
word, my pet aversion. She tells me 'Eric' is not a suitable name for
me. I should be reserved, quiet and a namby-pamby, apron-string
type. Apparently I am too abrupt, although how she can talk I do not
know, as she verges on being dictatorial! But I like her all the same.

A telegram arrived from Mrs Jones, stating her daughter
Kathleen would meet me tomorrow.

How I would love to visit Pall Mall, Nelson's Statue, Marble
Arch, Piccadilly Circus, the Strand, etc. with Dot one day.

Wednesday 16th May 1917

Went to meet Kathleen at Corner House, Strand, and what a surprise! For some reason I was expecting a fairly tall, fair and fat girl.
She is small, dark and anything but fat. Awfully nice, although a bit
affected at times. She's engaged, worse luck. She talks well and has a
nice free manner. Says she's shy, but I reckon she thinks a good deal
of herself. Had a fine lunch together and I kept her late for her
office, but she said it didn't matter at all.

Did London Bridge, Pall Mall, Buckingham Palace and the Tower
of London. The latter was most interesting. I enjoyed it immensely.

Met Kathleen again at 5 pm and proceeded to Chiswick Park,
where I was introduced to Mrs Jones, who was very nice
although rather nervous. Kathleen steadily improved during the
day and at one point gave a character sketch of me – a poor one.
She says I am a cynic, thinks I am a philosopher and different
from any boy she has ever met. Said I was the only one she did-
n't get bored with occasionally. She guessed my age, too. Mrs
Jones thought it was between twenty-two and twenty-five, and a

friend there said twenty-nine. Ha! Ha! Later that evening her sister returned home and we played music and sang till 11 pm, when I left to stay at the Union Jack Club.

Kathleen should make a jolly companion, although quite hard work. Doesn't like walking. Dotes on 'the River'. I wonder what her fiancé is like?

Thursday 17th May 1917

Buses are still on strike and there is talk of sympathetic strikes on trams and trains. Had lunch with Kathleen and decided I really like her. Tried to persuade her to come to a matinee with me but it couldn't be arranged, so I took an affectionate farewell! I went to the matinee *Maid of the Mountains*, comic opera. A really beautiful piece. I must send the score to Dot.

I forgot to mention I posted some badges home to Dot in the morning.

After leaving the theatre, I passed an awfully well-dressed and pretty girl who, as she walked by, said 'Hello'! I was interested, turned about and caught her up. She was even nicer than I at first supposed, but it soon became clear she was a prostitute! I can well understand why many of our poor lads fall into the snare set. A beautiful girl on the street and the glad eye, an unsuspecting youth and a few moments of pleasure. A return to camp and in a fortnight – the hospital at Bulford. Alas for the unsuspecting and uninitiated. I can see the great sense in the lectures that our lads get before going on leave even more than before.

Well, to continue. She said perhaps I wanted tea and so we went to a restaurant. I was particularly interested but told her I was not a probable customer and asked her about herself. The usual tale, of course, that one reads in books and very few believe.

She left home three years ago and now she cannot leave her awful work. She is careful and does well at the game, is pretty and well dressed and doubtless thus lures many of the unsuspecting. What a temptation and a fall at seventeen! Whether her tale was true or not I cannot say, but that is exactly as she told me of herself. She was quite confiding and I feel inclined to believe her. I left her outside the café at 6.30 pm and got a taxi to Paddington. The whole episode has left quite an impression on me.

And so finished my London leave. I spent about £10 altogether and thoroughly enjoyed the whole trip. Friedman, Walsh and Edgar have just arrived back and are full of stories of their exploits. Walsh's stories are somewhat more elaborate than the others, as is to be expected.

Saturday 19th May 1917

Machine-gun school again today. Dealt with stripping mechanism and stoppages. Had a chat to young Gordon Winn on various subjects – prostitution, marriage, drink and its side effects, lewd jokes and their effect on a healthy mind, the comradeship possible between man and wife or between a boy and a girl pal, etc. Awfully interesting. I like Winn and shall certainly cultivate and keep his acquaintance.

There's a sergeants' dance on tonight and I am surrounded by much heavy drinking. Walsh is already too drunk to stand. Edgar, meanwhile, is busy gambling away what remaining pennies he has. I can foresee some lively times in the next few hours. As I write, Sergeant Hall, blind drunk, is wandering around with a rifle and bayonet pointing at all empty beds. I don't approve of it at all. There's bound to be an accident someday.

Later: The dance was a fiasco. The drink ran out before the ladies arrived and some of the men behaved in a less than gentlemanly conduct. A fight broke out between sergeants from rival battalions and I am afraid the whole thing was called off soon after eleven. The officers are livid and I am hardly surprised, although one woman apparently told Edgar that it was the most exciting non-alcoholic party she had ever been to!

Tuesday 22nd May 1917

I proceed on draft on the 24th! This Thursday! Of course I have jumped at the offer. The longer I wait the more difficult will it be for promotion. I must make a will and write some letters in case I 'go west'.

Altogether I am entirely ready and don't at all mind the prospect. It should certainly mean some quick promotion. News of the draft has heightened both my sense of excitement but also my feelings for Dorothy. I really must be in love. The more I think of it, the more convinced I become of the fact. I tell Dorothy everything – far more than I ever tell Mother and my pals Hep and Russell. I dream of her and think of her all the time. I am really lost without her, and more conclusive proof of the great regard I have for her cannot be found than the fact that I have posted to her my diary – my thoughts and myself, pure and simple. I hope she does appreciate them, even if sometimes their contents hurt. I feel that I have nothing to hide from her. I have unburdened my soul to her. I do hope we never fall apart.

Tonight I am going to the moving pictures with Winn and Friedman.

Wednesday 23rd May 1917

Was only ten seconds off the record strip at the machine-gun school. Not bad, eh?!

Later was marked dentally and medically fit. This afternoon I went to bombing and threw three live grenades, which the orders demand before a man is allowed to go on draft. We were all made to wear shrapnel helmets. The test is remarkably easy, providing one is confident.

The officer taking the exercise was rather cautious, as there had been a nasty accident a couple of weeks ago. A soldier had pulled the pin, fumbled and dropped it onto the floor of the bunker he was standing in. The result was, by all accounts, a far from pretty sight. The poor chap was only eighteen. The truth is that nervousness has been the sole cause of any accidents which have eventuated here.

Learnt some useful stuff. 'Just remember,' the official said, 'if a grenade is thrown in your direction, get down on the ground quick, lie flat, have a quick prayer and you'll have a decent chance of seeing another day. A grenade explodes upwards and outwards so get down. Oh, and Lucas, you look the kind of hero type who thinks they can pick it up and hurl it back. Don't bother. Your mates won't thank you when they're picking up your remains, and nor will your mother.' We all laughed, as it hadn't taken the officer long to realise his character.

Thursday 24th May 1917

No sign of us leaving. We have now spent nearly six weeks preparing and the lads are getting pretty restless, especially Lucas! This afternoon there was a great stunt which was watched by all the 'heads'. I was in charge of the machine guns during an advance to consolidate a mine crater.

On my return to camp, I was greeted with four letters, two from Dot and one each from Mother and Raymond. I picked up Dot's and opened it and then I stopped, although it was a terrible effort to put it down. But I left it and went and had a bath, changed my clothes, then had tea and now I have just finished reading the mail in a clean condition and I have appreciated it all the more for having exercised the restraint. Thank you ever so much, Dorothy dear! What a brick you are. She tells me that from the day of my arrival in Australia on January 10th 1916 to the day of my departure on February 7th 1917, 425 days, I saw her 223 days! Well, well!

> Eric, how I wish I could see you now. I spend far too many hours day-dreaming and life is boring without my bronzed lifeguard to go to tea, films and dances with. I got used to playing the piano in front of an attentive and good-looking audience, and now even my practices seem dull. I hope you are making some attempt to ward off those English girls, although I can't blame them for their taste in men. All I ask is that you don't forget me and come back safe and well.

Oh darling, Dot. I'll never forget my girl. I did, I admit, have a good laugh about her slipping up on her way to the stage at the Red Cross concert.

I cannot find a match for this diary and I am afraid I'll have to take the best that offers, which, as far as I can see, means an ordinary common thick-paper affair, like a 'penny notebook'. I can have such as this one made in three to four weeks, I am informed by W.E. Smith & Son, but of course that is far too long. I really don't know what to do, as I shouldn't like to spoil the diary by getting an ordinary notebook. I should have foreseen difficulty when I purchased the books. I had an idea these two books would last about six months each at least!

I have everything practically in order now, except for writing a few letters before I go. Still no news as to when we are to move off. This fooling around is no good to me at all. I am impatient.

This is a copy of my will in case of accident:

In the event of my death I give the whole of my property and effects, including all monies due and amount to my credit in a/c no. 146253 in the Commonwealth Bank of Australia, to my mother, Alice Emily Evans, of 88 Berkley Road, Manly.

Eric S. Evans
Sgt no. 847, 13th Bn AIF, Codford, 23/5/17

Sunday 27th May 1917

Yesterday Major Hanis caught me with coat, hat and belt off, but I made a joke and he laughed and forgot about me. He is a sarcastic and mean man, though, a contemptible chap for all his smiling and his pleasantries. I shouldn't like to be in his bad books. I saw him later on and he talked for about an hour about himself and his reputation in the battalion. He told me he knew he was the most hated man in the battalion. He said, 'I stand alone and I am set on all the people who don't know their jobs.' Conceited not half.

I inadvertently let slip that my ankle was bad, to which he said, 'You shan't go then.' He actually made the tears come to my eyes, the brute. Later, he tried to make it up and cry quits but I wouldn't shake hands and he was quite surprised. I must have made an awful ass of myself and he must have laughed at me, even if not outwardly. Fortunately, the entry of Captain Koch cut short our conversation.

There are fifteen from the 13th Battalion on draft, including myself. Among the others are Walsh, Edgar, Friedman, Lucas, Winn and, of course, Hanis. It has been raining hard all day and this afternoon I have been writing a letter to Dot.

I have written a farewell letter to Mother, Father and Dot to be pasted in the back of my paybook and sent on should I be killed.

Latest word about our draft is that it won't sail till the day after tomorrow. Hang it!

Tuesday 29th May 1917

Goodbye Codford! Rumours had been floating around that the draft was cancelled and I have alternately been depressed and jolly, happy and lonely for the past twenty-four hours. My nerves have been near breaking point and everything's been annoying me.

With full pack and forty-eight hours' rations we marched out at 9 am. Oh! The handshakes. I was wished good luck for hours it seemed, and my hand was tired with handshakes.

My, what a feeling, marching with the band ahead of us, playing 'Blighty' with our heads up and chests out, and hearts nearly bursting. My whole body felt aglow and was tingling with excitement and pride. It's great, that feeling. What man does it not affect? Why, he that denies the feeling is not human. It's simply great. I felt fantastic as I marched along – proud to show myself as a soldier who is going to France to do 'his bit'. I don't just want to do 'my bit'. I want to come back again with honours and glory.

And now I realise as I sit here the chances of 'life'. They are good, but still I have to think of the realities. I wonder how it would affect them all at home if I was killed. How would my dear little comrade take it? Oh, happy days that I've had with her. May I be spared to enjoy many more!

But I am allowing my thoughts to wander somewhat.

Of the train journey I don't remember a great deal, as I fell asleep for most of the way. We drew into the docks at 1 pm amid much flag-waving and cheering, marched half a mile to our wharf and we are now in company with perhaps half a thousand Australians and the same number of Tommies.

What a contrast there is between Australians and the Tommies here. The Australian, with his devil-may-care expression and the Tommy with his parade-ground, disciplined manner. The Tommy doesn't attempt to break bounds, or at least when the sentry stops him, he is content, but the Australian isn't content. He argues. As a result, we are on a wharf and are piqueted in, in order that some of our men cannot get away. This is necessary not just because we have some rotters who don't want to go to France, but because many of the lads would go on the bust and lose the boat.

At 5 pm, we boarded a Channel boat, *La Marguerite*, a little two-funnelled, paddle-wheeled steamer. Every man has been issued with a life belt, which we must wear continuously, and our packs have been hung below. It is horrifically cramped, 1500 persons simply piled on top of one another, but I managed to sleep until 7.30 pm when we moved out. I am told the actual travelling will take six hours – Southampton to Le Havre. Our boat is a fast little thing capable of about 18 knots and we have destroyers escorting all the way. At about 9 pm rations, consisting of biscuits, cheese and jam and bully, were issued and tea was made available. The issuing was deplorable, not least because the Tommies managed to do theirs in perfect order.

This is a journey that I am not likely to forget. The swearing men and the stuffy atmosphere is pretty near killing me. The men gamble most of the time – cards, crown and anchor, and two-up. I won 30/- in the latter two games. Edgar lost again but remains cheerful. My tunic is absolutely filthy, as I have been lying in the dirt, but I don't give a hang. Dot's watch still keeps fine time and I don't know what I would do without it. God bless her.

CHAPTER 3

THE BULLRING

Wednesday 30th May 1917

Le Havre reminded me of Cairo somewhat. It was dirty and stinking in the part I saw and I felt quite disappointed. No pretty French lassies throwing kisses and hanging around my neck. No cheering and shouting. I think we all feel a little disappointed. Just a march along the cobbled streets with a few old women and old men passively watching, and hosts of little children begging for pennies, 'souvenit,' 'bully-bif,' and 'bisquit'. 'Some bloody reception,' Walsh said as we made our way through town. I guess we've been spoilt by our treatment elsewhere. Further along, we saw a few Belgian and French soldiers guarding German prisoners who were working along the road. They looked on with apparent interest.

During the two halts on our 6-mile march to camp, Belgian women selling oranges and chocolates swarmed around us. We cheered and waved to anyone and anything as we marched. One woman gave me a glass of water. 'New boys?' she asked.

I replied we had just arrived over from England. She looked weary and, with an unsurprised nod, she replied in poor English: 'Yes, I thought so. It is always the same. Happy, hopeful, young faces.' I paused and looked around me and realised the absurdity of it all. Here were our boys singing and chatting freely. I wondered how many soldiers these women had seen wandering merrily down the same road.

I am told that the training in 'the bullring', which is 3 miles from here, is very stiff. I really thought I would be sent straight to my battalion, but have been told that everyone has to do at least ten days in the bullring as a sort of hardening and tempering process.

Must ask Frances Wood for some tussore silk shorts to use as underpants. These are necessary to prevent chafing and also for hygienic reasons. There's a sparse supply of water in the camp and it's difficult to get a satisfying wash. Cleanliness is vital to keep away those disgustingly filthy body lice. It's easier here than in the line, where one necessarily expects that state of affairs.

The fun and games are over, and the lads know it. There's still plenty of good humour and the jokers are still at it, but we all know that the next few months will be a test of all our characters.

Thursday 31st May 1917

We're just outside the village of Rouelles, 6 miles from Le Havre. It's a pretty spot for a camp, but everywhere seems to be out of bounds. There's plenty of room, cheap canteens, hot and cold showers, a plentiful supply of water and washing accommodation. The Canadians who were here before us say it is the best base in France, yet, for all these relative comforts, I couldn't sleep for the cold. One blanket wasn't enough, so I'll have to forage for another, I think.

Had a pretty rough medical inspection before dinner. The doctor just walked down our line as we stood completely naked. It seems that its chief purpose was to discover cases of VD. One poor red-faced lad was singled out to report to the medical quarters amid much cheering.

We were then marched in clean fatigue, and with our box respirators, to the celebrated bullring – a place where staff sergeants bully and drill the very soul out of one. Some of the boys won't know what has hit them! The first thing one notices are lines upon lines of trench systems, entanglements and obstacles. There are gas rooms, physical training grounds and running tracks. Here we will take part in bayonet-fighting courses, musketry courses, bombing courses, and such like. The whole of the area is covered with smartly moving bodies of khaki-clad men carrying on their particular training to the harsh music of a sergeant major.

All the instructors are specialists in their branch and the best obtainable. 'There is no place for the shirker or for the unfit man here,' we were told. Every man is kept going at full pressure the whole time with few breaks. The malingerer quickly has his heart broken and the unfit man is soon sent to hospital.

On returning to the camp, we were informed that General Birdwood had made an unexpected inspection. We missed him, which was a shame, as I wanted to see the commander of the Anzac Corps. Walsh was less bothered, and has a point when he said, 'Why the hell have we got a Pom leading our army, anyway?' Granted, it does seem a little strange and even Edgar, who rarely gets vociferous, thought it to be a poor show.

Have just finished having a long chat with Private Doyle, an original, who updated me on battalion news. Nearly all the originals are dead now. The Bullecourt stunt killed off all but a couple of, until then, the lucky ones. After the battle, roll call gave us something like 300. Doyle recalled how the inhabitants of Ribemont, where the battalion had been posted before the stunt, were heartbroken at the sight of our depleted troops returning. The battalion is now resting there and trying to make up its strength.

Must write to Dorothy.

Friday 1st June 1917

The bullring today. I had quite a heavy heart when I put up my full pack and a heavier one when I got my lunch – a small cheese sandwich! We might be about to face bullets, but we could do without facing starvation. It makes me quite angry when I think that there was plentiful food back in Blighty.

On arrival we were all taken to the gas room, which was then filled with weeping gas, to test both us and the helmets. Those with faulty helmets were easily found as they wept copiously. It's a suffocating feeling and we all had a great desire to throw our helmets off. To do so or to have a leaky one would mean death, of course, in a gas attack. Three were found to be faulty, much to their wearers' discomfort. My helmet was good but I was glad to get it off after half an hour. The peg that grips the nose to ensure one breathes through the mouth makes one's nostrils quite sore.

Later on, we had lectures on advancing under artillery fire and using the tin hats as complete and efficient cover from shrapnel. Real good idea, too. These were followed by practising hip firing on the charge – a dodge learnt from the Germans.

The instructors are from all over the empire. Tommies (mostly guards regiments), Australians, Canadians, and they come here for two-month spells and take the subject they are most interested in. I suppose there are about 8000 troops in our bullring. All are supposed to be fully trained before coming over and this is just a touch-up in little matters, new things just up from the front.

However, the 'ring didn't prove so bad. Quite the worst of the training is the march up the hill to the 'ring. Had a sponge-down on return.

Saturday 2nd June 1917

Bayonet fighting this morning was taken by a bloodthirsty NCO guardsman by the name of Kelly. We all arrived and rather expected an easy morning, but were soon put in our place. 'Right lads, the holiday's over,' he bellowed. 'You may have come over here to see a few French sights and to sample wine and women. Well, let me tell you that in the next few months, if you haven't killed a German it'll mean you're 5 feet under. Kill or be killed. This is more than just a bayonet class; it's a lesson in self-preservation. Chances are that your bayonet will be the best friend you ever had.'

He proceeded to demonstrate the most effective way of using it by charging at a suspended sack of straw. His screams as he approached were such that a few of the boys couldn't contain their laughter. Realising that if he noticed, we would be probable replacements for the object he was bayoneting, I made an attempt to shut them up. The truth was that I was struggling to hold back the giggles myself as, with saliva dripping from his mouth, he repeated the demonstration with even more ferocity. This time he thrust into it with such force that the rope from which the sack was hanging snapped.

Efforts to control our laughter were futile and, as a result, we were put through a most torrid day of exercise. It finished with a run over an obstacle course involving vaults, water jumps, trip wires, trenches, embankments and ending with a 10-foot wooden wall. If truth be known, I rather enjoyed it! The older men, on the other hand, had great difficulty in even surmounting some of the obstacles, much less racing over them. 'I'll never laugh at a guardsman again' was all Edgar could say on returning to camp!

Sunday 3rd June 1917

Church parade. The chaplain, who is a peculiar chap, informed us that today was Trinity Sunday. He dealt with God as the Father, Son and Holy Ghost, and then told us to respect the respectable women and to keep away from the unrespectable women for the sake of our own respectability. Sound advice, too. I enjoyed the service and one phrase has stuck and has been running in my mind ever since – 'God is Love.'

Perhaps I have put too worldly a meaning on the word 'love' but this I know and am sure of. I absolutely live now on the most beautiful of all my thoughts. My love for the dearest girl on earth – I think, I hope, it is true and honest and good love. It is certainly very concrete.

Got a pass to go to Le Havre at midday and took a stinking little tram into the town with Edgar and Friedman. It is a rotten hole and I don't think I'll go in again. Hot and dirty for the most part and full of soldiers.

I was pulled up by an Australian major for not saluting. 'What's your name?' he asked. I told him and his reaction was one of astonishment. 'Good God! I don't believe it. I was warned to look out for you by a certain Dorothy Wright, who has written about you on numerous occasions. My name's Alf Hatton.' The name instantly rang a bell. Dot had often referred to Alf in conversation. It seems that their families were very close and Alf had been a virtual brother to her when they were growing up. What a remarkable coincidence!

We had a good laugh about it and he insisted on taking the three of us out to lunch. 'I am sorry I was such a silly frump getting you to salute, but we officers have been ordered to insist on it. Australian troops don't have the best reputation for abiding with military etiquette.' I apologised and we soon got down to talking about life in Australia and, of course, Dot. 'You seem to have made quite an impression on the girl. She's always going on about you in her letters,' he said. I blushed as Friedman and Edgar gave me knowing smiles, but privately felt rather chuffed. After lunch, Alf had to return to his regiment. Good luck to him. I must write to Dorothy to tell her about this chance encounter.

The rest of the day was spent wandering around the town. No pretty French girls with big eyes to be seen. Nothing but an army of sallow, uninteresting ones. We had dinner in a café, where we further gorged ourselves with fish, grilled steak and strawberries and cream. Quite a decent feed, eh! It was washed down with old French red wine, but it was sour and horrible. Ugh! I admit to making eyes at a very pretty and alluring French piece and silently 'toasted' her. She nodded and just at that moment an RAMC captain sat down, leant over and said, 'That girl is interested in you, be careful, old chap.' His name was Captain Clarke and he meant well. A Scotsman and a fine chap, he is a medical officer in Camp 13. He sat down and we all had a fine talk. He told me that of 5000 cases of VD in hospital here, only sixty had been traced to licensed houses! One can now see the reason for him warning me against the girl in the café.

I intend to visit the licensed brothel area, Rue des Gallions, merely for education. The state of immorality here is awful but the military authorities recognise this as a necessary evil, so they try to prevent VD by systematic daily examination of the prostitutes in the licensed houses, and by the establishment of early treatment depots. This is the best plan, but to think it necessary! The captain told me that he had heard there were actually houses run by the

Australian government for the AIF!?! I was amazed and of course contradicted him. How can a man who has a girl in Australia and who expects her to remain true to him possibly stoop to such connections with a harlot? Thank God I have never offered such an insult to my 'little comrade'.

Wednesday 6th June 1917

I had a dream last night and awoke as a lieutenant. I had both stars on my shoulders and stripes on my arm.

A rash is breaking out in a big way on my seat. It's mighty unpleasant. I wish those underpants would turn up. I suspect I have that uncomfortable complaint of 'crabs'. Got some calomine ointment but it's not done much good.

There's a big German internment camp at the bullring. The German prisoners look on at our training and appear suitably impressed. Bayonet and bombing are the only phases of our training they are allowed to see. Some of them only look about sixteen. The Huns must be getting desperate. Let's hope so, anyway.

I talked to an officer about the next expected stunt on the Messines Ridge. I learnt a lot that is inadvisable to write here, but he reckons it's going to be a big push. The 4th Division is now nearly up to full strength, having received reinforcement from both the 3rd and 6th divisions.

Edgar has gone to hospital – piles.

Friday 8th June 1917

The planned offensive I talked of began yesterday and we've all been reading about the capture of Messines. What a fine piece of work, and far easier than expected, too. A big list of VCs is also published. I do envy the recipients. Some soldiers reported a large explosion in the early hours, but I slept through it. Morale has been lifted by the news and even Sergeant Major Jabson thinks 'the Huns might be on the run'.

Torrential rain all day and we spent most of it being lectured to in makeshift tents. One of the talks was given by an imperial captain, obviously a ranker, who has been wounded four times. He urged us to force the pace, saying: 'If the Germans are quiet, wake them up; give them hell; kill them. The more you linger the longer the war will go on; you'll be here when the war babies come out.' He went on to give us the old saying, 'If you are told the opposing factor are Saxons — Saxons are not the most humane and quiet of the Germans — don't be content and quiet too — kill him, for the only good German is a dead one, be he Saxon or Bavarian.'

I've just been speaking to a Tommy officer who observed that the most common word he hears among the Australian troops is 'bastard'. I couldn't disagree. Talking of which, my pack is some load. Here is an inventory of all my kit, my whole belongings: slouch hat, steel helmet, jacket, breeches, putties, boots, five pairs of socks, three shirts, four handkerchiefs, cap comforter, towel and soap, shaving gear, greatcoat, full equipment, rifle and sling, pH helmet and box respirator, and lastly a sheet and blanket. Total weight is 60–70 lbs. It is a deuce of a march to the bullring carrying all this lot every day.

I am dying for a mail and I want Dot here to play the piano for me. This evening I have been dreaming of her and Manly. What a time I'll have on my return.

Sunday 10th June 1917

Went swimming in Le Havre with Edgar and Friedman. Had the bad luck to strike my head on a rock while diving. It made a nasty mess of my forehead and nose. Dot would have been horrified. I bled a great deal and the crowd was interested. I tried to appear unconcerned but didn't feel it. When I had recovered and been dressed, we went downtown and had something to eat. There, I saw some US soldiers and no doubt about it, they look smart. Beautifully tailored uniforms with soft felt hats and tassels. Some dog.

Afterwards, we went to the Rue des Gallions quarter. I only went into one brothel, no. 8, which had nothing to recommend it from the outside. Inside, though, it was well furnished and we were led into a big, tiled lobby filled with soldiers drinking beer at a franc a glass. The drinks were served by the girls, who had nothing on except a very open lace overall affair cut very low and not coming down as far as the knees, silk stockings and shoes. Some music was playing and the boys were singing or smoking, laughing and playing with these poor girls. The housekeeper, a fat old woman, stood by and received the money for the drinks and also for the other matter. After the money was handed over, the girl would take the soldier up the stairs to a bedroom. Rather disgusting, one may say, but still interesting.

It was quite the nicest-looking brothel I have ever been in, and apparently a fine type of good, clean girl, if one may use the words for such a person. Some were most alluring and a number were wearing next to nothing. 'Allo soldier. You would like a girl for the night?' they would say. I was sitting at the bar when one young vixen, somehow different from the rest, approached me. She couldn't have been more than eighteen. 'I have been watching you.' She went on. 'You are different from the usual men that come in.' My mind couldn't help but think of drunks like Walsh. To them she was just another victim of their intoxicated lust. She had short blonde hair and a sweet smile – a real beaut. Maybe she had chosen to solicit or maybe circumstance had led her to it – either way, I felt an intrinsic pity for her. We talked about Australia and she asked me about what life was like there, but before we had much of a chance to answer, some Aussie digger barged in. 'This isn't just a talking shop, mate. Is she yours or what?' Before I had thought of a reply, she got up with the words 'I must go. Bon chance.' The last I saw of her was as she disappeared up the stairs under the watchful eye of the housekeeper.

What an awful life, I say, and yet in France it is deemed an absolute necessity. Prostitution is but a profession and is simply viewed as a necessary evil. Even Edgar admitted he was terribly tempted. But I've said enough.

As we walked down the street a large brawl was taking place, seemingly between some Tommies and Australians. The military police were soon on the scene and, would you believe it, the two offending groups both turned on them! I wouldn't be an MP for any price. They are constantly called names and get no credit from our lads. All the boys seem to have a great prejudice against them perhaps warranted, perhaps not. If the tales circulated are true, then it's certainly the former, but I cannot bring myself to believe such rumours. Anyway, these poor redcaps are given a deuce of a time. If it's a Tommy, the Australians whistle 'Pretty Joey', and if an Anzac mounted policeman ever passes by, they coerce and jeer.

My head is still aching and I feel sick. All the lads want to know who knocked me. They think I've had a fight.

Wednesday 13th June 1917

The bullring is getting monotonous. I was in charge of a group defending a frontline trench against 'enemy' raids. Having no bombs, we used dirt and did quite respectable damage on the back and necks of the unsuspecting patrols. Some of the language was pretty ripe, I can tell you. By accident they caught one of my lads with a smoke bomb and severely burnt him. He went to hospital. It made things quite exciting. The boys like a little touch of realism, it's the sauce to the meat.

I was just about to go to the pictures tonight, when I heard a band playing some old Manly tunes. I lay on the grass, closed my eyes and pretended I was with dearest Dot. Later, a chaplain, very witty and a great chap with the boys, assisted with amusing speeches and competitions, such as perverted proverbs and verse making. He gave tins of fruit and tobacco, etc. for prizes. It was an enjoyable and spontaneous evening. The best since that day in Le Havre.

Monday 18th June 1917

I expect to leave in two days' time. My kit is all ready. I was passed by the medical officer and have been issued with 120 rounds. It looks like war. Just written eight Australian letters and one to Frances Wood. Oh yes, I got a letter from Father and also the parcel containing some more underpants, which are great. I feel the benefit of wearing them already.

It's been damnably hot and the compulsory bath parade this afternoon was much needed, as the huts are getting very pungent. After tea we played some cricket. I haven't handled a ball for about three years and it was noticeable. My reputation as a sportsman will never be the same again! There's a night-time exercise at the bullring and the persistent rattle of machine guns is causing a fair amount of excitement, although it's probably just a night exercise. The flares are like brilliant arc lamps.

Wednesday 20th June 1917

Goodbye bullring! We fell in at 9 am and about an hour later began our march into Le Havre. The lads sang the first third of the journey and were silent for the rest of the way. It was quite a strain.

Stopped at the station for three hours. A number of men began looking for beer and water, but the military police prevented us from leaving the station and soon our chaps were giving the passers-by their francs to buy beer and 'vin blanc and rot'. The redcaps once again stepped in, but not before some of the local boys had run off with young Lucas's 10 francs. Lucas swore to kill them if they returned, but they were shrewd enough never to be seen again. I could understand his anger. It was pretty rotten behaviour given that we are about to risk our lives for their country's freedom.

I had more success and managed to get a loaf of bread as well as a tin of raspberry jam. Some other sergeants have a supply of butter, some sardines and salmon – so we should be okay for the whole train journey. The train is about 600 yards long, or so it seems, and is composed mostly of horse trucks and some first-class carriages. The former were marked 'Hommes 40/Cheveux 8'.

Groups of forty unfortunates were packed into carriages about 20 feet by 8 feet. An unholy crush, I may say. There were some first-class carriages marked '2nd Anzac Corps', which we 4th Brigade sergeants commanded until turned out by the corps officers. As a consequence we had to take refuge in a truck, but we saw to it that only about thirty men were detailed to travel in it. Thank goodness, because it was bad enough even then.

The officers' accommodation was outrageous – four were detailed to every first-class carriage, which ordinarily in civilian traffic holds six, and they reclined at ease while their men were herded like cattle. I don't usually criticise this but I think the distinction here was altogether 'over the fence'. Anyhow, I was glad to see the officers portering their own gear to their carriage, and amused to observe some dignified and painfully new second lieutenant of the Imperial Army mincing along and pushing a barrow with his gear on as he went. Our lads, some of whom were already drunk, laughed out loud and I don't blame them. Thankfully, none of the drunks are in our carriage!

Our train crawled out at 3.15 pm and continued to crawl with Sunday stops every ten minutes or so. Conversation was at first purely centred on the remarkably unimpressive speed of the train, but rapidly degenerated to the same old sergeants' talk. 'Bloody hell, we're going to miss the war at this rate ...' 'Oh, that's a shame ...' 'No, I need to get some medals to impress the wife ...' 'Didn't seem too bothered about her in London with that shop girl ...' 'Give over. Shut up about that.' 'Who's got the whisky?' 'Hey, who drank it all?' 'I paid for at least half a share of that.' And so it goes on.

Later: It's getting dark now and things have quietened down. Some of the boys are smoking and reflecting, no doubt, on what lies ahead. Others are talking quietly to their mates or writing the odd letter, and although it's not easy to get enough space to even do that, some of the lads are playing cards. There's a sense of nervous excitement all around – a feeling that the adventure of our lives is about to begin.

CHAPTER 4

THE REUNION

Thursday 21st June 1917

The train journey was terrible – moving slowly at an average rate of about 15 miles per hour with intermittent halts. Came through Etaples at about 7 am and continued via Calais, Boulogne, St Malo, Hazebrouck at the same old dogtrot. Most of the lads were awake all the time. At every halt our chaps descended to the rails and stretched their limbs, with one party playing two-up at every opportunity. In our truck, we played cards and there was some pretty serious gambling. We all had great difficulty getting to sleep with thirty chaps squeezed in. Lord only knows how forty managed it. The only good thing was that we were too tightly packed to feel any cold.

The first visible signs of German bombardment were spotted at St Malo, where a church lay in ruins. It was here we passed a hospital train full of wounded going south. It was a sobering reminder of the reality of war. Soon after, there was another stop and I took the opportunity to have a wash in a horse trough as well as a shave, as I hadn't shaved for three days. My beard was surprisingly thick. I am toying with the idea of growing a moustache. It would certainly add a few years.

We continued on and stops became more numerous, as did the

aero-sheds, dumps of iron and shell destruction. Detrained at Steenwerck at 4 pm, and marched 6–8 miles; passing camp after camp, shell hole after shell hole and dump after dump. We could hear the burst of the enemy's shells ahead of us and aeroplanes buzzed overhead. There was no turning back now. This was the real thing.

At last we reached 13th Battalion headquarters, comprising a few tents hidden away under trees. The draft was split up among the various companies and I went to C Company as usual. Major Hanis is to become the company commander (just my luck!). Lieutenant Brierly is my officer in 10 Platoon and my flat sergeant is Sergeant Jerry Oswald, a brute of a man, tall, muscular and untidy. He is the only man I've met who has a beard hours after shaving. I don't know him well, as he was serving with a different company at Gallipoli, where his exploits were legendary, but if memory serves me right, you'd rather face a hail of bullets than Jerry's sarcasm. He's got a good sense of humour, though, and I can't think of a chap I would feel safer going into battle with. 'I am afraid we're about the only faces you're going to recognise when you meet the rest of the company,' Jerry Oswald warned me, and he wasn't wrong.

The old hands were nowhere to be seen and I realised what a long time two years is in war. He gave me a place to bed down under a little tarpaulin shelter, but I felt much too excited to contemplate sleeping.

Just as I was about to go on a wander Colonel Durant and Captain 'Mad Harry' Murray (of great fame after his winning the VC and getting a bar to his DSO) came up and shook me warmly by the hand. Colonel Durant, 'old Dolly' as he is fondly known, was amazed: 'What, you Evans? I thought Gallipoli would be the last we saw of you. Good on you. I am afraid it's no picnic over here, either, but you'll be right.' He indicated that I would be sent for officer training in the near future, but I made it clear that I'd rather a commission on the field rather than have to go through the officer training in Oxford. The signs that I'll get a commission are at least positive. It would be great.

My, they were pleased to see me and surprised, too. They made me feel quite at home. I cannot express how glad I am to be with the battalion again. I am walking on air and feel as lively as a cricket.

Nolan got news that I had arrived and came over to see me. He was on top form. 'Welcome to hell, mate! You can throw away all you've just been taught. This war's not something I've seen in any military manual. The only thing you've got to remember is to keep that gas mask close at hand. Fritz is rather keen on the stuff at the moment. Oh, and congratulations on your timing. The attack on the ridge (at Messines) was a hell of a stunt.'

Poor old 'Lew' McIntyre was badly wounded and his brother was killed. Paddy tells me the battalion took an active part in the last stages of the battle, preventing any possibility of counterattacks and enlarging the area gained by the first waves of troops, despite strong opposition. The boys have been out of the line four days. We're about 5 miles behind the front with the celebrated ridge some 3 miles ahead of us. It is utterly destitute of any tree or shrub, and the village of Messines can be seen as a heap of mess. The battalion is in a bad way for men – C Company has four officers, three platoons and 130 men, instead of 240-odd. It badly needs a big reinforcement.

The roar of the guns can be heard in the distance. In a strange way they provide the music to set my restless spirit at rest. After all the travelling and training, and in the company of my old comrades, I am now fully ready to do my bit. I feel content.

Friday 22nd June 1917

Fritz has been shelling all night – they've been dropping about 400 yards from here. He blew up a few ammunition dumps around here today and has been shelling Messines village and ridge pretty vigorously. I can hear the whine of shells searching for a battery not far away. It's a rude awakening for some of the new lads, but they seem to be coping well: they don't seem too affected. Lucas is as cheery as ever, Winn and Purcell continue to philosophise, and Edgar seems to be at home gambling with his new acquaintances ... and losing on the last count!

Saturday 23rd June 1917

Moved to a new camp called Regina today – west of Ploegsteert village. It's about 2 miles to the right and slightly further forward than the old one. At one point we came across a series of small wooden crucifixes. Some were named, others were not. The scene had the effect of silencing our whistling and singing, until one of the sergeants broke the tension with a crude joke. I saw numerous soldiers' graves on the peninsula but for some reason it brought home to me the fact that, while fighting for a just cause is honourable, there is something terribly dishonourable about being buried in such a makeshift and unmarked manner in some anonymous muddy field in France. It is, of course, the shells that make identification difficult. I must avoid dwelling on such morbid thoughts.

This new billet is some distance away from the front line, but it is in the centre of a nest of battery 'possies' – big stuff such as 6-inch howitzers and 2-inch guns, which the German artillery pays a lot of attention to. The noise of our guns firing is incredible. The whole place seems to shake. It is a remarkable sight, seeing them blazing away with tongues of fire leaping from their barrels.

Our fatigue involves laying 2000 yards of cable 6 feet underground from divisional headquarters at Steenwerck up to the firing line. A party was immediately ordered to begin the work. They returned a few hours later with three casualties from shellfire.

I didn't get any letters today and was quite disappointed, but received a fine pair of socks from Dot yesterday. Good old Dot, I was in serious need of them. Bed now with my gas helmet close by as Fritz is sending gas shells over.

Sunday 24th June 1917

This is an extremely unhealthy spot and I'd rather be in the old billet. The Germans search this district with their big guns all day. I went out on to the fatigue today at 9 am and we were home again by 1.45 pm. No shells lobbed nearer than 500 yards today, but several fragments came quite close enough to be unpleasant. Shells are too inconsistent to ever feel safe around here.

Had the rest of the day off and, in between a game of poker, managed a respectable wash in a pond. I later had a feed of red and black currants from a deserted garden and I am, as a consequence, beginning to have an uncomfortable pain in the lower regions! Serves me right! At least I am one of the very few not 'lousy' yet, but it can't be long coming now though. It's impossible to prevent the condition.

Still no Australian mail! I wonder how all are at home? I'm just dying to hear from Dot – fancy, it's over a month since my last letter from her! They'll all come in a bunch, I suppose. I am sending off some Field Service postcards tonight.

Oh yes, there was an interesting air fight this morning. Five Bosch machines, flying high, attacked our observation balloons and got three, in spite of our anti-aircraft guns. The observers were compelled to parachute to ground. The Hun machines, with shrapnel puffs all around them, turned the balloons into burning masses. It was a grand sight. I hear we got two of their balloons and a plane in return. Every afternoon our battle planes come out and fly over, searching, and our new fast tri-planes come out and sport too, but no Hun seems to take to the air at this time. Lucky for them. At present there's a violent anti-aircraft shelling going on and our dashed fools of machine-gunners are wasting good ammunition firing a Lewis gun at Fritz who, is about 15 000 feet above us.

Later: Fritz is sending off more gas shells tonight. Sleeping in gas helmets is virtually impossible, but those who choose not to do so at their peril.

Word has gone around that we are to move into the line on the 29th. There is still a lot of shelling, but hopefully it will ease off soon, as all our heavy stuff (artillery) and dumps are being shifted from this area. This should make things a bit healthier for us as Fritz likes to target them. I've got quite used to the noise again and have mastered the desire to 'duck' when they come over. Nolan seems to be totally unaffected by the explosions and Edgar's also coping admirably. Some of the other chaps are, however, feeling the strain and while they don't show it openly, some take refuge in their dugouts at any given opportunity.

Wednesday 27th June 1917

Watched a battery being shelled out about 600 yards to our right and we were all laughing at the unfortunate gunners running at the double across the wheatfields, when suddenly a piece of shell lobbed between myself and the orderly officer. In the end the joke was on me. Nolan claims he has never seen someone's emotions change quicker!

Another little excitement was caused by a big high-explosive shell exploding under one of our wagons taking off a wheel and causing a runaway. No-one was hurt and the horses were eventually brought to a stop. It was a marvellous escape.

Some time later a Flemish lady, who wore a pair of soldier's boots and looked like a sack of straw, came over to complain about the behaviour of our troops. I listened with amusement as Private Purcell, who had been called over to do some translation work, explained her grievance to Colonel Durant. 'It seems, sir, that some of the boys have been stealing her peas.' The colonel, unable to mask a smile, was instantly subjected to a tirade of aggressive French. 'What's she saying, Private?' he asked. Purcell replied that he didn't want to face a court martial for translating the abuse. 'Well, just tell her that we will do our best to avoid going near her peas in future and inform her we'll also try to warn the Germans not to shell near them, either.'

I was then ordered to escort the woman away, which involved going over the parade ground with her. This provided the lads with a good deal of fun and coarse jesting. 'Well, Sergeant, is she backshee?' 'How much, Sergeant?' 'Sleep well but don't get a coupon', etc. These civilians should not be allowed in the forward area at all. It's a great mistake and they cause a damn lot of trouble.

Part of the battalion is on fatigue work tonight. I believe they are to dig some new support breastworks on our frontline trenches. It is a dangerous 'stunt', as Fritz is lobbing his shells close by. There appears to be a great deal of machine-gun activity ahead. And it will be moonlight! We expect a good deal of casualties.

Thursday 28th June 1917

Four casualties last night. The shelling was incessant and it was too close to hope that we would all pull through. The ground shook with the power of the barrage. For the first time I saw a few nerves breaking under the endless bombardment. Only the occasional cry of 'Stretcher-bearers!' broke the horrific monotony of whining and crashing shells. There was little we could do but wait in our huts and hope that it would end soon. In such moments I try to think of the reasons I have to live, and one person in particular brings tranquillity to my thoughts – Dot. How grateful I am for your love and companionship.

Oswald is at least good company with all his jokes. The man knows no fear. Told me a funny story about how, as the battalion was leaving Messines, word was passed around that one of the generals was heading up to meet them. Jerry was in such a state, having lost his puttees and helmet, that it was decided he should be placed with the Hun prisoners they were marching along with. The scheme worked!

Pouring shells have been replaced by pouring rain this morning. The heavens have opened up with a vengeance and many of the huts are swamped out. Had a gas lecture this morning. The Germans seem to be receiving a greater amount of gas than they give us. We are using a new secret chemical. Let's hope it is efficient.

Nolan and I were in mid-conversation following the gas talk, when a single shot rang out just outside the hut, closely followed by a blood-curdling cry of 'I'm hit!' Seconds later we saw a chap running hell for leather towards the doctor holding a bloody wrist. Evidence seems to prove that it was a purposely self-inflicted wound and he could be in serious trouble. Poor chap.

Self-inflicted wounds are by all accounts not uncommon. Troops are coming out with the most ingenious ways of injuring themselves, from drinking salt water in order to induce vomiting to rubbing cordite in their eyes. If caught they are treated very badly – long-term stints in prison are the best they can hope for.

Friday 29th June 1917

We dumped our packs, greatcoats, hats, etc. at 7 am and moved off to our 'possie' at about 10 am carrying blankets and waterproofs, shaving gear, etc. We had about 2 miles to go along shell-riddled ground and duckboards along a route known as 'the Strand' to some breastworks in the centre of the wood known to the boys as 'Plugstreet Wood' (the official name is Ploegsteert). Battalions are all around us and Fritz sends over HE, shrapnel and gas shells all day, making a most frightful din.

My first sight on entering the wood was a graveyard blown to pieces, with the dead, decomposing bodies lying on the surface. Legs, arms and bodies strewn all over the path and smelling something frightful. Gruesome certainly, but this is war. It certainly brings home realities. We soldiers must try to rid such horrific sights from our minds if we are to retain our sanity.

Bits of shell have been flying around today, a few pieces lobbing close to me, but we have had no casualties. The shelling is most trying. We have taken over from the New Zealanders, who tell us they have had 20 per cent casualties. They have been working on a frontline trench at night.

I have today seen a most interesting and secret map of the position and although I'd like to, I don't think I should enter up the information gained. On this front we have semi-open warfare and we hold the line in 'strong' points.

There is no sign of wildlife, although the wood is in some ways still beautiful with its long, historic avenues, all of which have been named after London's streets. Smoke seems to hover above charred, blackened stumps of trees and mangled wire. I haven't seen or heard a bird anywhere. They are the sensible ones. Only rats, lice and humans are foolish enough to inhabit the place now. Despite the location, morale is still high and there is no shortage of jokes. A chap said to me today as we marched, 'Kiss me Sergeant and make me sick, then I'll get Blighty.' The same wit as we marched off fully loaded remarked: 'What is a mule? … A mule is a 13th Battalion man moving to the line.' I had to laugh.

I have a good dugout. Entirely splinter-proof but not shell-proof.

Certainly the 6- and 8- inch 'gazumps' lobbed here would wreck the whole joint. We have comfortable bunks put in by some excellent soldier. It's a bit dark and stuffy but still it gives one a more comfortable feeling when the shells come than a more open, fresh-air one. Luckily I have three blankets. One I brought; the other two were left here by a casualty, probably – so I am comfortable tonight.

This evening we heard a big barrage being put over somewhere and almost immediately they put them over here. The ground shook as the shells exploded, some landing within a few yards of our possie. It awoke all and so we talked to assure each other that we hadn't the wind up. Such circumstances turn soldiers into comrades.

Sunday 1st July 1917

Last night my platoon was assigned to clear up a communication trench from the old Fritz line up to our new one. On finishing the job in the early morning, our guide led us across the old no-man's-land into Fritz barbed wire! Here we were, stranded for twenty minutes with Fritz flares serving to throw us out in bold relief.

They must have spotted us and I expected some high explosives over, but they never came, thank God! Every flare made us dive for cover and sporadic machine-gun fire kept us pinned down for minutes. I could hear the dull thud of clumps of mud being thrown up by these devil sprinklers.

For some of the troops this was their first experience at being shot at and, although we kept totally quiet, the sound of the lads' heavy breathing could be heard all around.

At one point I got caught, with half my putties and a leg of my breeches hanging on the wire. I expected to feel a searing pain at any moment. It was a terrible time. I just couldn't move for fear of alerting the Huns and so had little option but to wait until there was a sufficient lull in the flare activity. Those damn flares constantly rising, hovering and fading, only to be replaced by yet more. Beautiful from a distance but deadly if caught by them in no-man's-land, as many a patrol has discovered. It was a chilly night but we were all dripping with sweat as we lay motionless and stranded. One thing was clear. We had to get out of this area, and get out fast, to avoid the first light of dawn. This we did by crawling slowly back in the direction that we had originally come in.

At last we found our road and, exhausted, began to make our way to 'Plugstreet'. Anyone who thought our evening adventures were over soon found themselves badly mistaken as, within minutes of reaching the road, Fritz put over a few sounds of shrapnel. It smartened us up a bit. Even Jerry Oswald looked a little shaky.

I went to the head of the line and led away to the right upon an open space when – plop! Bang! An HE landed 20 yards to my right. Again, far left, and then ahead. We hurried on when suddenly there was a plop! Right at my feet. I went down with a rush and awaited the bang. There I lay, my face in the mud, for what seemed like minutes, waiting for the explosion that would almost certainly kill me. I waited and waited, but nothing happened. It must have been a dud. It saved my life! The incident, I confess, totally put the wind up me and although I strove not to show it, I was shaking so much I could hardly put one leg in front of the other.

The lads in the rear also had a bad time, but incurred no casualties. My knees absolutely gave way every time a shell landed. This happened at least fifteen times and the furthest off wasn't above 50 yards away! My, I was glad to get away from that area.

Incredibly, we reached camp with just one casualty. Winn had got a hit in the ankle by a piece of shrapnel, but had only begun to feel some pain once he had reached camp. On sitting down he realised that he couldn't get up, so I carried him to the dressing station. A 3-inch piece of metal was discovered firmly embedded in his right ankle and he was evacuated to a clearing station. Finally got to bed at 4 am after a drink of cocoa.

It's a hell of a place for Fritz shells. There are battalions all around us and they tell us it is a quiet period! I would hate to witness a noisy one as Fritz HE, shrapnel and gas shells have made a most frightful din all day.

Managed to sleep a little this afternoon until 4 pm, when I was given a marvellous wake-up call. Eight letters for this chicken! Imagine it! I have read and re-read them – especially Dot's fourteenth. It was dated 21 April and I hope to get the 26 April one in a day or two. I got three from home, including one from Harold and two English ones as well. The one from Harold said: 'Why not take on the machine guns? It's a great cop!' By far a greater cop than I wish to take, thank you!

I have just heard that the premier, Mr Holman, may be around here tomorrow. What on earth for? I'll have to stop as I have to mend the various rents on my clothes after last night's escapades.

Monday 2nd July 1917

Mr Holman was due here at 12 noon and we all shaved and cleaned our gear for him. Fritz was shelling a bit and we had visions of newspaper headings – Mr Holman visits front line – calm under fierce artillery bombardment – chats with the gallant Anzacs – etc. But he didn't come!

General Holmes was killed yesterday. Alas, and he was well liked, too. Anyhow, that stopped Holman and his visit is apparently deferred.

I am working tonight. I believe we have two more nights to do, then six in the frontline, then back for a good spell.

Later: Our work tonight was not difficult – carrying duckboards to an advanced position – and we were home by midnight. A little bit of shrapnel and HE occasionally made things unpleasant.

Wednesday 4th July 1917

Fritz has been shelling the wood tirelessly. The feeling of crouching, enduring and hoping is terrible. Time stands still. There are the brief lulls, which provide lapses of optimism. 'Looks like the Huns are packing it in for the night,' one of the lads will say. And then it starts up again.

It came as some relief when six of us were given the job of inspecting the section of the front line that the battalion is about to move forward to. It's an old Fritz reserve and some of the concrete dugouts are a marvel of strength. The trench has originally been lit with electric light. A fair amount of Fritz gear was about here, which we salvaged, of course.

The captain who showed us over the position was drunk, very drunk, and he quarrelled with our Lieutenant Brierly throughout. A deplorable state of affairs. One of the 16th men tells me he is always drunk in the line. He ought to be kicked out, in my opinion.

The chaps tell us everything is quiet there and there's only sporadic shelling. One of their sergeants told us they'd only had a few casualties. Although there is a fair amount of patrolling done, the Germans are a healthy 2000 yards away. What a no-man's-land! 'Your only real problem, apart from bumping into a German patrol, is the smell. A number of decomposing Fritzes make it pretty pungent around here,' he warned us. On the way back we found the remains of a strafed aeroplane in ruins and collected some Hun ammunition to see if it would work on one of their rifles that we have in our dugout. Got back about 5 am.

After a much-needed sleep, I wrote to Dot, Mother and Minnie today and put my letters to be censored. Blytheman never reads my letters, just asks 'Anything censurable?' and when I say 'No' he affixes his signature. I like him.

The mail arrived late today and there were five letters for me – three from my 'little comrade', including the 26 April one. I was sorry that Dot's cable didn't reach her in time for her birthday. She's a brick, but an awfully catty one! Ever heard of a 'catty brick' before? She promises she will wait for the man she loves – good!

I hope you rest secure in the knowledge that I will remain forever faithful and true to you, Eric. Never think that time can change anything. If anything, it will only make my love grow stronger. Take care wherever you may be. Don't be a reckless hero. You are too precious for that.

I feel awfully happy, but such a letter can make one think too much. I do hope to be home for 26 April 1918 – our second anniversary since our first meeting. Won't it be grand?!

Sunday 8th July 1917
One of our machine-gun possies was blown out yesterday – one killed, one wounded.

The battalion moved off to the front line at 1 am with Fritz sending over shrapnel and high explosives on our path. We only had one casualty, though. I led with some difficulty as it was pitch- dark. However, we struck the sap which led to our support line. My platoon took over this while the remainder of the company took the front line. After the usual blundering and messing around, not helped by Hanis's incompetence, we were detailed to dugouts.

We're in an old German frontline breastwork. Electric light, concrete dugouts, etc. He held this line for two years or so before evacuating.

The difficulty we have is that his parados – our parapet – is very poor and all the dugout entrances are facing Fritz. This cannot be helped. Mine has had a couple of direct hits on it which have managed to displace concrete from the roof. However, it is splinter-proof and watertight – about 10 feet by 4½ feet by 5 feet high and boarded inside. I share with Sergeant Oswald and we sleep on the floor. The ventilation is non-existent and the smell of sweat and urine is overpowering. Smoking has, as a result, become mandatory for anyone who wishes to come in.

The fatigue party has just come back and it has begun to pour dash it! I've just had a warm drink of tea in a vain attempt to keep warm. My clothes are soaking. Now I must try to get some sleep as it's getting light – that is if Jerry Oswald will stop cursing and swearing at being soaked through. The place is in an awful mess now – all slushy.

Later: 12 noon – I have just been awakened by the arrival of tea. Everyone is swearing very loudly and all are wet. I am luckier than most though, although Jerry has muddied our entire dugout. I am detailed to do permanent ration fatigue, which means I have to do trips back to 'Plugstreet' at 11 pm, 3 am, and 12 noon to get company supplies (food, mostly). It's only about a 2-mile round journey, but involves carrying a load for an elephant!

Thankfully it has stopped raining and we are endeavouring to rig up a shelter over our trench in front of the dugout.

Monday 9th July 1917

I have just returned from the first ration fatigue. My God! How we swam, waded, slipped and cursed on that last journey. Somehow we didn't spill the rations, but Fritz was shelling us incessantly. It is 1.30 am. Fritz has the wind up him and has put over a barrage. He has scored a direct hit on company HQ. Two badly wounded. We all have the wind up, too, or at least I have. My knees are shaking and it's time to go to the cookhouse again. I'll wait a while, I think.

My heart is pounding at a great rate. There have been about six 'whizz-bangs' within 10 yards of the dugout. All I can do is to just think as hard as I can about the happiest and most interesting thing in my life. It is the only thing that keeps me from being a total coward and cringing in a corner of my dugout. Oh Dorothy! My thoughts of you are such a comfort to me! I think of the happy times we spent together at Manly and long to be back there in the sun. I think of the surf and the games we played on the beach. How I long to hear your music and to sing along. How can life be so fickle as to reveal such wonderful moments, only to reveal such terrible ones as these.

I must go now for another swim through the mud for more rations. The noise is incredible and a few men are struggling to cope. Friedman has got noticeably windy and could hardly hold his dixie of tea for all the shakes.

Later: I have returned again from my last trip – the time is about 3.30 am and I am dog-tired. Fritz has lifted his barrage. The hit on company HQ made an awful mess. Paddy and a party of three others were given the job of clearing it up. A ghastly business. He hasn't said a word since returning.

It's still raining and doesn't look like clearing off. Sergeant Oswald, in deepening our dugout, has discovered a man buried by a shell. He dug him out and took the papers to HQ. A poor 16th Battalion chap. That may partially account for the terrible smell.

Every night our scouts crawl through the enemy wire and make a reconnaissance of the area. Their attempts to examine the refinery and farms on the banks of the Lys have recently attracted a good deal of attention from enemy parties and casualties have been sustained. Tonight there is to be a raid led by 'Mad Harry' Murray on the 'possie' which opened on one of our patrols a few days ago. The mission involves ten men from the fighting patrol and their objective, I understand, is a blockhouse about 800 yards ahead. It is a dangerous operation and I feel extremely relieved not to be included. I can foresee a big barrage tonight, and more casualties.

Must get some sleep now and hope to have some sweet dreams about my dear little comrade.

Tuesday 10th July 1917

I have just received thirteen letters – two from Dot! What a joy! I think Dot's verse most appropriate:

> As I review
> My days with you,
> I find not one with sadness.
> But I recall
> Them each and all
> As blessed with loving gladness.

I'm glad Dot got the photos. I am now feeling deliriously happy, but such mail also just makes me wish I were home again. I believe I will soon be an out-and-out fatalist. I'm not quite, as I think life too sweet and I am afraid to die. Yes, afraid to die. I've tried to delude myself that I'm not, but I am afraid all right. I pray nightly for courage to carry me through any stunt I may be called on to perform and I pray also for my little comrade. She does help me a lot!

The patrol stunt I mentioned yesterday was a failure. They left at 2 am and only half of them have returned. It is now some twelve hours later. There was a terrific firefight. 'Mad Harry' returned okay, but they must have come up against awful resistance. A search party is going out tonight.

I have just been told that I, too, am going to have to go out into no-man's-land. Dash it! Along with five others, I am going to have to put wire out to protect our front line from attack. I am in charge of the group. Oswald is also included. 'It's a bastard! We don't get much money, but, my God, we do see life,' he's just said. Awfully true, I think.

Later: I have done two trips with wire to the front line. I nearly killed myself and the party, too, at the pace we went. Had no wish to be caught in no-man's-land with a Fritz barrage of machine guns and artillery. Flares were going up the whole time and we were all pretty windy. On the second occasion Private Harris was carrying some 6-foot pickets which we banged into the ground using muffled mallets. The dull thud of the mallet must have alerted a sniper, because all of a sudden a shot rang out and Harris fell. 'Bloody hell, Sarge, I'm hit! I'm hit!' he yelled. The man was obviously panic-stricken. 'I'm going to die,' he blurted out. Oswald and I crawled over through the mud and the slime. I held my hand over his mouth.

'Okay, Harris, but for God's sake shut up. Just tell me where you've been wounded.'

'I don't want to die,' he whimpered.

'Nor do we. Now snap out of it,' I breathlessly told him, 'and just tell me where you've been hit.'

'I don't know, Sarge,' he whispered, still in shock. Seconds later, he recovered enough composure to point down in the direction of his right leg. In the faint moonlight, it was possible to see a trickle of blood running down just below his thigh.

'Jesus, man, you're not going to die. You've got a bloody graze,' Oswald informed him less than politely. 'Now let's get the hell out of here before we really are for it.'

Wrapping his arms round either side of us, we darted low back to the frontline trench with the others following close behind. The distance was a mere 30 yards, but the weight of Harris combined with the heavy terrain made it seem like an eternity before we reached the parapet. Further shots fired out into the darkness but no more casualties were sustained. We tumbled into the trench and Oswald, on recovering his breath, proceeded to give him an almighty earbashing.

'You may have been bloody wounded, you may even have been dying, but if you ever dare scream out like that again, I swear I'll put a bullet in you to finish you off. You damn near woke the Kaiser with that noise. Now get some attention for that leg. It looks like a Blighty. You lucky bastard.' Harris had only joined two days ago.

Wednesday 11th July 1917

I have done one of my trips to the cookhouse and one to the front line and I am now waiting on my second, with Fritz looking uncomfortably close. Note the shaky writing. I'm writing to keep my pecker up as I am alone in a none-too-safe dugout.

Each day brings a few casualties and the shelling is beginning to take its toll. We burnt four of the dead tonight. A horrible job. I hear the shell lobbed right on our MQ and killed the crew all bar one man. The men were beginning to decompose, too. The smell was terrible. It's the smell that is most abhorrent on the front line. I can't describe it, but death is all around you.

I wish they'd stop shelling! If I get another chance to get away from the line to attend the OTC course, or anywhere from this shelling, I'll jump at the idea. And they tell me this is quiet compared with the Somme, Messines, etc. My nerves are not as good as they might be. Some of the Fritz planes were over here this afternoon, so low that you could almost knock the pilots out with a stick. We lay low, of course, but I suppose this shelling is the result of their observations.

I hear we are being relieved on the 14th. That will give me the opportunity to design and make some little souvenir for Dot. I have already collected a Hun nose cap.

Alas! I am infested with lice. It's frightful, but I can't do anything about it. We all are in the same way, no matter how clean we have tried to be. I can sleep with the constant sound of shelling booming around me. I can cope with Oswald's incessant snoring, but to sleep with chats gnawing away is impossible. They are tireless brutes. My skin is already red with scratching. It is impossible to resist the temptation and yet it does nothing to ease the misery.

I've been running a lit candle along the seams of my clothes and derive considerable satisfaction from the popping sound of burning them. But, like the Huns, they don't know when to give up.

I like Oswald's company, but have no desire to share with him again. He is completely chat-ridden and when he takes his boots off even the rats run for cover. Conditions are far from easy, I know, but Oswald's hygiene levels are remarkable. I pity his wife.

Thursday 12th July 1917

Today I took back dead men's spare equipment to the cookhouse. There, the quartermaster and I emptied the webbing. In one of the pouches was a crumpled family photograph. They seemed a nice family – lots of smiling faces. He was evidently the eldest and his doting sisters had their arms wrapped around him, while his proud parents looked on, amused. I found the whole scene tragic given what had just happened to him. Thank God they never saw nor will hear, I hope, about the crude cremation we had to give him and his three comrades.

The photograph has affected me badly and I wish I hadn't found it.

The rest of the day has been spent mending our duckboards and the trench where it was blown in last night. Major Hanis is too hard on the men. They are exhausted and quite unable to do another wire trip into no-man's-land tonight. One or two have had their nerves shattered.

Anyhow, I have just come back from my first cookhouse trip and have decided that I'm not going to make Hanis's proposed working party take any more wire. I suppose I'll be severely censured if I am found out, but still, I must consider the men and anyhow I have taken more wire and pickets than our party will use.

We are being relieved by 49th Battalion tomorrow at about midnight. I will be glad. Damn it, I'm itchy. My skin is red-raw. These lice are relentless. It is a wonder that any of us are still alive and I'm not talking about Fritz. Water oozes from diseased pools and the whole place is contaminated and stinking, especially Fritz's old trenches.

Word is going around that 'Mad Harry' made his way through the enemy posts to examine the river itself last night. Some are even saying he swam across it to examine the other side. Nothing surprises me about the man. He is the most complete soldier I have ever encountered.

Saturday 14th July 1917

Back in reserve, having left the wood last night at 10.30 pm. We made our way out at a great pace, I can tell you. It was almost a run and I perspired freely. We were sufficiently lucky not to have a single shot or gazump all the way! It was a great relief, I can vouch. A deathly silence among the lads said all that needed to be said. No-one spoke at all. There was nothing anyone could say. Only the clod of boots along the slimy duckboards and an occasional sound of retching as we passed the rotting remains of bodies broke the evil tranquillity of the scene around us. The journey was a classic example of how orders come down the duckboards in tense times.

One order, 'Steady in front', soon became 'Quicken up'. We marched, no, trotted, until I was fit to drop — I was absolutely dead-beat when we pulled up at our camp. It's a full 6 miles from the line, but we got a dixie of fine stew on reaching the tents. I was soon asleep but was awakened by some Hun aerial raiders dropping bombs quite close. I was too tired to get up, but couldn't get to sleep again due to the body lice.

Changed my clothes and washed the dirty ones, and then had a good sluice and washed myself. After parade this afternoon I managed to get a haircut.

We were issued with green envelopes today, so I'll be able to write Dot a letter which is not regimentally censored. Our battalion has gone to pieces, I'm afraid. They've been under shellfire too long and they've got the wind up pretty badly. Reinforcements, including my old mate Ted Hall, arrive soon. We need them.

The battalion band played this afternoon. It made me overflow with joy. Few originals are still in the band, but the new recruits did a grand job. The music has a great effect on me.

I had a good old chat with Paddy Nolan today. Apparently

Mumford, who is in his company, proved perfectly useless in the line and, for all his brazen toughness, was windy virtually all the time. He's all talk.

Wednesday 18th July 1917

It's a thousand days today since I first left Australia!

Last night I was on guard duty and had to keep pretty alert, as they were really bad eggs. Having said this, I don't approve of the way they are treated re rations and blankets. Major Hanis absolutely refuses to issue the latter and it was a beastly cold night.

Been feeling pretty low today. Orders and counter-orders every few minutes. No-one knows what on earth is going on early tomorrow. Men's morale is low. At least one piece of good news is that Captain Browning thinks my commission is imminent. This evening I played fly until I was too stiff to move. I can't sleep owing to everyone coming home drunk. How I do hate these drunken bouts!

This little piece of poetry on the eternal war on 'chats' has come my way today:

Little Pilgrims of the Night

When you've several army corps
On your body forming fours
Always on a night attack
Making charges up your back
Then you shout with all your might
Straf the Pilgrims of the Night.

Though some hundreds you may kill
You will find there's thousands still
Yes, they hide behind each other
And are smart in taking cover
Then they have an awful bite
Plus a shocking appetite.
There are families in dozens

Uncles, mothers, sisters, cousins
And they have their married quarters
Where they rear their sons and daughters
And they take a lot of catching
And cause an awful lot of scratching.

When you're getting off to sleep
Then they're forming up two deep
When you're in the land of nod
Then they're forming up in squad
And you'll find it most annoying
When the sections start deploying.

Then at last there comes the day
When you throw your shirt away
You'd like to cast your trousers too
If the powers would let you do
And adopt the ancient style
Of wearing nothing but a smile.

It's rather good, I think.

Friday 20th July 1917

Yesterday, we moved to new billets at Steent-je (called 'Stingy' by the lads) — a couple of miles from Bailleul.

The sergeants kept me awake half the night. As usual, they were drunk and noisy. Had an unfortunate row with one Sergeant Keep last night! He was drunk enough to be quarrelsome and, without any reason, rounded on me: 'Oh here's the glory boy NCO who thinks he ought to be an officer. Think you're a real bloody hero. You're only a bloody teenager, aren't you?' He was out of his mind and began to try to pick a fight. Nolan told him to back off and I was attempting to ignore his ridiculous comments, but he continued to provoke me. After half an hour of this baiting I decided to shut him up once and for all. I launched myself at him, but we were quickly separated and he withdrew, still hurling insults. The whole incident fills me with disgust. I think I like him less than any other NCO in the company, and they are all a pretty putrid lot as far as I am concerned. Good in the line, no doubt, but too uncouth, uneducated and unclean for me. Oh, to get away from their presence and to escape from the army altogether. The drunkenness, the dirt, the filth – oh it makes me feel so miserable. I've never felt it so much as tonight. Slang it, I must straighten up.

Oh! I got a letter from Frances Wood today. She actually admitted she missed me! For Frances that is quite an admission. Must write to Dot. Hope I won't bore her. I have come off guard and feel tired. It is at least a joy to be some distance away from the foul smells, lice and rats of the front line.

Monday 23rd July 1917

Yesterday's service was pretty rotten, but one thing struck me. 'There is really only one virtue: unselfishness. The others are mere offshoots.' The padre also said, 'Love can be measured by the sacrifices we are prepared to make for the object of our love.' How I would sacrifice everything for my Dorothy.

The bombardment we heard the other day and night proved a preliminary bombardment before a 'hopover' at Warneton. I hear the NZs gained all objectives and have consolidated the position. Good on them.

Oh! I have promised Captain Browning that there will be no friction between Sergeant Keep and myself. We have both been put in 11 Platoon. He is my junior, of course, and I detest him. I do hope I can stick to this rather rash promise to the captain.

Later: Major Hanis and Captain Browning gave some soldier yarns this evening which were excellent, but too dirty to record. Lieutenant Brierly also got involved and has risen 50 per cent in the men's estimations as the result of his turn. Since then, the sergeants got into some hard drinking. Jerry is already drunk, but paid me a great compliment: 'I've a great deal of time for you, son. The way you coped on the front was an example to all the men. The lads respect you. You showed a hell of a lot of courage out there,' he said. That, from a rough diamond like Jerry, is more than a compliment. He went on: 'By the way, forget about that incident with Sergeant Keep. He's all right really, but this war affects people in different ways and he's a bit of a nightmare when he's drunk a few. You're not the first he's got into trouble with. The truth is some of the sergeants are jealous about how a young lad like you has been promoted so quickly. It's just envy, that's all.' I appreciate his comments and will try to give Keep the benefit of the doubt.

I am thinking a lot of home tonight and am about to write to Dot. Rumour has it two boats have been sunk, so goodbye mail for a time.

Thursday 26th July 1917

Our conference today was on the review tomorrow by General Plumer commanding the Second Army. We are to march to Vieux Berquin, about 9 miles. It's an altogether rotten idea from my point of view, although I'd like to see the man. At least he achieved more at Messines than most of the other generals put together in the war. He's a soldiers' general and is well liked by most of the boys.

I've just spent two hours sorting out my new platoon's rations. We were two rations short. God knows, the men get little enough – three to a small loaf and six to a tin of jam for the day. In the end I bought a loaf and took my ration of jam for them. Poor coots, I pity them awfully sometimes. I always get my ration and can source if I don't, but if they don't receive their quota they go hungry unless I scavenge from somewhere. Is the army in such a bad way that it can't even feed its frontline troops? I hope not.

Australian mail in today but the important letters must have gone to Codford. I got one from Father, Flip and Olive, with no news except that Flip escorted my little comrade to the unveiling of our honour roll at Turner Hall. He tells me that she receives a lot of attention. I ought to be jealous, but I'm not in this instance. He tells me not to be, saying: 'You've got some girl. She is as sharp as a razor if any chap gets too friendly, and talks about you all the time. Only the other day she was telling me that you're the only chap who understands her.' Good, I'm glad.

Friday 27th July 1917

The review came off all right, although there's been a continuous downpour all day. The old white-haired General Plumer reviewed the 4th Brigade at Vieux Berquin as arranged. That moustache of his is something else. Nolan, knowing I had been contemplating growing one myself, teased me on the way back, saying, 'You'll have to smother your face in fertiliser before you achieve a growth like that.' On returning, I had to conduct a foot inspection before a good dinner – roast rabbit.

It looks like we're about to move back to the front for a big push. A Roman Catholic confessional was held yesterday, which is an absolute indication that we will be going into some serious action soon. Ironically, we were also supplied with Brasso to polish our equipment! The first time in battalion history. The boys don't even know how to use the stuff. I can't imagine what the heads are thinking of, as we'll have to dull it before we go into line again.

The sergeants came in drunk tonight. I didn't know they had any money.

No letters – I feel awfully disappointed.

CHAPTER 5

YPRES

Tuesday 31st July 1917

Rain, rain and more rain during these past few days. A big push has again begun and we have done well. This accounts for the continuous bombardment we have been hearing. I suppose we will be well into it in a week ourselves. I hope for the best, myself.

Just had a lecture by Archdeacon Ward on sexual intercourse. It was following by a lecture by our division senior medical officer on VD, its causes, symptoms, treatment and precautions. The archdeacon spoke with dramatic effect, striking while the iron was hot, opening up smiling and working up to anger. His address seems to have reached the hearts of all our men. Any man who deliberately satisfies his own animal lust and robs a girl of her greatest possession – her purity – was, he swore, 'a bloody skunk'.

I think we all agreed. How unworthy we soldiers are of the love of our dear ones left way back in Australia! The talk has certainly made a great impression on the boys, although probably only temporarily, as soldiers will always be slaves to their immediate surroundings.

Quite a commotion this morning was caused by a Fritz dropping bombs. It woke us all up. I hear the 14th Battalion lost six horses and had a number of casualties. They are about 1½ miles from here.

Last night some of the company made a raid upon some vegeta-
bles – potatoes – for our mess. About 60 pounds must have been
gathered. Another mess accumulated three fowls, onions, beans and
peas, potatoes and carrots! As a result, Hanis has just given us a rather
half-hearted speech on the sins of pinching. I don't think he really
regards it as a great crime at all, but warned us he would 'sock to
leg' anyone caught. He claimed we had quite a reputation, for which
no wonder. I got the impression he was vaguely proud of our wily
exploits! Anyhow, I believe some of our mess made a raid tonight. I
wonder what we will have for dinner tomorrow.

This slush, rain and wind is no fun. I want some music. I do
wish I had Dot here just to play for me, but alas that isn't possible.

Friday 3rd August 1917

It's been raining like the deuce.

Left camp yesterday morning in the pelting rain. Amid much
cursing, we waded on via Steenwerck, in the direction of Neuve
Eglise, and came a frightful cropper for the way was feet-deep in
muck and water. Mud everywhere, wet and hungry. It was
absolutely awful mud! – Slush! More mud! Rain! No shelter when
we arrived. Slept in a little lone muddy tarpaulin shelter and a
muddy bed with the symphony of guns blazing in the distance.

The brigadier assembled us at 10 am this morning and warned
us quite strongly about trench feet. The battalion we are relieving
has suffered badly. He went on: 'Right, lads. This is what you've
joined the army for. You're in for a rough spin, but I know that you
are more than capable of coping with whatever Jerry throws at you.
You've done it before. You are Australians fighting for your country's honour. Do your nation proud. Do your battalion proud. Do
yourself proud. This could be the breakthrough we need. You are
making history. Good luck.' By all accounts, we've got ten days in
support with plenty of work near the dreaded Messines Ridge. We
are ready to go and there is a nervous excitement among the lads.
Even Munday looks as if he is at last ready for war. Our main tasks
will be roadmaking, digging, wiring, salvaging and cable laying, and
we are expecting to do all this in the face of heavy shelling.

Later: Approached Messines by mid-afternoon. The whole way was pitted with shell holes. And mud! The last half a mile was frightful, absolutely up to our knees and were it not for the sandbags we had around our legs, it would have been pretty rotten. Passed dead mules, smelling awfully, and also some 16th Battalion men returning wounded. Hardly encouraging!

The trenches have water 2 foot deep in places and the place is alive with frogs. We have tried pumping the water out but still the water rises steadily above the duckboards. It is a most frustrating business. I don't think it will hurt to mention that we are over the ridge just to the left of Messines. Sergeant Keep has found me a pair of waders – big rubber thigh-boots. A peace offering perhaps? They make a lot of difference, but can easily be lost in the sludge if one is not careful. We – Sergeant Keep and I – thought we had a good, dry possie but, just after we got in, it cracked and half caved in. On one side a dugout completely fell in. We gave it a clean-out and by 8 pm it was habitable. By then it was too dark and I was too tired to do any more work on it.

I'm writing this with my head facing outward so that if it collapsed it would only fall on my legs and body. Can't be bothered to change for bed and will sleep in muddy waders, wet clothes and all. Fritz has just had the indecency to shell us as a welcome to our new position. Most of the shells seem to be falling to the front and rear of our positions, the former on our front line and the latter searching for batteries. Nevertheless, I'll be extremely glad when daylight comes.

Very hard to write in these conditions.

Saturday 4th August 1917

My third anniversary! Three years of war! When will it end?

At it all day, filling and laying sandbags, digging drains, carrying iron, duckboards, etc. until I am fair finished and dog-tired. Keep and myself have totally remade our dugout. It is now beautifully secure, waterproof and shrapnel-proof, I hope. We've just had a celebratory cup of tea and are feeling rather proud of it. In order to improve their dugouts, men had to climb onto the roofs of their trench. As a result, about an hour ago Fritz sent over a load of whizz-bangs. One officer was badly hit in the head.

It's been a beautifully warm day and, thankfully, the sun has dried up everything. At present, I am lying in a pair of silk under-pants and a pair of socks. The shells are still falling, which may explain my writing – it's awful, I know. Last night's barrage found me awfully nervous and I couldn't stop trembling. I don't know what is up with me. The sight and smell of death is all around me. This is a very dangerous area and one just has to hope that the shell doesn't have your name on it. I have ridden my luck so far. Long may it continue! I still have so much to live for. Dorothy, you are always in my thoughts.

We've just had cold roast chicken for dinner! Stolen, but that made it all the sweeter. The two of us finished every particle of it along with half a loaf of bread and half a tin of jam, so we didn't do too badly at all. But I think we deserved it, we've worked like pack mules all day. I have revised my opinion of Keep. He's not a bad sort, after all. We have patched up any feelings of animosity we had for each other earlier on this month. Undoubtedly a heavy drinker and a bit of a bruiser, but there's more to him than meets the eye. A family man – only this morning he was saying that the only thing that keeps him going is his wife and two daughters. Never complains and inspires respect from the boys, although this may be because they're scared of him. Certainly, I am glad I am fighting with him than against him. I talked to him about Dot and he said that I would be a fool not to marry her when I get back. Says that he did at my age and it was the best decision he ever made.

Later: It's 7 o'clock. Two hours until fatigue. Keep's humour, this diary and the thought of my darling back home are the only rea-sons for my continued sanity. The din really is upsetting. The 16th Battalion got quite a lot of casualties last night. I hope it is not our turn. I pray I may be given the strength to stand anything I may get in the way of work or shelling! The latter is certainly begin-ning to affect the men's nerves. One or two of them are suffering under the strain of this constant inferno. Poor old Lucas is one of them, I am sorry to say. His youthful exuberance and vitality for life has visibly eroded over the past month. No longer is he the warrior whose boxing bouts caused such mirth on the boat. He mopes around, seemingly in another world.

This afternoon I called out for him and another one of the boys to help sort out the overflowing latrine buckets, which the previous battalion had selfishly left for us. It is a filthy job but by using a rota we all do our fair share. I was informed that Lucas was refusing to come out of his dugout. Thinking that this was just insubordination, I stormed over there and was just about to give him a piece of my mind when I heard the sounds of heavy sobbing from it. Shells were still raining in around us and so I climbed in. 'Lucas, you've been given an order and I expect you to follow it,' I told him in no uncertain terms. Sometimes it is best to be harsh, even if it hurts, in order to snap them out of it.

'I can't do it. I just can't do it,' he whimpered.

'What the bloody hell do you mean, you can't do it? I am only asking you to empty the buckets.' At that point a shell burst nearby, and Lucas recoiled his body into a ball. He looked a broken man, trembling and shaking.

'Don't make me go outside, Sergeant.' It was a devastating moment. Here was the boy who had been perhaps the most war-hungry of all the chaps on the boat coming over. He was in many ways my outstanding private. A good shot, a courageous and sociable chap, who had never hesitated to follow orders whatever they were. And yet the shelling had got to him. We talked for an hour and I think I calmed him down a little. Once outside, his spirits perked up and he carried out his duties. He will need to be watched, though. This war can be so cruel. It is imperative that he does not give up and he must be kept active. The platoon is just about to go on fatigue and Lucas is definitely coming with us.

Haven't got time to write to Dot. I wonder what she is doing?

Sunday 5th August 1917

Fatigue last night consisted of carrying more duckboards about half a mile back from an advanced post, where some asses had dumped them. A guide led us about a mile through slush to the

16th line in front. Everything was as muddy as it is possible to imagine. Did two trips, Fritz catching us with HE at the dump on both occasions. We had no casualties, but some got the wind up and some of the lads were too shaky to even pick up their load, until Keep and myself got to grips with them. Lucas was exemplary throughout. Got back about 1 am. Hanis roared at me for leading them home on a different and better path than we led out on. He's detestable and has got it in for me.

Oh! I almost forgot! I met an old schoolmate, Frank Laws, on the line last night. It was hard to talk as shells were falling thick and fast, but I spoke to him enough to notice he had changed a lot. I hardly knew him. Never smiled at all and seemed totally distant.

I'm doing a most unusual thing – smoking – not for pleasure, but just to keep away hoards of flies and mosquitoes, which are troubling a great deal.

Lieutenant Brierly is not providing the men in this platoon with much confidence. He's a returned 13th man, so I know him quite well and will certainly stick up for him. Undoubtedly a fine chap, but he is not the type to be a good soldier. Rather undersized and a physical weakling, which hardly inspires respect. One cannot take liberties with him, however, as many of the men will find out to their cost. He is strict, but just. His main fault is that he is not well up in his work and always refers me to Major Hanis if I ask him something. Needs more confidence in this respect and should spend more time in looking after the comforts of the lads. He trusts me, though, and doesn't interfere. Altogether he is a strange chap, a mixture – would make a good friend but a weak enemy. A man in his sentiments, but never a soldier. The men, for the most part, don't seem to like him. I do.

Monday 6th August 1917

At about 9.30 last night, we were given the order to 'stand to', so we donned our equipment, fixed bayonets and loaded our rifles and waited for movement on our sector. At this moment Fritz sent up red and green flares, his SOS, I presume, which spectacularly lit up the sky. Soon after, his guns and all our guns began belching and thundering, illuminating the horizon with their flashes. We waited for orders to advance but none came. Instead, we ended up just sitting on our parapets and watched Fritz performing the most marvellous fireworks display as he sent up signals, star shells, beautiful golden rockets, etc. This continued for about an hour and then ebbed in intensity. Soon after, we were given the order to stand down.

Today I saw a man with the wind up, much worse than Lucas. He was totally unable to walk and shaking like a leaf. I had a good talk to him and he straightened up a bit. I pity him. He just couldn't take any more of it.

Our platoon is falling away fast. I can only put twenty men fit to work. Fourteen men in the company went sick today – some with trench foot, others with dysentery. The little water we have is filthy. We need those reinforcements badly. I wish they'd hurry up.

Sergeant Keep and I had another stolen chicken today. Oh, it was lovely! We chatted for hours about our plans when we return to Australia.

I'm afraid the Huns have this trench well registered. They put in some accurate ones at about 2 am and also counterattacked on our left. I understand they were unsuccessful in retaking the line they lost last night.

I haven't been able to write home this week I must make an effort tomorrow. I am feeling very sentimental. Gee – that was close. A shell just lobbed outside!

The first inspection of the 13th Battalion by Colonel Monash in Liverpool, NSW, 1913. (AWM H00520)

SS *Wiltshire* at sea, circa 1915. This ship carried Eric from Australia on his second trip to the Western Front in February 1917. (AWM A04186)

'D' Company, 13th Battalion, on board HMT *Ulysses* on
1 January 1915. This is the ship on which Eric and other
'1914 men' first left Australia for Gallipoli. (AWM J06499)

Ypres, 12 October 1917. Troops of the 5th Division walking along a winding duckboard, known as Jabber Track, through the waterlogged and sodden valleys in Albania Woods. It was here in the Ypres sector that Eric spent his third anniversary since joining the Allied war effort. (AWM E00985)

Ypres, 25 September 1917. Australian artillery limbers loaded with ammunition proceeding along the Ypres Road. (AWM E00829)

Ypres, 18 October 1917. Ypres Cathedral and the
Cloth Hall in ruins after massive damage – 'the place
is full of the horrors of war,' Eric wrote at the time.
(AWM E04652)

Ploegsteert ('Plugstreet', as Eric referred to it), Belgium, circa 1917. British Army soldiers in a frontline trench at a corner of Ploegsteert Wood. One soldier is using a periscope to observe German Army trenches. (AWM H09027)

Belgium, circa 1917. Two soldiers beside a sign reading 'Piccadilly' on a track in Ploegsteert Wood. Although Sydney – or particularly Manly – was never far from his thoughts, Eric must have longed to be in that rather more civilised Piccadilly, London's similarly titled thoroughfare. (AWM H02093)

Ploegsteert, Belgium, circa 1917. British Army soldiers in a trench protected by barbed wire near a corner of Ploegsteert Wood. (AWM H09032)

Zonnebeke, 12 October 1917. A view of the swamps of Zonnebeke on the day of the First Battle of Passchendaele.
(AWM E01200)

France, circa 1917. A group portrait of the members of the 13th Battalion Band AIF. Eric sent the sheet music for the band's regimental march back to Dot, his piano-playing sweetheart. (AWM H00565)

The music and lyrics of the 13th Battalion's regimental march. This was pasted into diary number seven with condensed milk!

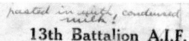

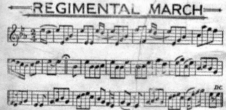

This is your Regimental March. Stand or March to Attention when you hear it played.

REMEMBER!

The good name of the Battalion is in your hands, especially when on leave or on detached duty.

The inhabitants of this country have suffered heavily as a result of this war.

Many homes have lost all their able-bodied men.

Remember this when you pass an Orchard or search for Firewood.

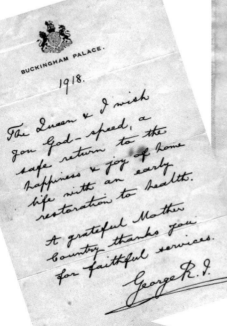

This letter was sent to Eric by King George V in 1918 and was personally handwritten and signed by King George V.

A collection of Eric Evans's mess-dress medals from World Wars I and II. From left to right: Member of the British Empire (MBE); 1914–1915 Star; British War Medal (1914–1918); Victory Medal; 1939–1945 Star; Africa Star; Defence Medal (British); War Medal (1939–1945); and Africa Service Medal.

CHAPTER 6

IN HOSPITAL

Thursday 8th August 1917

I'm wounded!

I write on the 8th after a most exciting past 30 hours. It happened at 2 pm. Sergeant Keep and I had just put some finishing touches to our dugout, filled in and re-vetted the trench about our possie. Less than a half hour before, Colonel Durant had passed with the old brigadier and favourably commented upon our work. But to continue:

Rations had just come up and Fritz began to shell us pretty heavily. This was our own fault as our men were persistently running and working on the top in full view of the enemy. Rations had just been dished out and I was holding a dixie of stew in my hand. All of a sudden one of the ration party made a dive into our dugout, where Sergeant Keep was eating. I didn't hear the shell coming – as a rule one can divine the shell will fall somewhere near – but there was a blinding flash, the dugout collapsed and out through the door was thrown the poor ration carrier's leg and all his entrails, clean into my face! Dirt and duckboard and splinters of shell, blood and muck hit me all over my legs and arms. I was stunned, my left hand completely numb.

I yelled 'Stretcher-bearers!' but I didn't dare look for Sergeant

Keep, when suddenly he burst out of the wreckage covered in mud and blood, right arm half torn off and legs badly hit. Oh my God! I shall never forget it. One man lying in pieces at my feet, Sergeant Keep more dead than alive, and me hardly able to stand with the shock.

Someone dressed my left hand but I wasn't in too much pain. There were a few specks of shell in my arm and I felt generally bruised all over. My head sang and I felt utterly silly. I had the presence of mind to ask for my coat, so thank goodness I have my pay-book and a few odds and ends. I have lost my whistle, shaving gear and, worst of all, my watch. But I am alive. Poor Sergeant Keep had a rough spin. He was less fortunate and was badly hit all over the body. Corporal Sturt conducted me to our medical where the doctor gave me a brandy while I waited to be dressed properly.

Well, from the medical, I walked and Keep was stretchered about half a mile along Wyshorte Ridge, which Fritz was shelling pretty continuously, until we struck an old road full of shell holes and ruts. Here an old horse ambulance was on hand to give us a lift.

Keep was in need of urgent attention but never once called out. In fact, he made no noise at all. Just stared upwards. At one point he mustered up the energy to look at me and, with an attempted smile, whispered, 'Well, Evans, I guess I'll get Blighty.'

I tried to respond but could think of nothing to say except: 'You'll be right. Think of home, mate.' The truth was that he looked terrible and, at one point, I nearly lost my temper at the length of time it took the ambulance men to mend a wheel.

To make matters worse, Steenwerck's wards were full up and we were directed on to Bailleul. Oh God! I shall never forget the nightmare of the ride. The driver got lost and we were forced to endure four-and-a-half hours in the joint, moving like a snail and jolting like the devil. Went about 10 miles instead of three.

This was okay for me but for a man in Sergeant Keep's predicament it was intolerable. Yet still he remained quiet and composed, wincing occasionally and sometimes whispering inaudibly. All I could do was hold his hand and stop him from lapsing into unconsciousness again. At least he was treated on arrival.

Don't think my wound will run to a Blighty. Am I happy, glad or sorry? A Blighty means ten days' leave! Anyway, I am lucky. I should be dead. That shell couldn't have been 2 feet away!

The bad luck is that I have got away just before a stunt – am I lucky!? I've certainly missed that chance of promotion. I haven't written home but think it better to wait until I am properly settled. I'm lying on a stretcher at present. Ah! Here comes the doc.

Thursday 9th August 1917

I didn't sleep too well on the stretcher. At least Keep spent last night in a decent ward. Fritz was putting put the wind up us by dropping big shells close by. I have been shifted today into a tent, hand dressed and marked with a red cross, which means ready for immediate evacuation. We expect a hospital train any time.

The major who attended me today is a rare old sport. I hope my next doctor is half as considerate. Hand is good but throbbing a little, certainly. The hit has broken open a lot of skin but I don't think any bones are broken.

Four deaths today. The cemetery is opposite my ward and I watched the burials. We all felt very mournful as the last post was played. Far too much time to reflect on recent events. When you're on the field, survival is the only object, but when one has time to mull things over, that is when you start to feel depressed. I will be glad to get further back where I'll have the opportunity to write home.

A few of the men in this ward are in a terrible state. One man has got terrible trench foot. His feet have swollen to triple their normal size and have burst open. It is a ghastly sight to see them and the smell is overpowering. Our forces must be in trouble if he remained on the front line in such a condition. Apparently there is a shortage of soap and antiseptic bandages. It is a disgrace.

A soldier is playing a flute. How soothing music can be to shattered nerves and frayed morale. It makes me think of Dorothy.

Sergeant Keep is in a critical condition but the doctor reassures me the operation went well last night.

Friday 10th August 1917

Hardly got any sleep last night. Late in the evening there was much frantic activity outside. A number of casualties were admitted and many had to be turned away. A nurse asked me if I would sleep on the floor and I soon understood why when I looked into one of the admittance tents. There in front of me was a sight that will live with me for the rest of my days. A mass of groaning men, dirty and stinking. Victims of another day of butchery. Young men, their barely lit, muddy faces, some expressionless, some wincing in agony, all awaiting treatment.

A few nurses hurried around in the darkness, carrying their lanterns, and trying to discern who were the most critical. While I tried to take in the hellish scene before me, stretcher-bearers who were rushed off their feet brought in yet more wounded men. Pleas of 'Nurse, give me an injection' and 'Water' could be heard and yet were rarely responded to. I made my way out and looked for water bottles. Having filled a few up, I made a vain attempt to alleviate the suffering. Some would not make it through the night.

As I was making my way across the duckboards carrying another couple of full bottles, I heard the sound of a woman whimpering. It was the matron. 'What's wrong?' I asked.

She continued to cry and sporadically repeated: 'I can't take any more of this. I can't do it. I just can't.' She slowly began to compose herself and apologised. I assured her that it was quite normal, to which she replied: 'I haven't slept for four days now, Sergeant. Even when I'm off duty I find myself writing to those relatives of the dangerously ill. It is all such a tragedy. I've just seen too much now.' There was little I could say to that.

Things have calmed down this morning but the whole place is overcrowded and the tents smell terrible. Dysentery has become a problem and the sooner I get out of this place the better. At least I've had my hand dressed and I am now just waiting for news as to when I get moved to a general hospital. I do wish I could get a decent meal. So far I have had bread and jam and tea, very sparing, too, and a little dob of marhonochie stew. I am hungry as a horse.

I wanted to visit Sergeant Keep today but wasn't allowed to.

Saturday 11th August 1917

Train left at 10 am and took till 2 am. We have only had a little stew, two mugs of cocoa and a little bread and jam on the journey. Pretty disgraceful, given our condition.

There was a very chicken-hearted chap in our carriage, slightly wounded in the foot. Like mine, it's only a couple-of-weeks' job. He talked of his wound all the way, moaned and made a great show. Rather insensitive, as Keep was in the same carriage and obviously still in a terrible condition. He also ran down the sister on the train and I told him off. He's a New Zealander, too, and should have better sense.

I have been landed in No. 47 General Hospital at Le Tréport on the coast of France. There, we got cocoa and biscuits and they sent those of us who were fit enough to bath.

I can't say I like the hospital so far. There's one sister, a ward orderly and two VAD nurses here. The latter know very little, are always conferring and disagreeing and generally drive me mad, although one would break a man's heart.

Sergeant Keep is in another ward, but should pull through by all accounts.

Sunday 12th August 1917

We haven't had much to eat today. I'm awfully hungry still. Five days since I was wounded and I haven't written home or to Dot yet. I'm afraid both will feel hurt about it, but I really couldn't write before. I'll get on to the letters 'tout suit'.

Had an X-ray but don't know the results. My hand certainly aches a great deal. The doc says that although it's puffed it's not septic. I've been having a rare old time telling the sisters all sorts of fibs. They've been in roars of laughter all day. They say I am the rowdiest in the ward.

Last night we told the jolly night nurse tales about rats until she was quite jumpy. The two VAD nurses, however, are very poor attendants and one has already got on my nerves with her manner.

She is a bit religious, too, and stated she thought the war was due to the sins in the world. Did I argue!

Wish I could visit Sergeant Keep. I believe he has just had another operation and that it went fine.

Monday 13th August 1917

Have just written to Dot and to Mother, and I feel much better, thank you. A most remarkable thing here is the fact that among thirty-nine patients only ten letters are allowed to be written – to save the censors, apparently. Damn the censors, I say. It's terrible that they should rob a soldier of his happiest moments. Thank goodness I still have two personal envelopes. I'll enclose about five letters in each and address to Base Censor.

The dining hall is another disgrace. There is always a great crush and bustle. It is a ridiculous spectacle seeing wounded men scrambling for totally inadequate food. There's no system and first come gets the lot. For tea I had a chunk of dry bread and cheese – rotten tucker for a sick man.

My hand still aches. Someone sat on it today. I've just been inoculated with anti-tetanus serum again. The sister squirted about a pint of fluid into me – or so it seemed. Feeling horrid.

Wednesday 15th August 1917

The feeding here is simply putrid and yet I overheard a Tommy remark: 'Gosh, we get fed well here, don't we? Certainly can't complain about the food.' He happened to be one of those big and hefty enough to be able to bustle for his food. He was surprised, even astonished, when I told him we were fed better in the line – I don't think he believed me.

I told one of the VAD nurses that I didn't get enough to eat. She replied, 'Why, you get enough bread and jam to fill up with!' I replied, 'Yes Sister, but, although you are not sick, I'll bet my bottom dollar if you were you'd feel as insulted as I am about being offered nothing but bread and jam, not forgetting the burnt and spoilt water disguised as tea!' 'You are a chronic grumbler,' she replied. Me? Ha! Ha! She is used to dealing with poor Tommies who are frightened to speak above a whisper even.

A doctor who came to see a sergeant with appendicitis roared at the poor chap for not saying 'Sir' and roused on him for moving his arm while being examined. I wanted to smash his jaw, the pig! I'm fed up with this hospital.

Sergeant Keep is, by all accounts, bearing up.

Thursday 16th August 1917

One of those VAD nurses is a little vixen – a tactless, inquisitive, irritating, nagging type with red hair and a weak chin. She really gives me the shivers when she comes near me. I'm feeling down in the dumps and am bored stiff. Today has also been very slow and I didn't get any letters, either.

Friday 17th August 1917

Sergeant Keep died today.

Monday 20th August 1917

Feeling frightfully lonely, somehow. I want to talk to someone.

A storm arose during the night and blew quite a number of tents down, broke guy ropes, uprooted tent pegs, split tents and broke tent poles, generally making things unpleasant and keeping me awake during the early hours of the morning. Every moment I expected the tent to come down, but it didn't. Gee it was cold.

Tuesday 21st August 1917

I have been thinking – should I really keep this diary going? It may land me into trouble if I lose it. I am pretty free with remarks sometimes, I know, and others might not like it. In fact, I never really knew I was so sentimental until – well, until 'the great event'. I wonder if I'll ever have the realisation of my dreams. Just me and my little comrade. Oh, after the war – who knows?

Things are getting more and more tiresome. I was in an ugly mood this morning and I'm afraid I was rude to the red-haired nurse. She deserved it, though, but I apologised later. We might be injured, but that doesn't mean we should be bossed around. I hate seeing these nurses treating the soldiers as though they were children. They forget that these are the same men who have endured hell on the front for months, even years.

My X-ray report says 'commination of 4th metacarpal' – whatever that may be. My right ankle is giving trouble. I think I must have been hit there as it's all bruised. My hand is recovering at a great rate.

I am definitely writing no more letters, except to Dot and home, until I get some. I did hope for one at least today. I've just been musing over my photographs. How comforting it is to see our loved ones even in a picture. Dot is lovelier and lovelier every time I look at her.

Wednesday 22nd August 1917

Couldn't get to sleep last night. All I could think of was home. An Australian sister came in at about midnight, sat on my bed and talked to me for over an hour. What a joy it was to have decent company. Such a sweet, kind and smiling face. I hope I didn't bore her. Told her about Sergeant Keep. She's the first person I have spoken to on a normal level since the injury. Awfully nice and I do hope she comes in again tonight!

Things are looking up. For breakfast we had some preserved eggs! They tasted awful but made a pleasant change from stale bread and tea. I wish I could be marked out for a convalescent home where I can buy food.

Went for a little walk today up to the cliffs and around about. This is evidently a very fashionable seaside resort. Many of the higher-class French people promenade along the cliffs and I spied some pretty girls. It's quite tantalising to see them there, and us bound in by barbed wire with the MP patrolling to keep us in bounds. Oh, how much would I give to be back in Australia.

I have seen some US nurses. They dress in white and wear a red cross on the front of their headgear. It looks good. The American privates are flash, too – riding breeches and a sort of canvas and leather gaiter, khaki shirts and felt hats worn cowboy fashion with a cord for a band and two acorns hanging from the cord ends. Flash! I should say so.

Friday 24th August 1917

Have just written to my little comrade.

I have been marked to base today – somewhat of a shock to me, as I expected convalescent camp for a while, as although my hand has healed, it's still very swollen and stiff. I suppose I'll be on light duty for a time at Le Havre.

Spent the afternoon on a jigsaw puzzle. Feeling pretty well bored to extinction.

Couldn't sleep at all last night and my little Australian nurse came over. We chatted for about an hour. It is so nice to be able to talk to an Australian girl. She's from Melbourne and has said I am welcome to visit her anytime. Says she thinks I'd get on very well with her parents. She is worried about going back in some ways: 'I fear everyone will think I've changed. I left innocent of what war is really like. Now I've forgotten what life is like without it.'

At present, there's a great commotion going on in the ward – a pillow fight. There was one on last night as well and I got well basted. Unfortunately, when I got out of bed to retaliate, the sister came in and caught me in mortal combat. Of course, I got all the blame and was told I ought to be ashamed of myself as a sergeant, but the nurse is a great sport and didn't mean it.

Feeling pretty hungry, so I think I'll go out and make a raid.

Saturday 25th August 1917

We have a new African nurse today in place of my red-haired vixen. Good riddance. The night nurse got me some pears tonight and three of us have just had a fine midnight feast comprising these along with some stolen bread, margarine and ham paste. I feel quite 'full'.

Some more Blightys left today – lucky devils!

Monday 27th August 1917

Had the good luck to get two letters from Australia – Dot's number nineteen and Mother's twelve. Mother tells me she dreams of me. I hope she isn't worrying. I did enjoy the reading, especially about Dot's episode in the divorce court. I'm glad to hear that

Phyllis Haver's husband did go through with the divorce. How awful it must have been to discover his wife was being unfaithful. I think of the trust and the hope he must have had in his girl and how he must have prayed for her and lived for her while away from Australia! Aye! In the same way as my own little comrade inspires me with faith and courage and a hope of a happy time with her after the war, so he have must have felt of his wife. Oh, may my little girl never thus deceive me, for that would forever destroy my faith in women.

Oh, I got a packet of six magazines from a lady I don't know. Her address, which I got off the parcel declaration form, was: Mrs Berkman, Cavendish Street, Stanmore, London. I must write and thank her for her kindness. Of course I can't read the magazines now that I'm leaving, but I'm sure the patients here will appreciate them.

General 'Someone or other' visited the hospital this morning and everyone got the wind up. It was the most flagrant display of stage fright I have ever seen. Our sister was simply awful. Running here and there, getting flustered, rousing if we sat on the beds and generally showing an absolute incompetence in the face of this 'great event'. Lord only knows what she'd be like if there was real cause for alarm.

I am leaving hospital tomorrow. Celebrated by buying a tin of chocolates and distributing them over the ward. I think I'm glad to be going, although I'll miss some of the men and nurses. If the Australian nurse – my favourite – doesn't come in tonight, I am going to her ward to say farewell.

Wednesday 29th August 1917

Well, I said goodbye to my very excellent and desirable Australian nurse. Stayed last night with some very hospitable Tommy soldiers, Welsh Fusiliers, in Dieppe. What a contrast to my treatment over the past three weeks.

Our first port of call was No. 5 Stationary Hospital (Australian) but we couldn't see any Australian sisters. They then took me around town, which was humming with life and full of soldiers, many wounded. Each 'star' seemed to have a fair damsel on his arm. When will I get my commission? Damn it.

There are ever so many of the 'Capes' – half-castes in the South African Labour Battalion. I hear they cause a lot of trouble and are constantly having rows with the Chinese workers, who are, alas, brought over here on contract for wharf labouring and road making. Both seem to be treated pretty badly from what I hear. One has to question the morality of imposing this war on such peoples.

Caught a train today at 6.46 am. My compartment was full of loud-mouthed, coarse French men and women. Arrived at Harfleur and made my way to base camp. I learn Colonel Dolly Durant is wounded, as is Major Pulling. Major Murray is now in command. The 13th Battalion is at St Omer on an expected two months' rest.

Such a surprise! Four letters from Australia. Dot's number twenty, oh so interesting. 'Eric, old chap,' she says, 'you're the dearest pal a girl could hope to have.' I'm so elated and I want to take her in my arms and hug her hard. I'm simply full up with joy at receiving such wonderful letters. It's great!

Thursday 30th August 1917

Saw the doctor today, who remarked that my case was one of premature discharge from hospital. 'You need time to improve that hand, Evans. It's your lucky day. All the A class men in this depot are being rounded up and sent to the front immediately. A big push must be imminent.' He recommended fourteen days' temporary base. Hurrah! I intend to have a real fine time. Drew 70 francs' pay today.

Dispatched a cable to Mother, stating: 'Wound healed – now at base, love.' I hope it reached its destination all serene. It should relieve Mother's anxiety somewhat. Also received a new uniform today. Some dog! The new boots look smart, but have given me blisters.

Oh, a tree fell on a tent here during a big storm the night before last and killed two and injured one man. It's as unsafe here as the line, I believe. It seems nowhere's safe in France!

Wednesday 5th September 1917

Ink again – I have bought this pen to oblige a friend who is broke, for 5 francs. It's an Onoto, too, and in good order. He wanted to sell his watch, too, but I didn't have enough money to do it without skimping myself for a trip into Le Havre for the weekend. I hope I retrieve my old watch. It means so much and I miss it terribly.

Tonight I've been sitting around with a load of soldiers talking about war and more war until we at last got tired of it and tried more pleasing subjects. Discussions were cut short by the arrival of Sergeant Walsh. Still an old, blustering talkative fool who spells 'ego' with a damn big 'E'. Needs to be taken down a peg in the battalion. He's a damn fool.

I have discovered a most curious and happy thing – I no longer write this diary for myself, I find myself hoping that my little comrade will enjoy reading it and I am writing it for her! Dorothy, I care more for you than I really want to admit!

Sunday 9th September 1917

Three years since I joined up! Oh that I could celebrate it with Dot. But, alas, conditions will not allow. This was brought home to me vividly this morning by being aroused at 6 am for a muster parade. At least I've received some good news! I have been informed that my watch, whistle and wallet from my blown-up dugout had been salvaged. I am so glad. That watch means everything to me.

Went to Le Havre today. Had a most delightful swim and promenaded the beach for a few hours watching the French mademoiselles bathing. I noticed ever so many of the Women's Auxiliary Battalion walking out with soldiers and apparently enjoying themselves. Much as I appreciate their spirit, I do not approve of their actions. They have become not the women we love but mere Amazons with a war fever. They look nice in their khaki, too, but I think it means the moral ruination of many of them. I don't like women dabbling in war and its everlasting danger! Is nursing not sufficient for our womenfolk?

Tiring of this, I walked to the Rue des Gallions and visited all the brothels, but I was soon heartily sick of the whole business. It's enough to make one's heart bleed at the immoral traffic and to curse the animal lust of the man. Met Walsh coming out of one. For once he was speechless! Claimed he just went in for a drink, but halfway through another one of his tall stories, he admitted that he had succumbed to temptation. For a moment he looked a little remorseful, but it didn't take him long to get back into his old blustering ways. What a consummate ass the man is — and yet I think I like him a little. Spent a few hours with him. His efforts to make up a conversation in French with a mademoiselle were screamingly funny.

We are to volunteer to return to the battalion at the end of the week. Am I mad?

CHAPTER 7

BACK IN ACTION

Sunday 16th September 1917

Terrible journey but at last I'm back with the battalion. For the life of me I can't say why I volunteered to go back. Even this morning I contemplated getting out of it, but refused to give in. Arrived in time for dinner – chicken – and greatly enjoyed meeting some old pals. We're in a village called Lisbourg. It's pretty dead, but very relaxing. The battalion moves out on Tuesday and they have been training for a stunt for weeks – it's going to be a big one by all accounts. Morale could be higher, but everyone is upset that the battalion hasn't seen the three months' recuperation it has expected after such a long period in the line.

Hurrah – I have just got some mail. One from Hep, one from Ray and Mother's unnumbered, dated 9 July, and a parcel of writing paper from Father – none from Dot! I am disappointed. I do hope there is no truth in the rumour that my diary has been lost!

Friday 21st September 1917

Yesterday we moved to new and pretty rotten billets at Steenvorde and I believe we'll stop here for a few days. There was a big hopover tonight and the flashes of the guns and the flares were plainly heard and seen between 9 and 10 o'clock. It is raining. It

always rains in a stunt. Anyhow, I hope our boys gain all our objectives. Fritz has been shelling Hazebrouck today with big stuff.
Hazebrouck is about 6 miles away, but the explosions sound much
closer.

Oh, letters, fourteen glorious Australian letters in one packet
today. I'm so happy – including Dot's twenty-three, twenty-four
and twenty-five, and four from home, all chock-full of news too.

Dot forgives me for my discussions of her on the boat. I am really so happy to have all the letters, but I really can't write much
tonight. I'm glad she got my ten-page birthday letter and that she has
enjoyed it. Ray is coming on somewhat. Gets letters from girls, does
he! And wants to squeeze Dot's hand! Ha! Ha! My boy's coming on.

Good news about the hopover early this morning. There's also
a rumour that the Germans have retired 3 miles away on the sector we were to have attacked. Hurrah!

There are quite a number of men being left out of this stunt to
come. I wonder what for. This evening as I was walking in the
pitch black around the back of my billet I had the misfortune to
fall into a slimy, filthy pond. When I reported to Major Hanis, he
had a good laugh. Yes, he shrieked with laughter at my sorry
plight, and all the other officers joined in! Oh, the stench was
awful. I have divested myself of all the clothing, but the smell still
clings. Ugh! I'll have to wash everything in the morning.

I have been given the outline of our stunt. It's a big affair and
I really don't like it. I mean, I have my doubts on it succeeding.
I'm not at all afraid for myself. Obviously I cannot write it all
here, but I understand the position has been attempted and
repulsed before by Scotty troops. Lord save us! I suppose it will
mean a lot of casualties.

Sunday 23rd September 1917

Arrived at noon yesterday in a shelter just behind Ypres (Belgium),
after passing through the battered town of Poperinghe. In fact, the
tail end of the 16th transport caught a shell coming through, with
nine casualties.

There's a lot of artillery activity in this sector, mostly ours, and plenty in the air. Just had an exciting minute or two watching an unsuccessful attack by a Fritz plane on our balloon overhead.

Later (3 pm): We are moving in an hour's time and the advance party has gone already.

I'll write of the hopover later, when it's through. We have forty-eight hours rations', wire cutters, Very pistols, duck guns, 200 rounds per man, two bombs, four sandbags each. Everything is ready.

Feeling restless. I wish we'd move. I have just re-read my letters and re-read them again, and somehow they've given me a 'tight' feeling. We all have our superstitions and lucky charms. I always carry the photo of Dot in my top pocket and, of course, have my watch. Nolan swears by his gold chain that he wears round his neck. He tells me it was his great-grandfather's. The funniest is Walsh, the most irreligious man I've ever met, who carries a little pocket-size Bible. He probably stole it!

Monday 24th September 1917

C Company got to its position last night without a casualty, although Fritz nearly caught us twice with heavy shelling, once just in front of Ypres and once as we reached a forward position, a former German line. Passing Ypres, I saw the Cloth Hall in ruins and most of the town in a terrible state (high explosives, mostly). From there the journey up to this possie was just one mess of shell holes, and in the low-lying places it is unbelievably muddy. I was bogged several times and needed to be hauled out by several lads.

We passed many dead bodies – some khaki-clad, others in the grey-green uniform of the enemy. They stunk abominably and as yet we have been unable to bury the fallen. It is too dangerous. To see the remains of fallen youth is a horror that cannot be put into words. Torsos, heads and limbs lying indiscriminately. It matters not that they be friend or foe. They are dead, and for their loved ones that is all that matters.

Relieved the 23rd Battalion in the front line at about 10.30 pm and 'stood to' all night to the accompanying music of Fritz shells and the light of his flares and rockets. One gets a very queer feeling on taking over such a possie as this, with a half-dug line and an uncertain front. Told to expect a Fritz counterattack at any time.

Morning broke with a thick mist and Fritz gave us a straight barrage for about half an hour. Our guns replied with interest. He shut up and everything was quiet, so Hanis suggested a fighting patrol should make a reconnaissance of our front.

My name wasn't called out, so I stood on sentry, while Jerry Oswald led a group out. Twenty minutes later our patrol loomed out of the mist with nine prisoners! They were a fatigue party of 39th Division Prussians looking for dead and I am told they were unarmed. Anyway, they shook at the knees and looked pleased when they were marched away under escort and unhurt. We managed to get some decent souvenirs – watches, cap badges, etc.

The patrol went out again and this time bought a fight with a resisting outpost. One of our men was badly wounded in the chest. Oswald got a hit by an egg bomb but wasn't seriously hurt. Just a few grazes on the arm. We accounted for about three Fritzs with rifle fire.

Fritz aeroplanes are active and are over in droves but we are lying low and as yet he hasn't exactly located our positions. Cries of 'Enemy plane' lead to frantic activity, with us sergeants bellowing orders to 'Put out those bloody fires!' Anyone caught smoking in the open is crimed on the spot.

A Hun plane came down today and has been the cause of much heated debate. Everybody claims the honour of the telling shot. It is all pretty lighthearted, although Walsh was vehement that he was the hero in question. This was until Brierly showed the surprising aptitude to ask Walsh if he could check to see if his rifle had been fired (by checking the barrel). Walsh withdrew, redfaced, much to the amusement of the accompanying crowd. Arguments continued for the rest of the afternoon. The fact the plane is about 1400 yards away in no-man's-land and apparently undamaged is ignored.

We are in a place called Albania Wood. No-man's-land is a miserable-looking area with trees, now just blackened, charred stumps. A patrol has just successfully occupied a pillbox some 100 yards out in front called 'Harper House'. From the amount of ammunition, machine guns and mortars here, there can be little doubt that we are in for a sizeable stunt soon.

Later: What a scare we had tonight. I was taking out a patrol and was in no-man's-land well beyond Harper House, when we suddenly encountered a Fritz fighting patrol. We would have practically walked into them had a flare not lit up our surroundings. As it did, about fifteen silhouettes stood out some 30 yards in front of us. My lads reacted first and there was a terrific gunfight.

Such was the speed of events that it is hard to describe what happened. Screams and shouts, flashes of rifle fire and the staccato thump of machine guns broke the morbid silence of no-man's-land. My rifle jammed and for a horrific moment I thought I was to be a feeble bystander. Thankfully, I remembered I still had two Mills bombs and lobbed them in quick succession in the general direction of the firing. They burst with dull thuds and must have had some effect, as the second one was met with a horrendous cry – a sound I shall never forget. The enemy patrol continued to fire, but the crack of their rifles became more distant. For a minute or two, the lads continued to shoot into the pitch-darkness and then Brierly ordered us to stop. After a while, all sound of gunfire petered out and, having called out a headcount, we withdrew with the disturbing sound of the wounded German slowly fading. I was perspiring freely, I can tell you.

On returning, exhilaration soon turned to just terrible thirst. I am famishing for a drink and none of us has any water. We've only had about a quarter of a pint per man today. Most of the men are desperately parched. I'm not so bad, as I have some chewing gum, which keeps my lips moist. It really is a crime that frontline troops cannot be provided with enough water. The stuff that comes from the 2-gallon tins tastes more like petrol than water, but tonight I would pay most handsomely for a glass of it.

Tuesday 25th September 1917

Usual frontline morning routine. The orderly sergeant (me this morning – worse luck) goes around the troops waking the lads up an hour before dawn and gives them the order to stand to. Amid much swearing, the men, half asleep, unwashed, shivering and hungry, crouch on the firing step with bayonets fixed. It's a necessary routine, as Fritz regularly attacks at this time, but the men hate it. After an hour they all stand down, with the exception of the duty sentries, and commence with a much-needed brew.

It's been pretty lively today. A sniper annoys us. Edgar is in a state of shock, having had one shot whistle past his head. 'For God's sake, keep your head low, Evans,' he hissed as I left his dugout. A further worry is that Fritz planes have flown low all day and must have spotted our possies. Consequently the Huns are putting up an enfilade fire from a whizz-bang battery. Poor Freddy Meadows, an original 13th, has gone south with one of our own shells – shrapnel fell short – he was a fine chap. Oh, that we could get some water: plenty of rations but no water. We are all parched.

We are reservists for tomorrow's hopover. Every man has been issued with 220 rounds and two rifle grenades for emergencies. A message has been passed along dealing with Hun treatment of prisoners, telling us he treats us kindly until he has all the information he wants, then the rough treatment starts. It could be a big job tonight. The 16th Battalion are to advance some 800 yards to the Red Line, where they are to build strongpoints. Meanwhile the 15th will advance through them a further 400 yards to the Blue Line. Our task is to act as back-up and to dig a trench linking our present front line to the Red Line. Complicated? I hope not. Must rest now. I am worn out, sleepy and, although I hate admitting it, this constant shelling is making me windy.

Wednesday 26th September 1917

The stunt is over and we are well dug in 1600 yards ahead. The battalions stuck to their jobs well. Zero time was 5.50 am. I was asleep when it began and it was misty and fairly dark. The barrage played on zero for three minutes and then lifted, advancing at a rate of 100 yards in four minutes and 100 yards in six minutes between the first and second objectives. I've never heard such a continuous roar. The noise of bursting shrapnel and high explosives was terrific and the ground shook with every explosion.

A couple of men were killed at the starting point, but most of the men successfully advanced in artillery formation and well under control. Fritz sent up no flares! Most remarkable! As a consequence, the return barrage was minimal. When it grew light enough our lads began digging a communication sap to the new position. Prisoners soon began arriving, some shell-shocked or wounded, others happy and well looking.

While most of the battalion was working like mad with picks and shovels, my party followed up the advance at about 7 am to help reinforce our attacking forces. We made four trips, taking 47 000 rounds altogether. Prior to going forward, rum was issued to all and I admit to feeling somewhat reckless after my ration. On one occasion, a shell lifted me clear off the ground, but I got only scratches for my pains and felt a bit windy. I brought back prisoners on two trips and we utilised them as stretcher-bearers. It's great sport, driving them on at revolver point. I didn't get a souvenir beyond two coat buttons. Other guys got watches before me. What a fool I am. Paddy Nolan has also somehow managed to souvenir a good deal of German stuff. Typical Paddy! He had a grin the size of the Salient this evening on showing me three Hun revolvers.

It was a fine sight seeing our boys working so tirelessly to build a line nearly 1000 yards long under such heavy shell and machine-gun fire. The only thing that stopped any of them was if they saw the chance to souvenir a few prisoners. I've just spent some time assisting the stretcher-bearers. There are some awful cases. Our task is made all the more difficult because there are two swamps we have to cross to get them back. I believe the captain made me drunk with the second lot of rum. I know it did me a lot of good. Hanis is pleased with my carrying work. It's been an exhausting day and I feel as mad as a meat axe!

Fritz is indulging in an airfight at present. We are putting it all over him. I am recommending Corporal Sturt for good work. He is brave and energetic and strong. Frightened of nothing. Damn the rain.

Friday 28th September 1917

I am writing in our old possie at Swan Chateau. Got completely lost last night and roamed all over the country, being redirected and misdirected all over the show. Oh, we were fair disgusted but too tired to object. Lieutenant Brierly didn't have a clue and nor did I. Walk, walk, walk until at last we decided to sit down and consider our position. Fortunately, at this moment our adjutant came by on a bicycle looking for C Company. It was a relief to see him and he walked alongside us, cheering us up ever so much. We have had twenty-five killed and ninety-seven wounded, greater than any other battalion and 25 per cent of our total strength.

Saturday 29th September 1917

I am pleased to say I got my watch and purse and whistle today from the 6th Battalion. I am a lucky devil, I know. Also got lots of letters – Dot's twenty-seven and twenty-nine, two from Mother, two Frances, two Harold and one Mrs Wright. Their news is so good and cheering. I am glad Dot got the diary and badges and Mother the photos. Dot says, 'And remember, I am always the same little comrade.' As if I want to forget! Hurrah, I have proved Dot's a flirt, she admits it and I'm jealous, too, but really I cannot blame my own little girl. I wish only that I was able to be home and look after her, my Fat Babe. Oh, I have a souvenir watch for my little comrade, too. I must now write a few letters. I have neglected them to play poker and have lost about 28 francs (£1). Serves me right!

I think Frances's VAD – 'Virgins, Absolutely, Desperate!' is a bit rough on the dear girls too. It's such a fine thing to be able to get such letters just after a decent turn in the line.

Later: I have just come from the dandiest show and have had some excitement. Fritz planes came over and dropped hundreds of bombs all over the place and our searchlights were playing all over the sky. When they found a plane it was great to see it dazzling white with the searchlights all focused upon it and to see its vain endeavours to dodge out of the beams of light. It was dangerous, too, for our descending pieces of shrapnel and machine-gun tracer bullets were falling all over the place and can do some damage if they hit you.

Monday 1st October 1917

A great deal has been made of the Australian advance at Zonnebeke in the paper today. It must have been some stunt, as Tommy and Scots troops had tried and failed three times. Old Fritz's morale vanishes when he knows we are coming. Even the prisoners admit it. Their pillbox defence is of no avail and the concrete dugouts are proving death traps.

Thursday 4th October 1917

Winter has set in and it's deuced cold.

Wrote seventeen letters today. Not bad, eh! Since then, I have been practically cleaned out at poker – done 100 francs altogether. It's bad luck for I was to buy Christmas presents with the money. I should be kicked, anyhow, for gambling. All the sergeants were drinking and with tongues loosened they talked, and now I know my conduct over the past week has earnt the approval, nay the admiration, of all! I am glad as I treasure a decoration for my work much less than I do my men's thoughts. The sergeants have also been jigging me about my diary and it's extremely difficult to write. 'What yarns are you spinning, Eric? … Are you writing about how you leaned against the barrage and lit your cigarette at the explosion?!', etc.

I wonder what Dot is doing tonight!? I have been sitting in a stinking little dugout playing cards by candlelight when I should have been in the bed dreaming of her.

Good news is through about our hopover. I believe our barrage caught Fritz as he came over for a counterattack and we absolutely massacred 900 and took 600 prisoners. The 3rd Division is held up, otherwise we have all objectives.

Saturday 6th October 1917

Received a batch of fourteen letters with Dot's twenty-eight, thirty and thirty-one, and four from home. Such grand news for me, too. I am pleased to know Dot got the diary. I do hope Mother doesn't ask to read it. I wish I hadn't told her that I was sending it to Dot. I hope she doesn't feel hurt.

I attended the court martial this morning at Steenvorde and gave evidence without a hitch. Lance Corporal Beattie was charged with desertion. I suppose this will mean another trouble later on. Poor chap. Later on, I wandered into Steenvorde with CSM Harper, Ted Hall and Private Flodstrom. Found a Tommy canteen, where the boys got pretty well tanked. Getting the CSM home was far from easy. He was drunk and I had to practically carry him the 3 miles to camp. He wanted to fight every chap we met and kicked up a hell of a row with his dancing and singing. Anyway, he's back now and sleeping soundly, thank the Lord. I have tried to get to sleep this afternoon but failed miserably on account of the cold. I think I'll write a few letters home and perhaps, with my mind in a state of contentment, I may have some luck. How I need a few hours to dream of my own little comrade. What a silly lovesick fool I am!

Tuesday 9th October 1917

I have been loafing all day. There was a big hopover this morning – the Kiwis, I believe. Terrible noise.

This water has turned me up – it is abominable and the chlorine makes it almost undrinkable.

Thursday 11th October 1917

I am writing in our old location at Montreal Camp after a pretty long and trying march of 15 miles, via Reninghelst, carrying all our gear. The pace was a cracker but not a man fell out. My feet were just getting tender for we were marching on cobbles most of the way. After the foot inspection – we always have to examine feet after a march – I gave them a good wash in some icy-cold water and felt much better. A shave and a decent tea of stew, bread and jam cheered my morale.

Oh, Walsh has been evacuated with scabies and a slight wound in the head (so he says). The lads say a tin hat fell and cut his forehead!

Friday 12th October 1917

Now in Ypres town centre quartered in dugouts or in portions of the old ruined infantry barracks. The place is in an awful state, not one house remaining whole. The place is full of the horrors of war. It is not hard to imagine the desperate conflicts in the early part of the war, the fight for the canal, which is now broken in and disused, and the hand-to-hand struggles in the streets, where the gallant Canadians suffered so heavily. The celebrated Cloth Hall, a mass of ruins, is within 400 yards of us.

Our billets, when we arrived, were filthy and we have been working really hard today to clean and drain the place.

There's no shelling, but one has to wear tin hats and box respirators at the 'alert' in case of gassing. Most of the platoon, including myself, is suffering from terrible diarrhoea at present.

Saturday 13th October 1917

We have heard bad news of our attack this morning – our division gained all objectives; the NZ troops were held up and lost the barrage but successfully attacked again. However, the Tommies on the flanks failed to leave the trenches! As a result we had to retire with losses. Alas, it's disheartening. Our flanks have let us down, not once or twice, but many times. Think of Bullecourt! Something is radically wrong with the Tommies. Is it leadership or is it the material? I'm not complaining, but we are given a damn lot of work in every hopover and we have earnt the name of 'shock' troops from our enemies.

Ordered some 'tres bien' Christmas cards today. There's a rum issue tonight and the boys are happy. They are all fixed for the night. Tonight we are leaving our comfortable billets in Ypres barracks and moving through the mud into reserve on Westhoek Ridge, near some places called Kit and Kat. It promises to be a dangerous time.

Monday 15th October 1917

I am suffering from the effects of a slight gassing of that deadly mustard gas. Nolan and I found a dent billet and I had little trouble going to sleep A1. But at about 1 am, I was awoken by a curious smell of garlic and mustard.

I stirred Nolan and he agreed it was the dreaded gas. The dull thud of gas shells bursting outside confirmed our fears. We roused all and spent an uncomfortable two hours with our box respirators on. A pain in the pit of my stomach asserted itself and my throat was dry and parched. All morning we have been troubled with his shells and the smell is rotten. I felt queer. Two men killed and about nine men evacuated as a result of these gas shells – blistered all over, blind in nearly all cases, sick, with headache and pains in the chest, throat and stomach. Many others have minor symptoms and I am one. I feel queer still.

Spent this morning on fatigue, digging a cable tunnel in front of Zonnebeke, an awful job, three hours' strenuous work. Constant heavy shelling, too, and we sustained one casualty. There were dead all along our path, both Fritz and our own men, in hundreds, all unburied, with their horrid, drawn faces and shrivelled-up brown hands, just skin on bone, grinning skulls, looking all most horrible. It's cold, so most do not offend one's sense of smell, but from some the stench is awful. Horses and mules are dead in their thousands – dead, dead everywhere. The Fritzes one doesn't mind so much, but to see our own dead unburied makes one think. Earlier today, I had to go through the pockets of one of the poor lads gassed this morning. He was a good-looking chap. I hardly knew him but had seen him around. He'd only just joined up with the battalion. Probably had a girl at home and a doting family. And yet he lay there dead with flies around his eyes. Not moving. At premature and horrible peace with himself. The faces of dead gas victims are always the worst.

I hope tonight we will live in peace without gas. If I get another sniff I'll be evacuated.

Saturday 20th October 1917

Conditions have prevented me from writing for five days. Suffice to say that we are on the front line.

Many of our lads have been evacuated, gassed. The shelling is relentless. I slept under the cellar of an old soda-water factory. I say 'slept' but I didn't for there were about sixty in the place and one couldn't sleep. The gas had me down, too, and I could hardly breathe.

From there, we moved to close support another 1000 yards on, where we have been until last night. We were gassed here and we are all suffering. Was a peculiar gas, irritating nose and throat. We all have the symptoms of heavy colds – pains in eyes, headache, difficulty in breathing and swallowing, sore, red, raw throats and chests, coughing and spitting up a slimy phlegm. Some are much worse off, with acute vomiting, blistered skin, and so on. All of us have a great desire to drink. It's awful and I am anxiously waiting to get out and go sick, but really can't go away now.

We only have two sergeants and about forty men out of 110 and are doing a full company's work. I have had an old German concrete dugout these last two days and so felt pretty safe. Last night, we moved up to this possie, taking over from 46th Battalion.

We have a wide front and not sufficient men for the work given us. We'd be in trouble if the Germans went on the offensive. Apparently, of the 415 men in the battalion who went into Zonnebeke six days ago, only about 300 are still with us.

Sunday 21st October 1917

I am just about alive but feeling terrible. We are to be relieved tonight by the 16th Battalion. Fritz planes have been working all the morning and a bombardment is expected at any time. Lieutenant Brierly seems close to breaking point. He's a good man, but the lads have lost the little confidence they had in him. I like him as a person, but am sorry to say that he has not proved himself a leader of men. I sincerely hope I never have to go into the line with him again. He is continually windy, has no spirit of leadership, inspires no confidence, is ignorant of his job and doesn't understand the boys at all. Harsh, I know, but true, and I am merely echoing the men's opinion.

I can't write much as I'm not up to it. I am ill enough to be evacuated but I have an opportunity perhaps of a star and mustn't lose my chance now. I'll stick to the last.

The 'chats' are causing us all much grief. Have worn this shirt of mine twenty-one days without a change and haven't had a wash for eight! No wonder I am crawling with them.

Monday 22nd October 1917

Little did I think I would ever experience such an awful period. Yesterday evening Fritz caught us just before we changed over – killing Major Hanis, Corporal Sturt and that fine worker Flodstrom in their machine-gun post some hundred yards in front. I was called on to take charge. Fritz is shelling like hell and I haven't run so fast in all my life. Several landed within 10 yards of me, but I got to the blown-out possie, where I saw the three killed lying there, half-buried and a further one badly wounded. The whole scene was devastating and at first I turned away from it. It was all too much.

Maybe I am not so callous, after all!

After regaining my composure I yelled for stretcher-bearers but no-one came. Clearly, I couldn't carry all of them back and so, after comforting and checking the pulse of the wounded man, I quickly went through the dead men, looking for treasured items, letters, watches, etc. to send to their loved ones. It was gruesome work.

Sturt's head was half off and everything was bloody. Major Hanis had been hit all about the breast and heart, with his pocketbook and paybook in pieces, and Flodstrom without a head at all! I vomited at least twice in the process. How sad the scene was. Three fine men who so deserved a more honourable end and whom I had no option but to leave unburied.

The wounded man had lost his left leg from the knee down. Another terrible sight. Occasionally he made a deep cry, but for the most part all he could whimper was the word 'Jesus' over and over again. I lifted him up, but so heavy were his muddied clothes that halfway across I had no option but to have a quick rest. My weakness is undoubtedly the result of gassing.

It was nigh on relief time when I got back to the trench and it wasn't long before the 16th came along to relieve us. By this time the wounded soldiers had been taken away, but I couldn't have provided them with a particularly welcoming sight. My clothes were caked in blood and mud, and I was still panting from my previous exploits. They themselves had had a rough time and already had casualties galore, but took over without a curse of any kind. I then led my boys out among the shells in search of a path that would take us away from the carnage and death surrounding us. Lieutenant Brierly was in a complete daze and quite unable to speak, let alone give the platoon orders, and so it was up to me to get them back. Lost most of the time, sick from the effects of gassing and numb with emotion, we trudged on through the slush for hours before eventually finding a track that led us away from the hell of the front line. We were deadbeat by the time we reached a YMCA joint, but a tin of cocoa perked up spirits somewhat. Rum was later handed out and I confess to having more than my fair share, before collapsing on a bench – half-drunk and hardly able to breathe.

Later: At noon today we moved to railway dugouts where the rest of my company are. It's awfully stuffy and stinking – foul air. I have been vomiting and feel awful. I am really ill.

These dugouts, built by Canadians, are miles in extent and the galleries and cuts run all over the place. I am told this was the drive from which the blowing-up of 'Hill 60' occurred. The whole structure is 40 foot underground, timbered and strutted with iron girders, absolutely proof from any shell, but as I said before, they are unsanitary and stinking. Electric light is laid on, but it went bung while we were here and we only had a few candles. I did nothing all day beyond rush up and down to get fresh air and to nearly stifle myself with coughing or vomiting.

Thoughts of that blown-out dugout continue to haunt me. Alas, poor chaps. Flodstrom was a bonny lad, as was Sturt. Such fine, laughing, jovial chaps! Even Hanis, who I admit I have not always seen eye-to-eye with, was a good man. I am sorry, awfully sorry and feel it terribly! What a way to die.

CHAPTER 8

BLIGHTY

On 23 October 1917 Eric was subjected to a further, much more serious, mustard-gas attack. While he was not blinded as so many victims were, he developed serious, and potentially fatal, respiratory difficulties. The next day Eric was put on an ambulance train and taken to 13th General Hospital in Boulogne, where he was observed. However, after showing no signs of improvement, it was deemed necessary to send him back to England as quickly as possible for further treatment. Three days later, on 29 October, Eric's birthday, he returned to Dover in a cot on board the hospital ship *St Andrew*. From there, a hospital train took him to Shrewsbury in Shropshire, where he was placed in Altingham Park Auxiliary Hospital, about 5 miles out of the town. There were some fifty other patients, many of whom were, like Eric, suffering from the effects of gas inhalation. The hospital was the residence of a millionairess and, unlike many of the places that treated wounded soldiers from the front, had a fine reputation.

Monday 4th February 1918
Well, it's been three months or so since my last diary entry and it feels quite strange starting it after such a long time. A lot to catch up on, but am now feeling sufficiently well to write again.

To say that this has been a difficult time is understating the obvious. I don't remember much about what happened, except that I was sleeping in a billet some miles from the front line when I was woken by the horrible and familiar stench of gas. I put my respirator on, but began vomiting and was forced to take it off at various intervals. When the all-clear was signalled, I continued to be sick and became besieged by bouts of severe coughing fits. It was terrifying. I couldn't get any breath. I really thought I was dying. The lads rushed for the doctor, who said I should be evacuated the next morning. My hair was shaved and I was washed down as the gas lingers anywhere it can. Spent a night in agony. Never have I felt so awful. All I can really remember is the doc telling me I'd be evacuated in the morning, with the words 'Evans, the war's probably over for you, my boy. Back to Blighty.' Yet I remember feeling no emotion. My God, I felt so sick. My condition was such that a feather could have knocked me down.

Since the gassing I have at times thought I wouldn't make it. Breathing difficulties, a racing heart, violent coughing and sneezing, nausea and diarrhoea. The doc says I've had a kind of chemically induced pneumonia. I would never have believed the full horrible nature of gas had I not suffered from the effects of it. That I have managed to pull through is to a large extent the result of the love that has been bestowed on me. Dot's letters have been a godsend. Where would I be without her words of love and affection? What I can be certain of is that my darling comrade has picked me up from an abyss of loneliness and despair. Lying in a hospital ward so far from home and from the people I cherish has tested every resolve. It's been a strange passage in my life and I must be thankful that I am coming through it hopefully a stronger and better person. One certainly views life from a different perspective when it becomes a fight to continue. I do hope that Mum and Dad, and everyone at home, are not worrying. To ease their fears I asked the lovely Nurse Densham to send a cable: 'In Blighty, slightly gassed, doing well, love, Eric.' I would have thought they may have heard already, but I didn't want any exaggerated reports to come back to them. Overall, the hospital has been first class and the treatment is royal, but it's a cold and miserable existence. A far cry from the sun, sand and surf of Sydney. The fire in the ward most evenings does at least provide some warmth and light to the chill and drab surroundings. Daylight hours are so short at the moment.

How I want to leave it, to run away from the constant coughs and splutters around me, the groans, the stench of chloroform, the sterile whitewashed walls, the cold wooden floor, the pitter-patter of nurses' feet, the helplessness of it all. I'm homesick. Christmas was particularly hard, although the hospital did its best to create some festive atmosphere. Decorations were put up and looked first class. Mistletoe hung everywhere and opportunities weren't lacking, but I didn't take advantage of it.

All I wanted was a kiss from my babe. It's an aching feeling that persists. We even had some local carol singers come in to sing to us and tears freely rolled down one or two of the patients' faces as they listened, and no doubt recalled past Christmases with family and friends. What a contrast!

The day itself was a merry occasion, although the English type of celebrating Christmas hardly appeals to me. The nurses, each with a lighted candle, woke us with traditional festive songs. Unfortunately I had had a sleepless night and was too tired to appreciate their efforts. Soon after, the commandant came around and wished us a happy day. There was a certain amount of bewailing the fact that there was no snow. My mate Glenister was particularly upset: 'Bloody hell! You come over from Australia, get a Blighty, and find yourself spending your festivities in a hospital ward in England. You'd think we might have been given a bloody white Christmas.' I remember jealously looking outside and watching some of the lads having some fine sport – dead leaf fights in particular. Any frivolity was, however, tempered by Sister Johnson (of whom more later) having a sense-of-humour failure when it was discovered that a certain amount of leaves had been shoved into Corporal Perry's bed.

I had received a little parcel from Dot a few weeks earlier and did not open it until the day. It was a lovely box of chocolates. Every one I ate I counted a kiss from my best beloved. Indeed, gormandising was the order of the day. I tried to persuade Nurse Densham to allow a few of us in the critical ward to be allowed to come down to the dining room. I succeeded and we were sat down on nicely laid tables with crackers, prize packets and apples. Each man was allocated a place with three presents. Mine were a cigarette case, a shaving (steel) mirror, and a khaki-covered pocket book. The nurses, sisters, children of the house, commandant and a visiting captain waited on us. There was beer! Also turkey and pork sausages, potatoes, turnips, brussels sprouts, with as many returns as necessary, followed by plum pudding containing silver coins. Unfortunately, at the end of this feast I had another serious coughing bout and had to be taken to bed. This meant missing the sisters' and nurses' concert. Nurse Densham was said to be simply marvellous, a real scream, as Clarence, the nervous wreck of an author. Speeches followed and a request was made not to play up. It was unnecessary, as the lads were dead-tired. Dreamt of Dot and home. How I would have loved to have been in their company.

Oh, I forgot. The Australian Red Cross or Comforts Fund, I'm not sure which, sent us all a Christmas parcel. A pipe and tobacco, six packets of Capstan cigarettes, a handkerchief, a matchbox, a packet of chocolate and an Xmas card. Jolly generous.

New Year's Eve I simply remember being as a day when I wanted letters desperately. The nurses must have wanted to hit me as I enquired again and again as to whether any post had arrived. I couldn't help thinking of the time I had last year with my darling. Our dancing, our resolutions and our New Year embrace.

1917 has now been and gone, and despite the way it ended, it's been a happy year. A year when I made a great pal who has helped me through the hard times, moulded me and made me a better chap. My only wish is that my love for my darling girl should remain constant and true. May peace come quickly to this, the war-weary world in 1918 so that we may be freed from great strife and cruelty forever.

I have been looking at my photos. I only wish I were closer than 13 000 miles to those featured in them. It's homesickness, all right, brought about by nothing to do and stagnation. There were no

Australian letters throughout virtually the whole of December and us lads were pretty near desperate by New Year. For some reason the mail was held up, but it did at least mean that January was a great month.

Paddy Nolan writes regularly from the front and updates me on how the boys are faring. Lord only knows how his letters pass the censors because he gives me some excellent information. The battalion left the Ypres sector a day after I got gassed. Just my luck! On being told they were in GHQ Reserve beyond Abbeville, based in a little village called Woincourt, they naturally expected a long rest, especially as the boys felt they had done more than their fair share on the front during the past months.

Hopes of a great Christmas were confirmed when orders read that they would have a long period 'to carry out thorough training'. Turkeys were bought, rooms and crockery ordered and all sorts of preparations were made when suddenly in early December another order came through that they should 'be ready to move at short notice'. A few days later, they were back in the Cambrai sector, where the Germans had broken the British line. Spirits were, by all accounts, very low and hardly improved on seeing a lonely billygoat, the mascot of a Welsh battalion that had been annihilated, wandering disconsolately across the frozen, battered fields. Paddy says it was so freezing that the mules and horses had to have their shoes spiked. So, after all their hopes for a great Christmas, they found themselves on a bleak hill in thin tents.

The band apparently played in the New Year and a few days later they were moved up north again to fill in defences. 'There is a feeling that we are in for a big attack. The top brass are taking our trench preparations even more seriously than normal and we are constantly going into no-man's-land in a bid to capture a few Huns, presumably so that we can interrogate them or find their plans. Huns are being more cautious than ever, though, and we haven't had any luck.' It feels terrible leaving the boys to fight the war while I am lying in a bed feeling useless. The truth is that I don't envy them at all but, as 'Dolly' Durant always says, the battalion becomes family. I often wonder how Lucas is faring. Edgar is apparently gambling away and enjoys his drink a little too much, while Jerry Oswald is 'still mad, although there is method in his madness'. Paddy's been given his star – I am glad and cannot think of anyone more deserving of the honour. I do however have the rotten, gnawing sensation of having missed my opportunity.

Alas, at the end of last month I heard some very bad news. Poor old Alf Hutton is dead. It happened some months ago, I believe. I heard this terrible news on enquiring how he was to a wounded sergeant in the 15th Battalion who got here yesterday. He pulled out a letter from an officer that mentioned Alf being killed at Ypres. What a shock. What will his poor mother think? I know Dot will be devastated, too, for she spoke very fondly of him. I don't look forward to writing her a letter about the tragic news, although I am sure she will have heard by the time it reaches her. I liked him but only met him that one time in Le Havre. I've written to the officer, Lieutenant L.C. Simpson, 15th Btn 5th FA, asking him to provide any details and shall send them on to his poor mother. I feel very much affected over the whole matter.

There is a lot of talk in the wards re the refuted Bible prophecy on the end of the war. I hope so, at any rate. I am dying to get back to my loved ones, although am rather less optimistic than some around me. The peace proposal at the end of last month fell through. The Huns don't seem to know when to give up. Indeed, they are even having air raids over London, and have, by all accounts, wrecked some parts of it.

The war news is generally pretty depressing at the moment. It's extraordinary that so much effort and death has resulted in so little gain. Just before Christmas we heard the news that Australia has turned down the conscription question once more. When the *Anzac Bulletin* published conscription figures, the 'No' majority was a stagger. The language among the boys in the hospital was quite ripe, I can tell you. Glenister was outraged. 'Anyone would think that the country isn't supporting the war. Do they want it to go on interminably?' he said, and I was inclined to agree. It's not exactly morale boosting to think that the folks back home are not fully behind an all-out effort to defeat the Huns. Thank God for the

Americans. At least their commitment might sway the balance our way. That is certainly more than I can say for the Clydeside workers. Their resolution is an eye-opener to me. They are both cowards and traitors. Do they think our four years of fighting is to go by the board for naught!? The curs, to desert us thus when we are in need of the really decisive push. I am very bitterly awakened from my dream of universal support from all classes. Well, well, 'tis war, I suppose, but I am sick of these curs!

Still coughing a lot and running a high temperature, but I now believe that I am fully on the road to recovery. I am glad to restart this diary, although I have virtually forgotten how to write!

Saturday 9th February 1918

I am feeling better and my voice and throat are much better. I have now been moved into what was formerly a beautiful dining room, perhaps 40 feet by 40 feet and 25 feet high – richly decorated, but of course all covered up now. I look out of a sunny window onto lawns and trees. Oh, so pleasant. I am very lucky. They treat us well here and Nurse Densham in particular has been wonderful to me. She has kept me sane with her company. We talk about everything from poetry to gardening. The highlights of my day (excluding letters from my darling comrade) over the past few months have been the talks we freely indulge in. During my darkest moments she consoled and talked to me and I am very much indebted to her. She has a brother over in France and is particularly sympathetic to what we boys have been through. 'He's everything to me. Oh, Eric, if anything should happen I don't know what I would do.' Like me, she's a mad-keen letter writer and writes to him religiously three times a week. 'Tell me what it's like out there. Is it as horrible as some of the soldiers say? Will he be different when he comes back?' Such big questions are, of course, impossible to answer. Somehow she is about the only person I have met apart from, of course, Paddy Nolan, since I arrived on the *Wiltshire* whom I have been able to properly confide in. Nurse Densham sometimes sits at my bedside after dark, always carrying the same old tatty lantern, and we just talk. She comes from a place in Wales called Llandudno and wants to set up a restaurant there. Tells me it's a beautiful town and has asked me to visit it sometime.

I have written to Captain Browning asking for a recommendation for the Officer Training Corps in Oxford, seeing that today I learnt that I have been marked B1A3 – only one step from draft. It seems the senior medical officer had played the dirty on me, as I really don't think it is a fair classification. If I go to Oxford I won't mind so much, though, as I'll be improving my position and having a dinkum good time.

The nurses are calling me 'the baby sergeant'! I wonder why. I've been told to put my stripes up on my 'blues'. They've put me in charge of all the patients and I am responsible for their order!

Tuesday 12th February 1918

Feel as good as gold today and have been reading. Had my fortune told, which involved a ring and proposal to a dark lady across the water. What ho.

The commandant of this place, also the owner, Mrs van Bergen, is fine to us lads. She gets 2 francs per day ration allowances for each one of us and all the rest comes out of her purse. I am on full diet now.

I'm afraid I am indulging in a very mild flirtation with Nurse Densham now that I am back with the land of the living. I am able to appreciate her loveliness. She's a beaut. Tall, elegant with a smile that makes all us lads melt. The boys all tease me and think she has a soft spot for me. I don't believe so. We are just friends who share much in common and like each other's company. It is certainly not as if I ever hide my feelings for Dot. In fact, we've spent many hours talking about my babe. I hope my darling comrade isn't upset. I don't think I'll be too harshly judged for my actions. I may casually mention I had my ears well boxed by Sister Johnson for distracting her too much from her work and for calling her Alice, when I am only meant to call her 'Nurse'. The sister has something against me. 'You're supposed to be a sergeant and it is about time you acted like one,' she scolded me yesterday. Who cares? Is it such a crime that a man should seek some conversation with a girl his age?

I have sent the diary, part four, and the Fritz watch away by registered post. I enclosed a note to Dot with the sad news about Alf, and took the opportunity to tell her how much I miss her and thanked her for her letters. For the first couple of months here I was really in no fit state to write to her and the few I did manage to get away were short and rather vague for obvious reasons. I often wonder how everything is going at home. I do hope Mother is not worrying.

Thursday 14th February 1918

I have just chanced on some more information about Alf from a 15th Battalion chap, who was actually present when he was killed. Alf had a leaky dugout, so gave orders for a new one to be made. This was done and he shifted his quarters. Some little time later a shell lobbed in the new dugout, killing him instantly. His head and arm were completely blown off. An officer, name unknown, in the dugout at the same time was, I am given to understand, unwounded. To make matters worse, Alf was due to leave that same day for a school of some description. His remains were collected and buried at or near Reninghelst in a cemetery several days later.

Friday 15th February 1918

Nurse Moore came back today from holiday. She's an old maid, well educated, speaks French and German, musical, but with an affected manner which causes the patients to mock and laugh at her. However, she has promised to play the piano for us when she is free. It's dashed good of her and I'll be very thankful, although she will, by all accounts, be rather tiresome to practise with. There's not enough music in this place and I plan to get some concerts going. The place needs cheering up. The nurses are all for it except for Sister Johnson, who warned: 'If it's too loud and boisterous I'll have to stop it, Sergeant. Do you realise this?' Yes, nurse, I do, but I'm only trying to perk up the lads' spirits.

The masseuse here wants taking down a peg or two. She's far too superior and cynical, constantly runs down NCOs and fair makes me annoyed. I especially dislike her treatment of those who are obviously in a bad way. The other day she was abusive to a chap who dropped his tray. She shouted at him and I could see tears running down his cheeks. I've a plan forming to even things up a bit. I won't accept any soldier who has been on the front being treated like that, I can tell you.

A few of the lads are clearly suffering from nervous dispositions. One man in particular shakes convulsively and has a blank expression for much of the day. He is being transferred, I believe, to a psychiatric hospital or something. Another suffers from terrible nightmares and can sometimes be heard down the corridor, screaming. It wakes everyone up. Poor chap. These people are the real victims of war. I am getting better – I only hope they can recover too. It is a terrible sight seeing once laughing and active men reduced to such a state.

Saturday 16th February 1918

Haven't had any letters for over a week. Organised our first singsong after tea and I think the lads quite enjoyed it. It was an effort to get them going, though. My throat and chest are still bad, and my singing was a little croaky.

The days are rather tiring and it's hard to find anything to do. Perhaps this is why I am becoming somewhat mischievous. Glenister and I decided to sneak out and pay a visit to the orchard. It was beautiful to suck in the fresh air, although it began to rain like the devil. Unfortunately we got well trounced by Sister Johnson for going out in slippers and getting soaking wet. To make matters worse, as we were being told off I saw a couple of nurses, one of whom was Alice, looking in through the window and I smiled at them. The sister thought I wasn't taking her talk seriously. I really didn't mean to be rude.

Spent the afternoon with a 16th Battalion chap. Duncan's his name. He's lost both his legs off at the thigh, both arms badly hit and his face smashed. He looks to be in his last stages and he told me he felt awful. 'I wish I were dead,' he said. He's a man of about thirty-four with a family. One of the nurses tells me he is just at the critical stage. 'He may live,' she said, 'but the balance is against him as he has septicaemia.'

War is responsible for some most horrible and cruel things!

Tuesday 19th February 1918

There has been an epidemic of handkerchief pinching going on. All the nurses have suffered, losing as many as two handkerchiefs per day. It's very funny to see the nurses and to hear them accusing everyone. We're constantly up to silly antics in the ward, making apple-pie beds, etc. I came in just in time to find two nurses interfering with my bed. Others were not so fortunate. It's dangerous to leave the room for a second. Morale is high among the lads and they are beginning to lose their shyness and singing better.

The commandant went away to Paris today and the lads assembled and gave her a cheer. We have a lot to thank her for, she's really kind and I am told she invites all colonials to spend furlough here if they wish.

Duncan's in a bad way, poor chap. It's awful to witness his agony. I gave him a shave and talked to him to take his mind off his wounds, but to tell the truth, I was awfully pleased to get away from his painful cries. He's losing the fight. Asked me to look up his wife and tell her how grateful he was for the happy times they had spent together. I told him to cast away such negative thoughts and urged him not to give up – to live for her. But once again he replied: 'Evans, I am not afraid to die. I feel quite ready. My only fear is that I hope Pam does not dwell on what might have been. I hope she begins a new life, has more children and finds happiness.' It was hard to listen to and harder still not to show any emotion. Later, I thought about his words and they made complete sense. It is hard to think of Dot with another man, but should I die, how terribly selfish it would be not to want her to get married and have a family with someone else. I must write to her to tell her. I think about my little comrade all the time and wonder when that news re Alf's death will come to hand. Soon, I hope!

Have just had a really good chat with the nurses and I am now very hoarse. It was an argument regarding Australians and their worth. Since then, we have been having a bit of fun pulling their legs with yarns and tricks. One of the nurses accused me of being married today!

Wednesday 20th February 1918

Had a dream I was in London with Dot during an air raid. Was awakened in the middle of it. I wonder how she is. I want to write tonight but somehow I cannot get the exact mood. I must get some letters soon. I am feeling very much in the blues at present and I'd like some nice, cheery letters from Dot and home.

I'd run amok, only one of the chaps has his parents visiting. We are expecting a convoy of new troops in tonight and so twelve of us have been moved onto the terrace. It's pretty cold, but we've plenty of blankets and I'll sleep well in the open air, I hope.

Rumour has it our battalion makes a raid tonight.

Duncan got his wish today. May he rest in peace. I must write to his wife.

Friday 22nd February 1918

British take Jericho, Palestine.

Hurrah! Some Australian mail! Small, certainly, but a letter from Dot, Mother, Elsie, Ray, Spider, Minnie and Russell. They weren't bad, but I sensed Dot wasn't in the best of spirits. My brief notes and the few cables I have written since the gassing have evidently given her many sleepless nights.

> *Although you say you are fine, I don't believe you. I know you too well for that. Eric, you are always in my thoughts and I wish I could do more to help you. It's a helpless feeling. Only the other day a neighbour, Mrs Thompson — I think you met her that time I played in the pantomime — received a letter that her son had died of wounds. There are too many stories like that being told and it's hard to listen to them. I'm longing to see you.*

I must write a long letter to confirm that I really am on the mend. I feel guilty that she has been worrying so. Evidently a number of my early letters from here didn't get back. I, too, have not received a number of hers. Damn this war.

The convoy was all colonial troops, mostly gas, and one chap is in a shocking state. Blind and coughing up blood. He can't even hold down any food. This gas is awful – a devil's weapon!

I am wondering what my love for Dorothy really means to me and how it will all turn out. Happy? I hope so.

Saturday 23rd February 1918

Had a rotten night and didn't get to sleep till 1 am. Thinking of all manner of things – home, war, surfing – everything.

There's a paragraph in the paper today regarding the honours of the 4th Australian Brigade. They are as follows:

VCs	4	MM	411
CB	6	Bar MM	16
CMG	4	MSM	3
DSO	19	Foreign Honours	26
Bar DSO	1	Min Dispatch	164
MC	73	Mentioned in Corps &	
Bar MC	3	Army Orders	88
DCM	70		

Bluegum Daily Mail, 9 February 1918

Many of these must be in the 13th. I think this really is a record to be proud of. It certainly can't be said that we Australians aren't doing our bit. We know that we are not the most disciplined out of the line, but we've got battle discipline. There is a spirit that is second to none.

I recall an incident that had occurred before I went over to France. The Huns had hung up their flag in no-man's-land against their own wire. A couple of the boys in the battalion took exception to this and viewed it as a challenge to capture it. Slowly they crept towards the German positions, but were spotted and subjected to a hail of bullets. After a brief wait they continued, creeping further and further on, despite the attentions of the enemy.

Then with a quick dash, one of them grabbed the flag.

Unfortunately, on their return, some Lewis-gunners of the 29th Battalion mistook these silhouettes rushing towards them as the enemy. Their luck had run out and they were shot. One was killed; the other had his left leg shot to pieces. On dragging himself to the trench, he was met by the colonel and proudly declared: 'I've got the flag, sir. But I'd rather have my leg.' That is Australian spirit.

Have been a bit upset and desperate for something to do. Spent most of the day unsuccessfully hoping for further Australian mail to cheer me up. I am very, very moody.

Monday 25th February 1918

Hurrah, three more letters from home – one from Mother, Dot and Hep, all brimful of news. At present Dot's family is looking after a blind boy and a DCM youth. She has heard of Alf's death and is very cut up about it, but I am glad she didn't cry. She feels guilty about the latter, but she shouldn't – I know how fond she was of Alf. Dot and Mother evidently see each other a lot and, by all accounts, get on famously. I am sure Mother appreciates it.

Well, I have had some mail, and such fine letters, so now I am content. I have written eight letters and I feel perfectly satisfied and will mount on the post office piquet with a glad heart. Somehow, I have been perfectly happy all day, evidently because of the home news, and the day passed oh, so quickly. There are plenty of antics going on in the ward. One leaves it at one's peril. My bed was short-sheeted tonight, but I found it out. They have all failed to catch me, so far. I have been asked to learn and to give some Shakespeare at a concert in a few days. I have a copy of *Macbeth* and have foolishly promised to play the murder scene.

Must write to the Red Cross re Alf's grave.

Nurse Densham brought me some chocolates. I'll be sick for sure now!

Tuesday 26th February 1918

Eating chocolate this morning, I had an accident. My gold crown broke clean away and my mouth has felt awful ever since. I am afraid

I'll have to get the offending tooth out now. Hang the chocolates.

Have also been unfortunate enough to have a row with a Canadian. He's so obstinate and I'm afraid I'll lose my block yet. He took my diary from my bed when I was out of the room and, on returning, threatened to read it. I was outraged and most unamused when no-one tried to help me.

He refuses to apologise, saying it was just a lark. Some joke! He's a great favourite of Sister Johnson's. I detest silly, petty squabbles, and must have a talk with him to straighten the whole thing out.

Received a postcard from Captain Browning, which I am keeping. It is a photo of all the silver cups won by the battalion and is a fine souvenir. The captain writes: 'I passed (and strongly recommended) your formal application for Officer Training to the CO and he has promised to do all he can in the matter. I hope the matter can be satisfactorily arranged.' I am well pleased about it. Had I been still with the battalion I'd have been CSM now. He says the boys are in good form.

Also had a letter from Hep awaiting me, a fine letter, and I was amused at his bewailing having to send best love from Dot to me. 'I reckon it is very rough for an attractive girl to ask a chap to send her love – best love, mark you – to another fellow,' he writes! The letter was dated December 23rd.

Thursday 28th February 1918

A great day today with letters galore – three from Dot, as well as one each from Mother, Elsie, Harold, Father and two from Hep. Dot's letters have taken me all day to digest and I have just finished writing an answer to her and also to Mother. They were spiffing letters and such fine photos. I do like that one of Dot on the fence. I think it's typical. Dot does look quite grown up in the snap of her playing with the kid. It's great that she gets on so well at home. I wonder if her prophecy that Mother and Father will get back together will ever be fulfilled. I rather fancy not, although I should think it most desirable. Poor Mother, I am awfully sorry for her. It must be terribly lonely. She says she'd be *quite* content if I were home, but I somehow doubt that. Her's is a hard, hard time.

I am so glad the second part of the diary had arrived, but I am afraid 'The Maid of the Mountains' score has gone to the bottom. I have missed four of Dot's letters in succession. Like Dot the other day, Father seems very worried over my condition and writes to say the word 'slightly' in my cable didn't carry any weight. More reassurance is evidently needed.

Also received a letter from the OC, Captain Synott, of the 15th Battery, re Alf's death.

To Sgt E.S. Evans

Lt. Simpson has also handed me the letter of 10th instant he received from you asking about Major Hatton. I have some photographs and proofs, which I am very pleased to be able to forward to his people through you.

With regard to his personal effects, I regret to say we were unable to recover anything from the dugout. His kit, I understand, was forwarded to Messieurs Thos Cook, but nothing has come to hand since his return from England, and I am communicating with them in regard to it.

I am sorry to say I was unable to find any trace of the Major's people to write to them, but I believe Colonel Lloyd, who was associated with him for a considerable time, has done so. The grave is in a little cemetery at Dickebusch near Ypres, so you may rest assured that it will always be looked after and easily located in after days.

We all feel that the Division has lost one of its most valuable officers and a man with a future ahead of him. Young as he was, and for all his sacrifice, the memory of his life is that of a splendid soldier and a perfect, gallant gentleman in these crowded days of great events.

And if it is any consolation to his old friends, I feel sure that they will meet many of his admirers among those of us who may some day return to tell the tale.

Yours sincerely
Raymond Synnot Capt.
15/2/18

What a letter! I'll send it, of course, to his mother and hope it will perhaps be some small consolation. The photos mentioned have not yet come to hand.

Friday 1st March 1918

Saw the doctor today and I am surprised at his verdict. I am not looking well enough yet! And I am to stay here some time longer. He sounded my chest and told sister something I didn't catch. Looks like I'll manage to sling here for another few weeks. Hurrah! I'm in no rush. Nurse Densham kindly sent a telegram back home: 'Evans practically recovered, now convalescent.'

This afternoon I took a short walk with Glenister and detailed to him the joys of surfing. The lads from the terrace made a grand raid this evening and managed to pull us all out of bed. Glenister and I got our revenge by locking them in a room for an hour or so. We are putting on some entertainment for when the commandant gets back from Paris. I have been given *Julius Caesar* tonight to learn the Brutus and Cassius quarrel scene. Nurse Moore gets on the lads' nerves frequently, but she's an old spinster and tries to entertain us, so I for one forgive her for her many faults. The music here gets awfully stale, though, at times.

Received Dot's number thirty-two. Sister Johnson has been making some personal remarks re my letters. Evidently her code of honour isn't too strict. I thought Brutus's farewell to Cassius rather appropriate as regards me and Dot: 'If not, farewell; and if we meet again, we shall smile.'

Sunday 3rd March 1918

I have heard the hospital has been asked if any Australians are ready to be shipped back to France. The answer was 'no' and I presume because they want us here to give the concert for Monday.

The commandant came home this morning. We put up flags and lined up and cheered her as she stepped from her motor and mounted the steps. She was pleased and said: 'Thank you so much, boys, for your warm welcome. I hope you have done well while I was away.' She's a fine sport. No false pride or patronising ways. I like her a lot. I am thinking of getting a little paperweight of bronze, a kangaroo with a tail as a paper knife, made for her.

Later: Well, the concert went off 'tres bien', I am glad to say, and I think everyone is satisfied. Even the bed patients were brought to the affair. My humble self gave a bit of 'Gunga Din', acted in a comedy duo – 'Shall Us, Let's'; was Cassius in *Julius Caesar* and sang a song. I smoked a pipe in one of my monologues and feel rather queer. My performances seemed to go down quite well and I got a decent round of applause. Glenister was a scream as Charlie Chaplin.

The commandant thanked us and told us it was worth coming from France for. Congratulations showered all round.

It's a job getting the burnt cork and vaseline off my face.

Thursday 7th March 1918

Was given permission to visit Benington War Hospital, as I had heard there were some boys from the battalion there, and I really have to make remarks on what I witnessed. It's an old workhouse and generally the most cheerless hole on earth. The way the poor lads are treated, the stringent rules, and the rotten food is a disgrace to civilisation. How must the poor wretches feel? There's nothing pleasant for them in their Blighty. Is that how a nation thanks its servicemen for their sacrifices? I had heard some awful tales of treatment there before my visit and our men here are continually warned to behave on the penalty of going to Benington – penalty, mark you. I didn't see anyone I knew and was only too glad to get out of the place. I feel outraged. Sister Johnson will regret it if I ever hear her threaten the patients here with the words 'Next time, Benington.'

I received a letter from Captain Browning today. It tells me to get better soon as I will be sent to OTC almost immediately if conscription is carried. Alas, it is not and my 'star' is as distant as ever, for he says that in event of 'no' being returned, there will be no more commissions for a long while. Always my luck!

I think I'll drop a little note to Dot. I feel rather lonely and I'd like to be with her in thoughts.

Friday 8th March 1918

Giddy, black spots before the eyes and a sickening sensation at the pit of the stomach. I lay down and felt better.

This afternoon I went on the river in a punt, got well wet endeavouring to make headway up the stream against a 4-knot current. We tried paddling – Glenister was with me – then I cut a sapling and tried punting until I felt too tired to go further. We drifted back, tied up and went for a walk and a chestnut hunt, getting some beauts and being severely pricked opening the burrs. He's excellent company and my one real mate here. Got gassed at Ypres like me, but his condition is more unstable and he is prone to terrible coughing fits even now. A young chap, nineteen, who was brought up somewhere in the outback on a fruit farm. By all accounts, the war provided him with the perfect opportunity to break away from a life that involved picking pears from morning to dusk: 'I thought I never wanted to see a piece of fruit again in my life. But you know what? This war's got my craving going again!' He's in no rush to go back, though. A fine chap who, although not educated, is excellent company and has a charm that even seems to work on Sister Johnson – sometimes. Always getting up to mischief, but he does it with style.

Nurse Densham still has her little jolly ways with me. She's promised to try and learn *Macbeth* to play the murder scene with me. She is a little worried, though, because she hasn't received a letter from her brother for some time. Told her I'd be a nervous wreck if I worried about not receiving regular letters. I know it's different because they are coming from Australia, but I think it eased her mind.

I've just frustrated an attempt on my bed by discovering holly leaves in my pillow and under the sheets in time, thus saving a rather painful time. Another chap wasn't so lucky and his bounce in and out of bed was ludicrous.

There was a bit of excitement tonight. One of the Canadians, a McCann, the chap I had a tiff with, went out on pass to Shrewsbury on a nurse's bicycle and got drunk. He was found at the foot of what is known as 'the Column', dead drunk, and we were telephoned to fetch him. Now 'Canada' is Sister Johnson's great favourite, even beyond Glenister, so she came and asked two others and me to go in the motor, fetch him home, and say nothing. We went and I enjoyed a really decent spin. Poor 'Canada' was found crying and babbling like a child. 'Don't send me back,' he kept saying. I think he'd got it in his mind that he was about to go to the front or something. There was little chance of that as he'd fallen from the bicycle and broken his ankle. We got him home and put him to bed, but it was cruel to hear him in his half-drunken state, crying. He's sobered up fairly quickly and is now just whimpering: 'Oh, the shame of it! The shame of it!' I feel sorry for him. He's a decent enough chap. Of course, he'll be sent away from here after that. Such is the way with drink!

Saturday 9th March 1918

Got Dot's number forty-one this morning. The photos in her letter are passable, but the dress doesn't suit either Dot or Elsie. I appreciate the heart setting and the love message to me from Dot. The girls must be camera-mad. Dot tells of Granny's death, poor bid, as well as Anne Fitzgerald's disengagement. Her catty remark, 'Now's your chance, Eric', was a little uncalled for, I feel. I have never understood why my darling comrade felt threatened by Anne and me. Silly girl! There was also a remark about my diary: 'There is one thing that pleased me in your diary, the number of times you thought what Dot was doing and what would please Dot. It was nice to know that in the middle of all your troubles and excitement you think of your little comrade.' Such a nice thought from my little comrade. I am quite glad she liked that, but it's true!

The day has been intensely cold and I have hardly stuck my nose out of doors, except to take a walk with a friend, Glenister, to Benington and to our discredit, we ate, between us, 1/- worth of cakes before coming back! Our quartermistress and chauffeur, Miss Tait, had a bit of an accident, hurt her leg and now she is quite bad and it necessitates taking a holiday for a month. The new chauffeur, Miss Holloway, of our Irish VAD's sisters, has arrived in her place. She's a sporty individual and awfully nice, but driving cars! Oh my! She took us up to the garage in the car, let her clutch in with gear in second, nearly jerked us out, failed to change quick enough into third, jerked along like a mad thing, then accelerated to cause the car to jump and generally give us a thrill. At one point we came within inches of running into a stone pillar, but we had no accidents. I wouldn't like to witness her joyriding!

We have lately been having a bout of larks, too, especially with the beds, short-sheeting, sewing up pyjamas, letting beds down, pillow fights, etc. It's rather exciting and some amusement for the boys. It makes a fearful mess of the sheets, etc. though, and the sister says it's got to stop. I am afraid I've offended friend Nurse Densham somewhat with my funny stories. She's quite cool with me now. Alas, poor me!

Sunday 10th March 1918

Had a new batch of gas cases arrive today. They were in an awful state. Ten of them were blinded – mustard gas. Alice and the other nurses spent the whole day tending to them. It was terrible to see these young men in such pain. Their blank, sometimes terrified, expressions said it all. A few let out the odd cry and plea for more attention but most said nothing. Life seemed to have been sapped out of them. Their only concern now was to rid themselves of the constant stinging, yet no amounts of morphia seemed to help them and the nurses just had to go up and down the ward bathing their eyes in bicarbonate of soda and inserting cocaine under their eyelids. By all accounts, they are leaving tomorrow for a more specialist place.

I don't feel at all like going to the church service, for I don't think much of the parson or his discourses, in spite of the fact I've been told by Sister Johnson I ought to go, if only to please the commandant. Since when has religion become a matter of complimenting a special lady? Ugh! What a horrid perception of religion. I don't want to become a hypocrite.

Tuesday 12th March 1918

A terrible day. No sooner had the concert got under way than Glenister whispered in my ear that Nurse Densham had received a telegram and was obviously upset. I broke away from the singing and went over to the hall, where poor Alice was sitting on a chair in obvious distress. A few nurses were attempting to console her and I was about to be ushered away by one of them when she looked up at me and said, 'Oh Eric, it's happened.' Tears welled in my eyes. I knew how much the dear girl had loved him. It was an awful moment. With the nurses there I felt inhibited to say anything, when she just got up from her chair and hugged me, sobbing uncontrollably. I'm so sorry for her, poor kid.

Wednesday 13th March 1918

Nurse Densham has gone back to Wales to stay with her parents. I miss her and feel more affected by the news than I ever thought possible. I am also feeling terribly homesick.

It is rumoured that the 13th Battalion has been badly cut up in a Fritz attack. They were caught changing over, I believe, and succeeded in beating Fritz back. I hear Captain Browning is seriously wounded with three bullets in his kidneys. He's a fine man and I hope he recovers. It's a funny thing, how these sorts of rumours travel, and this one is probably correct. I suppose I should consider myself lucky in not being there, but still – there were decorations and promotion to be got. I covet both of them.

The blind cases left today.

Monday 18th March 1918

Two lads – an Australian and a Tommy – failed to return from Shrewsbury last night and have still not come back. Sister Johnson is very concerned. They'll turn up all right. They have either had an accident, are drunk, or have met some loose-moralled women and are putting in the night. We'll probably lose all our chances of privileges here, though. Someone has just set off in the car to look for them.

I have heard a little more about the fate of Captain Browning and some of the other 13th boys. Most of the battalion had departed from the front when the German attack began. Browning and about six others, who were in an outpost, had not left yet, and were soon surrounded by about 100 Germans. Still, he did not surrender, and some tremendous fighting occurred. On his left flank a Lewis-gunner from another regiment saw this wave of Germans attacking and fired on them, killing a good deal of the enemy, who began to retreat. Sadly, the Lewis gun also killed some of our number and severely wounded Captain Browning.

Later: Well, our absentees have turned up. It appears the Australian, who is wounded in the head, got drunk and became unmanageable, so the Tommy stood by him until a policeman escorted them to the nearest hospital, where they slept the night. They are in disgrace. Of course, they'll be sent out of here. The silly fools.

Tuesday 19th March 1918

The two disgraced soldiers left us today. I was sorry to see them both go to Benington.

Sister Johnson has just done a very mean thing. I made an innocent remark about the inability of certain persons to keep their mouths shut. She construed it to refer to her and said: 'That's a dirty remark meant for me. Shame on you that you're not game enough to say it to me direct, even though you are an NCO.' That's not true, Sister, but it is indeed a mean thing for you to say such a statement before these men and then to hide behind your sex. I was rather wild. She then proceeded to withhold one of my letters – evidently thinking this was a source of amusement. I made it clear she had exceeded the bounds of good manners and that I detested anyone fooling with private correspondence. Everyone in the ward smiled a broad smile and she looked taken aback. I am sick of her attempted playfulness and, as she is no longer in charge, I don't have to be so careful. She later today boxed my ears for saying 'devil' in her presence. She is a silly ass. It was too funny for words. I'm having my revenge now, all right.

Fed up, stagnant, depressed, call it what you will. Sick in the stomach, too, no energy, tired, etc. I can't think what is the matter. I fancy music but one chap is recovering from chloroform. The reek has made me feel pretty ill.

Thursday 21st March 1918

Nurse Densham is back. Very quiet and evidently still in shock, poor girl. Trying desperately hard to cope and even signified she was still willing to go on with *Macbeth*. I won't put it in the next concert, though – just in case.

There's another big operation going on at present. The smell of chloroform is very strong indeed.

Saturday 23rd March 1918

Glenister and I were forced to walk into Shrewsbury. Rotten luck, as the only car to pass us was being driven by a fierce aristocratic man who made no reply to our request for a lift. The mean beast. A common soldier couldn't possibly ride next to him, I suppose.

Nurse Densham gave me a book of views from Llandudno yesterday, so I went and bought a copy of 'Indian Love Lyrics' as a present to her. I also bought some hair dye for the concert. I was politely asked if I wanted it for myself. How embarrassing!

Went to the theatre and saw *A Tale of Two Cities* and it wasn't too bad for a change. The place was crowded, but we got chairs in the aisle.

We then went to our usual place and were informed by our waitress that a lady sitting at another table would pay our bill, but we were not to thank her as she didn't wish her husband to know! It was dashed generous but rather embarrassing. I began wondering about my appearance. Do I happen to look like a destitute, friendless, poor soldier? It rather spoilt our meal, for I didn't like to order what I wanted and I couldn't look over at the lady for fear of blushing.

Feeling somewhat uncomfortable, we hurried over the meal and were just about to leave when the immaculately attired woman came over. 'I do hope that you don't think it presumptuous of me to pay, but you remind me oh so much of my boy.' She looked at me. 'Your smile is exactly the same and your hair. I loved him so much and so didn't want him to join the war. He didn't have to. He was a seventeen-year-old who was still at school.' We daren't ask her what happened when she said: 'I got a telegram "Missing, presumed dead" but I never believed it. That was seven months ago.' At this point she began crying. 'I'm sorry, so sorry. It's the last thing you wanted to hear but sometimes I just can't help it.' There was little that we could say. No words could come out. All I could muster was our gratitude at her generosity. It was an awful scene and I was glad to get out. She meant well, poor soul, and all I could feel was immense sorrow for this mother who had lost her one real treasure. I thought about Mother at home and for a moment had a terrible sense of guilt. How could I so selfishly join a war with the idea that I was embarking on an adventure while leaving her at home with little to ponder apart from my welfare. Was I right to join? I have had few doubts, but this one incident made me question whether any war is worthy of a parent's grief.

Oh yes, the kangaroo arrived today. It's splendid and I hope the commandant likes it.

Monday 25th March 1918

A colonel was here, looking over the hospital and commenting thereon. He's a decent old bird and said 'Good day' to me. He made a point of speaking to every single one of us. 'The sister tells me you got a lungful of gas.' I confirmed this rather vague prognosis. 'Bloody awful stuff,' he went on. 'Well, I hope you know that we are proud of the job you Australians are doing over there. The spirit you boys have shown is an example to us all. Speedy recovery, old boy.'

Have just been arguing on the rival merits of steak and onions vs cakes for a person's tea. Seems to me cakes are in the majority for favour here. Can't understand some people. My word, we must be bored! Nurse Densham is much more like her old self now and entered into the discussion.

The doctor has marked me out to convalescent camp today. I am both glad and sorry. Glad to be moving to fresh fields and sorry to leave such a nice place. I will miss Nurse Densham, but no doubt we'll write.

One Booker, an unprincipled, evil-tempered soldier, who alleges to have lost his purse with 25/-, has spoilt the evening. Very few believe it has been lost. I think it's a put-up game to try to wheedle money from the commandant.

Wednesday 27th March 1918

Today we are expecting a general here and are all madly sprucing
the place up for him – washing floors, blanching our coats, getting
clean collars and doing hair. Why all this fuss for a mere general?

Had a letter from the Red Cross concerning Alf's death:

Australian Red Cross
36 Grosvenor Place
London SW1

21/3/18

Dear Sir

We beg to inform you that we have received an unofficial report,
respecting Major A.J. Hatton, 5th Brigade, AFA, and trust it will be
of some assistance to you.

No. 3484 Gnr L. Westcott of the same battery reports that he saw
him killed by a shell in the battery position at Tokio, in the front of
Anzac Ridge at 7.10 on November 9th, 1917. He was taken back to
the wagon lines to be buried, but General Westcott can give no par-
ticulars of burial.

We are continuing enquiries and will advise you of any further
information we may receive.

Yours faithfully

Sgt Vera Deakin
Secretary

I will send Alf's photo of his family, three Australian postcards and
some fine proofs of photos he had taken on arriving in England
back to his mother, along with a letter. The other photos I won't
send until there's no risk from submarines. I think that will be best.

Booker went away today. Good job, I say.

Later: At last I have discovered about the truth about the general; it was a hoax to make us all clean up. It succeeded admirably and the nurses are enjoying the fact that they've managed to get one over on us.

Monday 1st April 1918

April Fools' Day.

I notice in orders the GOC has asked all ranks to hurry back to France and to forego leave! Things are serious, evidently. I don't like discussing the war but really things are most distressing to say the least of it all. It's rather a remarkable order, I think; perhaps the like of it has never before been heard of. Certainly I know all A class personnel and staff are drafted always and B2 C class are taking their place. There must be at least 100 000 Australians in England at present.

One of the 13th boys, Keen Late, a corporal in the 24th, brought another of the lads, Maitland, down to see me and we had a really fine chat. I learn Gordon Winn has been evacuated ill. Perhaps I shall see him in a day or two. It was quite nice to hear of the lads. Poor Kates is dead, also many more of the boys.

Things are changing here. Drastic changes, I'm afraid. Sister Johnson is clearing us all out and evidently intends to make the place more military and disciplined when we are gone.

Glenister is a scream. He is now blamed for all practical jokes here and is fetched out of bed as many as four times a night by irate recipients of some form of practical jokes, short sheets, holly leaves, sewn pyjamas, etc. So far I haven't been blamed for any, though I've had a hand in a few. We planned a raid tonight on the upstairs mob, but think they have rumbled it.

I have been told my heart is affected bad enough to warrant discharge. I wouldn't let my mother know for the world. Of course it may not be as bad as all that. It would account, no doubt, for my weakness and lack of breath. I hope it isn't true and yet it must be, I am afraid. It's no use worrying, I suppose, but Mother mustn't know till I get home anyhow. Of course I'll let Dorothy know as soon as I have found out the truth of the matter.

CHAPTER 9

ON THE MEND

Wednesday 3rd April 1918

Writing in London on leave!

Pretty sudden! Last night I was just getting to sleep when Nurse Densham came over to my bed, lantern in hand. 'Eric! Eric, wake up!' She was obviously rather flustered and I asked her what was wrong. 'You're leaving tomorrow. I've just heard.' The news was obviously enough to make me fully wide awake. In some ways I should have felt relief, but I had spent the last five months in the hospital and had almost come to regard it as home from home.

We started to talk but, fearing we might wake someone up with our excited whispering, decided to creep out. I got out of bed, put my dressing gown and slippers on, and the two of us tiptoed and out down the stairs. Neither questioned our actions. We just instinctively followed one another. I followed Alice out of one of the back doors and we just talked, and walked around the grounds. There seemed so much to say and yet the news had come with such a shock that it was difficult to know where to begin. She'd been so wonderful to me in what were undoubtedly very troubled times and I think I had in some ways provided her with the support she'd needed after the news of her brother. The bond between us was real and yet we both realised that for as long as I remained in the hospital we had taken it for granted. I had so needed a friend and she had been that person. On we strolled, until the first signs of dawn began to appear. I never once forgot about my darling comrade but felt an overwhelming longing to embrace the beautiful girl in front of me who had done so much to keep me from sliding into the depths of despair. 'You'd better go inside,' she said. I could see she was struggling to hold back tears and I admit I wasn't finding it easy, either.

'You're right. God knows what would happen if Sister Johnson saw us out here.' We laughed and at that point kissed. It felt right and while I know that my darling girl might be scornful of such actions, I also know that she would understand it.

Left hospital at 10 am and arrived in London at 4 pm or thereabouts. Went to Horseferry Road, where I was asked by the doctor if I felt well enough for leave. Said yes and here I am with £20 in my pocket and dead tired. I'll go out and see Frances Wood tomorrow, I think. She'll be awfully surprised. Maybe I was a fool to take leave at once, but there you are. My leave commences tonight at midnight and expires 11 pm Wednesday next week. I'm exhausted. I'll put my money and my gear away, and go to bed to sleep soundly, I hope.

Thursday 4th April 1918

Well, today I have obtained respectable diggings at the Charing Cross Hotel, being too tired last night to go further than the nearest soldiers' hostel. It's a decent hotel and I created quite a stir when I marched in among a crowd of officers carrying a muddy white kit bag over my shoulder, asking for a room. The girl eyed me and asked, 'Any luggage?' I lifted up the dirty kit bag and said 'Only this.' She smiled and gave me a form to fill in, all particulars about myself, which I thought pretty rough, and I was given room 281. A decent little room, nicely furnished, with phone, etc. The food restrictions don't allow a poor soldier to have a meal of greater value than 3/6! Here am I, with £20 to spend and I am not allowed to do as I like.

The following appeared today:

Australian Corps
B.E.F. France
26 March 1918

Boys,
The time has now come when we must take the strain. I think I need
hardly say more. Everyone fully realises what this means and I know
that I can confidently appeal to every single individual in the A.I.F
to realise that it is up to him personally to take the strain for the sake
of his country and everything he holds dear.

Remember that personal determination to attain victory at what-
ever self-sacrifice, by every individual, is what counts, and it may well
be that this spirit on the part of even a few men may be the deciding
factor of the great battle in which we are now engaged.

Remember what they are thinking of us in Australia now, and
remember the lasting traditions which the force has made for itself.

R.W. Birdwood
KCB, KCSI, KCMG, CIE, DSO, ADC

This is just a little of 'Birdy's' flattery, but it's interesting and has
some bearing on the present offensive.

Friday 5th April 1918

It's cold and snowing some. I went to Chu Chin Chow last night.
Very good, but I was alone. Oh for Dot! Today I arose at 11 am or
thereabouts feeling unwell. Had nothing to eat. Strolled down Pall
Mall to Buckingham Palace and saw the King's Stables. Met an
Irish officer of the Dublin Fusiliers, late an NCO in the Irish
Guards. An awfully nice fellow. He gave me a Scots Guard green
shoulder badge and a button of the same regiment. I'll have to
send these to Dorothy.

We went on to Trafalgar Square and, while listening to a boys'
band, the Queen Mother passed by in a car! Though fairly old, she
is still quite nice looking. In the crowd I met a Canadian girl, but
I didn't like her much so I just bunked after talking to her for a

few minutes. I may be doing her an injustice, but I fear she was loose moralled.

I had an overwhelming desire to smoke a pipe, so I got my Red Cross issue and some 'baccie and lit up. Turned into a phrenologist's, where for the sum of 2/6 I was told my characteristics, etc. and also a lot of rubbish. It's amusing and pretty correct. I'll send Dot a copy and wonder if she'll recognise me. Some of it is wrong, much right. It may be worth remembering and will certainly amuse Dot.

Came over all queer in the afternoon and could hardly walk. Oh, so sick.

Tuesday 9th April 1918

Still suffering from a terrible headache. Sunday was our anniversary: two years ago since I first met my darling girl. I seem to have known her forever and yet in some ways it seems like only yesterday. But what a lonely way to celebrate. Sick in a hotel room on the other side of the world.

Determined not to mope around feeling like a sick prawn for another day, I rang up Frances yesterday morning and we had lunch together. I wasn't really feeling in the mood to eat, however, but I did want company badly and it quite bucked me up. I was vastly amused with the talk of one of the 'aristocracy' at the next table. He was an 'eyeglass' gentleman and was most amusing. He related a story of some 'awfully jolly' Australian officers who went into shrieks of laughter over his eyeglass.

Took Frances to *Arlette* at the Shaftesbury Theatre. It was a great comedy and very enjoyable. We had a bit of a tiff going home, though. She tried to lecture me on the train, but I wasn't having any of it. Frances went on to say a chap had told her she was much like the Australian type of girl. I said that it was a compliment entirely undeserved. Of course she was offended although I was only teasing, and wouldn't take my arm. This rather amused me. She then said I was obstinate when I wouldn't take hers! The other people in the carriage were much amused and so was I.

On getting home we sat and talked seriously till about 4 am. She had a bottle of whisky, which she had won in a Red Cross raffle, and for some unknown reason we began drinking it. Thinking about it, that might be why I still have my headache! It was foul stuff but certainly had the effect of making us talk on all matters. She told me of herself and her doings, family troubles, etc., and I told her how homesick I was. She's an understanding wench, and sympathetic. She agreed I was old before my time and the war was responsible for a lot of unhappiness. Said I was difficult to know and understand, but said she liked me a lot. Alice and my darling comrade have been such wonderful confidantes but it was great to unburden my mind on such subjects. I know Dot would understand.

Debated this afternoon whether to go to a theatre tonight or go back to the hotel and sleep. Decided to walk up and down Piccadilly, with all sorts of street girls giving the glad eye on the kerb, and quite a nice girl spoke to me. I learnt she was waiting for a girlfriend who was late. Asked her to dine with me. She refused, but I pressed and she reluctantly agreed. We went to Lyons where there was a decent crowd and music, etc. She was a nice, quiet girl. Rather shy and frightened, too. A little ill at ease at the start, but she became quite friendly. We went to a revue, *Any Old Thing*, together. I didn't like it much. Tried to get a taxi after the show and failed, so saw her home in the wet. She kissed me and thanked me. I wanted to kiss her, too, but I remembered Dot and didn't — only squeezed her hand and left her.

Wednesday 10th April 1918

A simply ripping day, quite an Australian sunny day, I mean. I think I have been very fortunate in having such beautiful days for my leave. I rose early and wandered over to the Serpentine, where I saw a WAAC looking lonely and rather nice, so I spoke to her. Her name was Yolande and she allowed me to take her for a row on the lake and I had a good time. We gave a slum kiddie a row for a time. He told us the school had been granted a holiday as one of the boys had won a medal. He was quite proud of the fact. She was a girl on the recruiting staff and not one of the type usually reckoned on as a WAAC. A country girl, rather nice to speak to, but no features deserving of being termed striking. She didn't smoke or drink. Her boy was killed in the war and she is distinctly honourable. I have promised to write to her, but of course there's nothing doing here. I love Dot and Dot only. Really when I begin to think of what I've done, I am not playing the game with my little comrade.

We went on to the wonderful Grafton Galleries to see the coloured war photos. It must be seen to be believed. There were some splendid examples and so realistic. I'm sending the catalogue to Dot. Seeing these pictures brings war to the door, all the honours and the humours of war are there, and the Coldstream Guards string band gives a musical program.

Checked to see if my extension was through. Alas! It was turned down. I was awfully disappointed, but I gathered up my gear, taxied with the WAAC to her hostel and thence to Waterloo Station to catch the 9.50 pm train. We had an embrace. But there, what's a kiss or a hug?! Before she cherishes any hopes I must write and tell her of my 'pal'. I wonder if Dot will mind me being so free. I hope not.

Thursday 11th April 1918

I am writing in the sergeants' mess at No. 11 Camp Hurcott, and it's a nice place as far as camps go. Could hardly believe my eyes on meeting Sergeant Walsh at the station. Still the old talk and boast. He carried my bag the 2 miles. He's been over here for about a month now, suffering from slight gassing. There are quite a number of 13th here; they are all being gathered in, our gassed cases chiefly. I asked how Paddy Nolan was. Walsh says he was all right when he left. To use his words, 'Paddy is as game as a piss ant.' A rather prevalent expression in the army, as mad as it seems. He went on to inform me of a terrible thing that happened while the battalion was at Neuve Eglise. Twelve of the strongest men had been picked to represent the 13th in the brigade tug-of-war championships and were doing some practice pulling when some 'rubber-heels' screeched over. One burst some 40 yards away from them, but was a grass-cutter and hurled its contents spitefully along the surface. When some of the boys rushed into the field they expected to find a casualty or two, but to their horror they discovered the whole team had been wiped out. Seven dead and the rest frightfully wounded.

Tuesday 16th April 1918

A telegram from the battalion today enquired urgently whether I was sick or fit for general service. Alas, the doc says I am not yet fit for general service and so I am afraid I've lost another opportunity. It is certainly hard luck. Still B1A2. My heart was very jumpy during the examination and the doctor says I am to report to him if any duty I am put on is too much for me. I won't act the martyr. Since then I have been mooching around like a sick prawn and I feel pretty fed up.

Oh, I wish I had Dot here to keep me company. I wonder how she is and what she is doing. Still no mail. I am badly in need of some. It is so disheartening, really.

This evening we had an organised debate in the mess on such subjects as 'Why did you enlist?', 'Should the bottom of the English Channel be tar-paved?', 'The venereal situation' and 'How will the shipping affect Australia after the war?' All were quite widely discussed. I spoke on 'Should the rum issue be abolished in the trenches?' and also on most of the other subjects. 'Why did you enlist?' was a favourite question and 'the venereal situation' provoked a great deal of argument. I spoke for fifteen minutes on both that and the shipping question. We are singularly fortunate in having a gentlemanly set of sergeants.

Friday 19th April 1918

As my 'no duty' pass was up, I went on parade today and was put in charge of the gardening fatigue. All the ground around the camp is cultivated and my men were digging in preparation for planting. It was an easy job, although it was a job to keep the men on the task. They were continually wanting to go to the latrine and forgetting to return. In the end I hit on a plan which made every man leave his hat behind, thus compelling him to come back.

Have written for the score of *Arlette* for Dot's birthday. I hope she likes it. Have been unsuccessfully roaming around the whole of No. 7 camp looking for any mail for me gone astray. I am feeling especially depressed at the moment. To make matters worse, the doc says the strychnine medicine has to be continued.

Walsh and I have spent much of the evening talking about girls over here and the troops' treatment of them. Walsh is a married man and yet was justifying his and other soldiers' indiscretions: 'Look at it from our perspective. We may love our wives. We may love our kids. But when you've been shot at, shelled at and face the prospect of more of the same, it's not altogether surprising that soldiers allow their morals to wander. I'm not saying it's an excuse, but it is a fact that when he has been away from the opposite sex for a matter of not just months, but years, he comes to Blighty with the sex impulse on top. Our animal feeling must be satisfied.' He made sense in many ways, although I preferred to disagree.

We then went on to talk about the amount of marriages that occur. The lads realise their ultimate end, in 20 per cent of cases, is death, so they pick up with a girl, and like it or not get her into trouble and then he marries her – there's no question of love in most instances. It is just to do the honourable thing by the girl he has imposed upon. Walsh agreed that this was a mistake: 'You've got to love her. I got my wife pregnant before we were married, but I'd known her for years and was sure it was the right thing. My only worry was if it was my kid, as she was no saint. I still wonder. The kid's got red hair and God knows where that came from.' I questioned if he would ever tell her about some of the things he had got up to. 'Tell her? Bloody hell. I value this little face of mine!'

I admit to having had the first feeling in several degrees myself and I hardly wonder at some men giving way before it. Certainly, were it not for the thought that in Australia a comrade is waiting for me and the promise I made to hurt no girl, I should have long 'ere thus fallen. I've had some rough times in Cairo, particularly, and I know how hard it is hard to keep away. Perhaps it's right, but it hurts me to see men who profess to having a girl in Australia, and are in many instances engaged or married, talking of the undesirable subject and picking up and keeping company with any and every girl. Having girlfriends is no sin, but most men of this type have but one object in view and the girl is often only too willing to give.

I am going to bed now – to dream of the mail I will get tomorrow from my little comrade.

Saturday 20th April 1918

At last I am rewarded with letters! I was in charge of the detention escort and after taking the prisoners for a short march, I was sitting in my hut when up came Reg Miles from No. 12 camp to tell me there was a bundle of mail in that camp for me. Three from Dot, three from Mother, two from Raymond, one from Harold, and one from Elsie, as well as several others. A nice haul and I have just finished reading them. Now I must start answering. I am feeling quite lighthearted over the mail. It's great.

Dot's letters were fantastic. In some ways I feel rather sorry for the quarantine boy, because the dearest little girl in the world has spurned him. Oh, Dot, why are you so attractive to men? That dumb waiter stunt of hers was characteristic of my darling, too. How funny – I wonder when she will grow up?

Also had a note from the Red Cross, thus:

We regret to inform you that we have received another unofficial report respecting Major A. T. Hatton 2128.

Gnr J. Madigan, 15FA Harefield Hospital, states:

He saw Major Hatton killed by a shell on the Zonnebeke Ridge. He was in a dugout, when he was killed instantly and his body was taken to Godesvaakde where he was buried. He had a fine funeral and a large cross was erected on his grave, but Gnr Madigan had not seen it himself.

We are continuing enquiries, and will advise you of any information we obtain and trust that it will be of some consolation to know that he was killed instantaneously.

With good wishes to yourself.

Yours faithfully
Vera Deakin
Secretary

A fine letter and I'll post it on to Dot.

Sunday 21st April 1918

Letter from Captain Browning. He is not dead, then, but is severely wounded and in London and he tells me of the appalling list of casualties. Poor Paddy Nolan was killed, and also Curley Harper. Poor Paddy! I feel empty. The enemy had broken through the British defences near Arras and the battalion was ordered to move forward into a small village called Hebuterne in order to halt the Hun advance. 'I have been informed that Lieutenant Nolan gallantly pushed on through the houses, cellars and streets of the village, despite constant enemy attention. He was shot, but, in spite of his painful and dying condition, remained cheerful and provided some valuable information before finally passing away.' The news has affected me very badly and I have been wandering around in a disconsolate daze for the whole day. At least he was given a proper burial: 'The boys got him away and buried him in a quiet cemetery, untouched by shells, just outside the village. They managed to find some plants and a cross was made and engraved. I know how close you were to him and hope this provides you with some consolation.'

Tuesday 23rd April 1918

Still in a state of shock over the news about Paddy. Detention guard this past few days hasn't helped because I've had too much time to reflect on it.

Received a letter from Mrs Valerie Reid, 26 Grosvenor Street, Neutral Bay, asking for further particulars of Lance Corporal Reid's death: 'If it is not too much trouble we would be most grateful if you could tell us a little more about the fate of Thomas.

It is so hard to come to terms with the full enormity of the news. Somehow, further information about his death might just set our minds, if not our hearts, at rest. I hope you understand.' Poor people, they feel it keenly. I wish I could tell them more, but the truth is that it was some eight months ago and I really didn't know him well. I'll get Dot to look up my entry in the diary about the end of July and see if there are any particulars in it. I'm afraid not, though. I'll also write for a photo of the grave, but he's buried in Steenwerck CCS and it's now in German hands.

Oh, I forgot to say that Captain Browning's letter informed me that 'Mad Harry' Murray has been made the commanding officer of the 4th Machine Gun Battalion, having risen from the ranks through sheer merit. He will be a sad loss to the 13th as he is undoubtedly our greatest-ever soldier, with a record for gallantry that no-one in the AIF nor in the rest of the Allied armies can rival.

Friday 26th April 1918
'Our' day.

Anzac celebrations yesterday passed off well and the dinner was a grand success. Most of the women arrived by charabanc. Unfortunately the Wilton ladies were prevented by the police from coming out in the motor cars we had provided and we had to get horse conveyances.

The lady I sat next to at dinner was a Miss Owen, and a very nice girl she was, too. Tall and dark, with freckles and a kind face. I thoroughly enjoyed her company. After dinner we adjourned to the dance hall and had a merry time talking and dancing. Unfortunately, when the canteens closed at 9 o'clock a crowd of drunk soldiers attracted by the music made a nuisance of themselves. Some pushed their way into the hall and we had to use force. A drunken sergeant, I'm sorry to say, used filthy language and abused me profusely. He was forcibly ejected. One chap hit me in the ribs. I returned it with interest square to the jaw and my friend made off. A stone was then thrown, which shattered a window. A dozen or so of us sergeants made a sally and most of the obnoxious cases retired. The remainder were told off and we were not troubled again. The dance went off well, but the floor was fairly crowded. I sat out several dances with my elegant companion and later on accompanied her to the ladies' room down the other end of the camp. She seemed to enjoy it and has promised to see me again. But she's not a patch on my own little comrade. I only wish she'd have been there for me to look after.

Walsh and the others have been chaffing me all day about my attentions to Miss Owen, but they don't understand about my little girl, 'our' day and the many happy memories of days gone by. Dot has been in my thoughts constantly.

Oh yes, there were several cases of prostitution during the progress of the dance, to my knowledge. It's unfortunate, as these things give our camp dances a bad name. I'm only glad that I had a nice companion. There's talk about the matter in the mess at the present moment. Anyway, this is no talk for 'our' day. I'll cut it. I wonder what my little girl is thinking now. I'd like to gather her in my arms and kiss her and talk to her. Our day! The day has brought back memories of a golden age. Let us only hope that next anniversary we shall spend together.

God bless you, Dot! I'll write my little note now.

Saturday 27th April 1918

Got a lovely letter from Dot. Glad to learn the Fritz watch is okay and that she is well. Poor dear, she says she is thoroughly tired of the war. I can sympathise as I have the same complaint.

> Eric darling, when is it all going to end? I am feeling thoroughly war sick. It seems an eternity since you left. I trust you are looking after yourself. Don't rush back to the fighting. You need as long a break as you can get and I can rest at ease with my emotions while you are not involved. I know that sounds selfish but it is how I feel. Day after day I seem to see more casualties around the town. You mean too much to me for anything to happen to you.

Darling Dot, you really are a treasure. I, too, am thoroughly tired of this beastly war and yearn for my return.

I also received this letter today, ref. A.A/7/3339:

> *In reply to your letter of 29th March 1918 in which you make a request for a photograph of the grave of Major Hatton, who is buried in Belgium Battery Corner Military Cemetery in Ypres and whose grave is registered in this office, I regret to have to inform you that at the present time it is not possible to take any photographs in this area.*
>
> *A note, however has been made of your application and should it be possible later on to operate in the area referred to, a photograph will be taken and the desired number of copies forwarded to you as soon as possible thereafter.*
>
> *Signed: H. Willis 2 / Lt*
>
> *War Office*
> *Winchester House*
> *St James Square*
> *London SW1*

Evidently our last information is a bit wrong and I am afraid the Germans are now close to overrunning this area. I hope the photo can be obtained, however. I'll post this letter to Dorothy, but I'm afraid the grave will not be recognisable afterwards.

I am on fire piquet at present – a duty that merely prevents me leaving camp, and in case of fire, I have a squad of thirty men to act as firemen. It's a good job.

Sunday 28th April 1918

The dirty misleading scoundrel! The doctor duped me! I thought I was marked fit, but was marked back at B1A2 instead of being put on draft. I am doomed to stay here for another couple of weeks now. This stagnation is doing me no good.

Went over to see Jack Walsh and we went for a walk. He is cock-sure about his commission. In spite of all the things I have said about him I believe I really like the man. We bumped into Pat

Purcell, in the 34th Battalion, who was evacuated on the 5th of this month. Apparently the Somme position is rotten generally, and the villages are all deserted. The people have all cleared out and the Tommies have been needlessly retiring. The Tommies are all windy and are coming down like flies from their positions. Australians are sent from point to point and are reinforcing anybody. I don't like the news. The Tommies have disgusted me. Many have their tails between their legs, I am told, and the Australians are being worked to death. I hear the 4th Division has been awarded the distinction of 'Royal'. Hurrah! The brigade evidently excelled at Hebuterne, where poor Paddy fell. Newspapers have been full of the way they won the village at the point of bayonet, cleared it and the fields beyond, fortified it and assaulted the enemy in his own trenches no fewer than twelve times. By all accounts the Huns threw everything at our positions and lost vast numbers of men in the process. A single line of diggers defeating an overwhelming German force is something to be proud of. Battalion losses were high though – over a quarter becoming casualties.

Wednesday 1st May 1918

Well the OTC stunt has 'gutsed'. There's an order out today that no more are to be held for some time and all the sergeants from this depot who were undergoing a course have been returned. It's rather unlucky, I am afraid.

I've now been five weeks on B1A2 class; I am wondering what will be my next move. I am really heartily sick of the whole turnout here. I want a flutter and a little bit of excitement.

There's currently a discussion here as to whether our girls are loyal to us or whether they are as inconsistent as us. I have no doubt that my girl is loyal but the general opinion is that they are as unfaithful as the men are. The sergeants seem to have that Epicurean motto, 'Eat, drink and be merry for tomorrow we may die.' I can't even blame them for this monotony, and the war makes one far too devil-may-care. The topic arose because one of our sergeants, a married man, not too well educated, went to Brighton on escort, slept the night with a woman, and he's now got the dreaded VD. He was most perturbed certainly and went to the early treatment hut for precautionary measures. Since then, the AMC sergeant in the hut has given him another wash-out with special preventatives and now that he thinks he is in the clear, he is laughing and joking about it! Just imagine that man and think of his wife. Why, even if such a thing has to be, why is he so joyful? His wife, alas, can have little place in his heart. What a wonderful influence my comrade has over me.

Saturday 4th May 1918

Had a bad spasm last night about 11 pm. Everything sort of seemed to be stopping. I got cold shivers, trembling in the face and knee joints, and a difficulty in breathing. An AMC sergeant, at present in the hut, a very kind-hearted and fine chap, did what he could for me, but I wouldn't have a doctor. The spasm only lasted about half an hour and I was all right afterwards. I went to sleep soon after and felt no more effects. The sergeant promised to keep quiet about the whole thing.

Medically reclassified again today, B1A3 I think. Alas, ordered to be a prisoner escort from Bulford today. Felt terrible. Even an MP on the station remarked on how ill I was looking. Had to wait till 3 pm for my prisoner. There are over 1000 VD cases – all Australians. There is a WAAC encampment here and I think it is an insult to the girls to be put in this district. Bulford and VD are synonymous in the soldiers' vocabulary and of course the girls suffer thereby. They should be moved from here. I got my prisoner, who seemed inoffensive enough, and we had to wait in Salisbury another hour for a connection. Got to Wilton and had to walk some 4 miles in the rain to camp. Arrived back deadbeat.

The following appeared in the *Anzac Bulletin* of April 26th and is worth entering. Speaking of the present offensive:

The Fourth Division holds the reputation throughout the force as the most travelled Australian division about France; it has fought in every field and invariably with the greatest distinction – one of the brigades went in to reinforce a tired British division. This brigade met with heavier fighting than the 3rd Division, especially at Albert and Demancourt on April 5th …

A splendid record for my beloved division! I am really proud of our honours.

Tuesday 7th May 1918

I am fortunate in getting more mail. Dot's number fifty was nice but she doesn't sound on good form. I don't think she should have got so involved in the argument about the war with that Mrs Rogers, although I agree that our politicians should be doing more to try and end the war diplomatically. Too much blood has already been shed. Certainly, there was provocation but – no, I don't like her meddling in such matters and I am glad nothing more serious came of the trouble. But how dare she call Dorothy a 'selfish siren'! Was a dirty low-down hit from an evil-minded woman!

Lately I have been thinking ever so much about home and my little comrade. Her letters are normally so cheery and welcome to me. How I'd like Dot with me now. I am in charge of the bar and after a pretty brisk trade, things have settled, so I'll write her a letter. B Company was paid today, so that accounts for the trade. Have had a couple of drunken sergeants about the mess and kicking up a row, but they've gone out now.

Had a rotten dream last night. I fell into a shell hole and lay beside a wounded German officer. We instantly began fighting but as I had no gun or knife, I was forced to strangle him. It was horrible.

Friday 10th May 1918

I've not enjoyed the past few days of bar work. The place is always full of drunks all day and it's enough to make one swear off drink forever. The dirty, filthy habits of drunks here are enough to drive one mad. Loud-mouthed, boastful, in a fighting mood, letting out secrets and suchlike. They fill up with drink, go outside, put their finger down their throat and bring up the lot, come in and start again. Oh, it's sickening.

Today it's been particularly hard owing to the obstreperous conduct of one Sergeant Wilkins, drunk, who wanted to fight me and invited me out, hurling insults galore at me. He's pretty uncouth when he's full of liquor. I stood it some time and at last got sick and came out, however the other sergeants stopped me and restored peace once more. Today I've been worrying about the matter as such disruption is rotten in the sergeants' mess, especially. However, the same chap is now in the mess again and he's forgotten all about the rumpus, so all is well.

Saturday 11th May 1918

Three letters from Dot! What cheery and fine messages they were, numbers fifty-two, fifty-three and fifty-four, the first being her anniversary number. It's great to have. I can just imagine Dot telling the people that her ambition is to have 'a husband, a home and wee babies'. Just like my chum. Perhaps some people would call that old-fashioned. To me it is perfectly natural and joyful. I am so glad Dot is of that mind. Would be better if all thought like that. Oh, how I do love you for that, dearest. I wish I were in the position to offer you more than I do now Dorothy, my chum!

Met a 13th lad, Manzies, today. Says the battery is being moved back and forth at furious pace and casualties are heavy but it's fighting now rather than just murder with big guns and heavy shells. I hear Munday is in 'the clink' charged with impersonating officers, etc.

Sunday 12th May 1918

Got a letter from the WAAC. She writes rather nicely. I am now going to shut the bar and write a few letters to Australia. I hope Dorothy won't think my carryings-on are proving me untrue to her.

What beautiful weather we are having. Lovely sunny and warm day, so like an Australian spring day. How I'd like to be in the surf! I slept most of the afternoon and I have just written home. In Father's letter I told him I didn't want the boys to enlist, but if they did and I was here, I'd see they didn't go overseas until they were nineteen.

Walsh, who was 'full', showed me the sentimental side of his character in the bar tonight. I never thought he could have such a love for his dead mother. He said, 'Eric lad, look after your mother, you'll miss her when it's too late.'

Wednesday 15th May 1918

Got a letter from Alice today, including a photo of herself in uniform. Not bad, is my remark. She also sent me an article in *Nash's Magazine* on the diary habit. Awfully good and true. It discussed the difficulty of being absolutely truthful in the narrative and also writing it for pleasure. It certainly is a pleasure to me, though I confess to having often been moody enough to vote it not worth the candle.

Friday 17th May 1918

Had a rotten dream last night. It started with me walking down the hill at Manly with my kit bag. I had just returned to Australia and there was no-one at home, so I went to look for Dot. I was sick and tired and leant up against a post. Dot came along, saw me and hesitated. Slowly she approached me but her expression was cold. She wouldn't let me kiss her and seemed annoyed. She left me to go and talk to a crowd of young fellows, and forgot me. I woke up crying! I don't want another like it.

My spirits perked up, though, with the arrival of a simply fine Aussie mail today with three from Dot, three Mother, one from each of the rest of the family and oh, loads of others. It was great to read my comrade's letters – they were full of news. Harold smokes a pipe! Part five of the diary is now reported received. A letter ending 'Yours till hell freezes' came today from Frances. She's a funny girl at times. Also received a note from the WAAC. I'm glad she's sensible enough to understand me.

Anyway, a funny thing happened while we were there. We met these two girls walking along the bank of the canal. Walsh was coming out with his usual banter, when all of a sudden one girl slipped, tottered on the bank for some seconds, clutched the nearest thing to her, which was Walsh, and both overbalanced into 4 feet of swift-running icy-cold water. 'Twas a sight for the gods. Anyhow, he is now getting hell about it in the mess.

A few Manly lads came to see me today and we had quite a

chat. A chap called Clive Muir knew Dorothy. I think he is rather keen on her. I liked him – he's open-faced and honest. We launched into a discussion of my little comrade. I was awfully pleased to unburden my soul a bit and to tell old stories. He's got that bonny snap of Dot that I love and somehow I am not grudging it. Asked me if I knew why Dot was so attractive. Mentioned she wouldn't kiss anybody and didn't like being kissed. I, of course, know better, but didn't say so. I don't know if he understands my affection for Dot. Anyway, we have a common object. We agree on most things in general and I can see some decent, old-time chats for some little time to come. He is enamoured over that snap of Dot on the grass with the seagull and wants a copy.

Later: I've just got over a bad turn this evening which has been coming on for some hours. It lasted about an hour. I'm still listless and my left eye is sore again. My throat is sore and swollen again, too. Pulse only 120. Hope I feel better soon as I am going on furlough to Llandudno to see Alice in a couple of days.

Monday 27th May 1918

I left my diary at camp and therefore have much to catch up on, having just spent a week staying with the Denshams at Llandudno.

Alice met me at the station and we sat in a cafe and talked for hours. We agreed that what had happened on the last night in hospital should not be repeated. She was so very understanding. 'Eric, it doesn't matter what my feelings are for you. You have Dorothy and when this beastly war is over she will be waiting for you in Australia. I couldn't even contemplate leaving my parents as they are getting old and both need lots of support.' I was glad she broached the subject, as I had been worrying about it ever since agreeing to come and stay.

The truth was that Alice had been wonderful to me while I was ill and I am eternally grateful to her for the companionship she showed me during those dark days, but there is only one girl in my life and that girl is Dot. Alice knew that, as I had never once hidden my feelings for my comrade. I hope she meets someone, for she will undoubtedly make him very happy.

Before we went to her house she warned me that her mother and father had not really accepted that Richard was definitely dead. This was despite the fact that his commanding officer had written to them expressing his condolences and informing them that he had been victim to a sniper's bullet, while taking a reconnaissance party into no-man's-land. 'They still think that there might have been some mistake and as nothing in the way of his personal possessions have been sent back, they refuse to contemplate the reality of the situation. Father spends most of the day reading the newspapers from cover to cover, hoping to find something that might tell him otherwise. Don't worry, we'll go for long walks and get out of the place a lot, but just be prepared for a possible scene. Mother will no doubt be reminded of him when she meets you.'

I was beginning to wonder whether I should have come down to stay with the Denshams. Here I was with a beautiful girl to whom I had vowed to be nothing more than a friend, and with her parents who were going to struggle having a young soldier in their house. Anyway, my initial worries proved unfounded and I think my stay, if anything, did the parents a fair amount of good. They hardly mentioned him and only once when I mentioned my love of surfing did Mrs Densham look watery-eyed. Alice told me later that Richard had been a keen sailor and loved anything to do with the sea.

Llandudno is a nice place, but fairly deserted. The pier is fine, with a concert pavilion on the end. The shops are many and varied. We had some very pleasant walks, but never made the effort to tackle the rugged high hills around the town, although they looked very inviting to climb. There was even some snow on some of the peaks. I should love to have a ramble in this place for a month with Dorothy. How nice it would be in the summer.

The whole week did me a lot of good. I've now got a touch of colour in my face and, strange to say, Alice says that she has never walked with anyone who provokes such smiles from female passers-by. Some compliment!

Apart from walking, we also went to the pictures a lot and Mrs

Densham cooked up some delicious dinners. Alice and I kept to our word, but did a fair amount of flirting – I wonder if Dot will be very jealous. She shouldn't be. Alice is still working at the hospital and left to return there when I left. I have so much to thank her for, but although I will certainly write to show my gratitude I think it best that we should not get in contact too much. She agrees. Sometimes it is better to close a good book rather than read on and get disappointed by it's finale. Negative, I know, but true.

Saturday 1st June 1918

The war news is absolutely rotten and disheartening. If it goes on much longer I shall be a pessimist.

Later: The drunks are about and I suppose we are bound for a rowdy night. At 11.20 pm the mob came around, headed by a Sergeant Wilkins. He should know better. Along with his eternal sidekick Goodwin, a dope of the highest order, he demanded that I should open the bar. I was in bed and nearly asleep, and refused. He withdrew but a few minutes later returned, shouting the words 'Out, you bastard!' Of course he was drunk, but I shall not forgive that insult. I will demand a public apology at least.

Monday 3rd June 1918

A mail today, two from Dot, and socks and some snaps, what snaps! I love the ones of Dot in the bathing costume. She looks great! I can just imagine her mother's horror when she learnt Dot was sending them to me. Thank goodness Dot isn't such a prude to think any wrong in it. How I hate this rotten false prudery.

Got another one from Yolande. Her fiancé, who had been reported killed in action, has just escaped from a prisoner-of-war camp in Germany. She is evidently fearfully pleased and excited, and not without cause, I say. It's indeed peculiar to bump against such happenings in life. They would suit some sensational fiction better.

Jack Walsh, Pat Purcell and Forrester came down to see me tonight. Walsh had a grand tale about being run over in London.

I am in the mood for a cuddle and a flirt.

Tuesday 4th June 1918

I had a letter from Nurse Densham today saying how much she had enjoyed my visit. Her parents have begun to come to terms with Richard's death. Life in hospital is less fun now, though, and apparently Sister Johnson is worse than ever. She ended her letter:

> *No longer is there any larking around. It is like a concentration camp and she scolds the nurses at every opportunity. We all miss you and Glenister terribly. Glenister left while we were at Llandudno. He never made enough recovery for him to be sent back to his Battalion and has subsequently been given what I think you boys call an 'Aussie'. Take care of yourself. I won't forget you and will write sometimes, but not too often.*

A new batch of whisky has arrived in the mess. It is particularly potent and I foresee problems tonight. Goodwin is already drunk and rowdy, as is his mentor, Wilkins. Others are just slurring. Their talk is lewd and indecent, and every second word is an oath. A woman to such a person is merely a creature sent to satisfy a lustful craving of the animal that is in a man.

Thursday 6th June 1918

A chap cut his throat yesterday in the wood at the bottom of the camp. He'd been very depressed and threatened to do it. No-one believed him and some even joked as to when he would do the deed. Well, he tried today and there is a certain amount of guilt in the mess that we didn't take heed of his warnings. Fortunately, one of the sergeants found him lying naked, covered in blood. He's been sent to hospital and will recover.

Wilkins has just got away on prisoner escort but is down for the next draft. Bet both he and Goodwin work off it. The cook is also meant to go back to France but has been put into isolation. Rumour has it he's shamming VD.

Saturday 8th June 1918

Another roaring-hot day and I feel pretty well washed out. I have been running perspiration all day. How I wished to be down at

Manly in the surf and with my comrade. Went sick this morning and got light duties! Went within an ace of throwing 'a sixer' in front of Major Taft.

Wilkins isn't back so is 'off draft', and I saw Goodwin doping a cigarette with sugar before SMO's parade. With men like that, the war will never be won.

Sunday 16th June 1918

At classification the SMO asked me how I felt and I told him I was fine. He then felt my pulse and said, 'You'll do.' So now I was marked A3 and I'll be on draft at any moment now. I am both glad and sorry, but I shan't bother very much about that part of it. Talking of drafts, Wilkins is under arrest and is for court martial tomorrow. He lost his prisoner and was five days adrift. I think it's a scheme he's been working.

Thursday 20th June 1918

I arrived in 12 Sergeants' Mess, OTB Sandhill Camp, Longbridge, Deverill, Warminster yesterday, and learnt my draft is due to sail on 2 July.

Just been out on a platoon in attack stunt and, while waiting, a machine gun put a burst among us and wounded two chaps. I bandaged one up. He had a bullet clean through his right hand, entering at the left just above his wrist and travelling diagonally out of the third joint of the index finger. He was dreadfully annoyed as he has a sure 'Aussie'. In the stunt I slipped jumping over a concealed trench and went head over heels rolling plomp into the trench, much to the amusement of the brigadier's staff. But not to mine!

I fired 120 rounds and my rifle was so hot that I badly burnt my thumbs on the ironwork and I was completely done on the finish of the stunt. Later this afternoon, we went through the gas chamber to test our masks. All my brasswork turned greeny black with the chlorine and the stink clinging to my clothing, and I can still smell it. However, it was well to get it over.

I see they have Jack Hardiman here at last. It's about time he declared war. He has swung it just about twelve months on a sprained ankle. The draft went today.

Sunday 23rd June 1918

A 15th corporal and I hired a bike and went for a spin to Trowbridge, a distance of 12 miles. Hooked two girls, at least the corporal did, and I had to take up with one of them. She wasn't at all to my fancy; the corporal being out for that which usually motivates our lads when on leave, and these type of girls usually walk together.

We went for a walk and I entertained my girl on a bit of 'straight' stuff until she became quite angry and said she'd go home. I was tired of her, so I agreed and mooched around from 8.30 pm until 10.30 pm waiting for the corporal. The place was dry and uninteresting – dead slow, to my mind – and the girls all stolid and unhealthy-looking. After a weary wait my cobber turned up and we hit the pace up home without lights – were almost ran down on one occasion by a car on the turn. He got all he wanted, so he informed me.

Tuesday 25th June 1918

The newspapers have been full of the recent anti-war massed meetings. I can't help wondering if peace can ever be achieved between our nations. Certainly, someone will win the war, but can there ever be true goodwill after all that has happened? I wonder. Only the other day when I was at Longleat, I got talking to a nice elderly couple about this. It became clear that people back home hate the Germans even more than troops in the trenches. One might even say that the soldiers have a kind of respect for the enemy, and the Saxons are generally deemed to be a fairly decent bunch. This couple recounted a story about a man who was arrested for being German, even though his son was actually fighting in a Tommy regiment. By all accounts he'd lived in England most of his life. Can you believe it?

So Dot has received my note about Alf. I'm glad Dot is satisfied with my letters. They're 'just you', she says, and it nearly made me cry to read her remarks on my statement, 'Upon my honour I have never loved anyone like I love Dot.' Oh, that I were worthy of Dorothy and her splendid nature! Dorothy, my comrade and pal. Poor Dot, she can't seem to manage other girls, especially if they talk in the same rotten way as some men do on sex matters, etc. I can hardly blame her. So glad that diary part isn't missing at all and even if she did disapprove of one or two things last leave. Dorothy isn't jealous of my carryings on and even if I fall in love with a girl here, she'll never be my pal, she says.

Wednesday 10th July 1918

I write once again, having been too ill to write a word during the past two weeks, not even my usual Sunday letter home. Of course this epidemic of Spanish 'flu' was responsible and I was put in isolation with a high temperature and feeling fit to die. I'm not quite sure how long I was ill in the hut, but I couldn't eat. Vomited and had a splitting headache, and awful throat, and found it difficult to move.

After a few days my temperature subsided somewhat but I still couldn't eat and felt oh so weak. Unable to sleep and when I did I had awful nightmares. The doctor said after about four days that I could go to my hut, but I literally couldn't rise! Thankfully I was well treated, but the food – well, for a stomach like mine it was impossible. I'm now in the Group Clearing Hospital and today I feel good enough and have had a bit of a walk. Have just gone on to full diet and have been hoping for some parcels to augment the ration.

I missed the draft, of course, but there's plenty of time to catch another. They go every week. Letters today – three from Dot, two from Father, one from Mother, Harold and Elsie, and two from Russell, among others. I really don't feel fit to review them here today, much as I should like to.

Friday 12th July 1918

Slept all the morning. My, I could eat a horse – I am certainly improving all right. Just finished sixteen pages to Dot and a note to Hep. It's too dark for more. I have had to use YMCA paper and envelopes as I am broke. I yielded to the temptation of a two-up ring and so it serves me right. I really want dear little Dorothy here to keep me away from these troubles, or I'll become a gambler pure and simple.

There has been quite a number of lady visitors in the ward, but none took pity on this chicken. However, I've been having a very fair time altogether with discussions on 'swinging it' with various members of the ward. They are all convinced I am so doing, but I am not, even though I may act the goat.

By the way, Father's letter would make anybody's head swell. One would think I was a blessed hero instead of a blinking failure with a hospital record as long as an arm, no promotions, only a lot of breezy words from a few officers in high places.

Sunday 14th July 1918

Am feeling pretty rotten, have very little strength today and I have been sleeping a lot. This is a rotten complaint and no mistake, I can't write further. Everybody has remarked how ill I look, although some accuse me of swinging the lead! The good news is that the doc could find nothing wrong with the heart, so evidently I've quite got over that trouble and now it is merely lack of control of my limbs and that tired feeling. Need a wash. It's rotten that we can only have a hot bath here on Tuesdays and Saturdays. Is it coal saving?

Have been discussing war tonight. We have a hut full of pessimists and I am afraid most of the NCOs are hopelessly stupid and scatterbrained.

Wednesday 17th July 1918

Tonight I went to a concert given by blind musicians in aid of St Dunstan's Blind Institution. It was really excellent and the audience, being in complete sympathy with the performers − most unusual in the AIF − received them very warmly and encored. It was pitiful to see the performers with their sightless eyes. All wore glasses. All the music was fine, mostly classical, and I thoroughly enjoyed the evening. It makes me realise how lucky I was to escape being blinded by that gas attack. The thought of losing my sight is too awful to contemplate. I admire how those boys are attempting to get on with their lives so manfully.

In Frances's letter she actually hopes I had a bad attack of flu! The beast, I'm sure she doesn't know what that really means. She's sort of instituted herself as my guardian angel and insists I shall tell her everything I get up to on leave and elsewhere.

There's a stunt on tomorrow. All men to parade in full kits at 5 am – a matter of getting back into practice. I can't understand the unearthly hour, though. Sir William Robertson, commander-in-chief of internal forces, is to conduct an inspection later and will no doubt make an utterly needless speech. He is at least quite interesting in that he has managed to rise from private to general.

Oh, I forgot to mention that Wilkins arrived yesterday and is already stirring things up. He's managed to acquire another entourage of unsavoury characters who follow him around and generally cause trouble.

Thursday 18th July 1918

The stunt is over, and all are loudly cussing. It was wet and everybody is in a bad humour.

Thursday 25th July 1918 — after a week of training

Preparing for war. Passed through gas to have box respirator tested. There was nearly a panic in the gas chamber when the place caught alight. A mad stampede followed, but the situation was swiftly dealt with and calm was restored soon after. I do, however, feel rather ill since coming out of the gas. It brought back bad memories.

There's just been a kit inspection and everything is now ready for overseas. The sooner we move, the better. The suspense of waiting is interminable and saps one's emotions.

Quite a lot of the 13th have arrived here in my absence. Pat Connors and Corporal Bales in particular brought with them great news about the deeds of the battalion in France. Earlier this month they executed a brilliant offensive which captured Hamel. Our losses were 126 out of 510 engaged, and the American troops attached to us lost fifty-seven out of 227. Poor Sergeant Hall was among those killed.

President Clemenceau hastened to visit and congratulate our boys. Pat showed me a cutting of the speech he gave: 'I shall go back tomorrow and say to my countrymen: "I have seen the Australians; I have looked into their eyes, I know that they, men who have fought great battles in the cause of freedom, will fight alongside us, till the freedom for which we are fighting is guaranteed for us and our children."' Quite something from the grand old man of France.

Today I have just rewritten my letters to Mother, Father and Dot to be posted in case of my death. I'm sending them to London this time. I feel quite heavy-hearted somehow now. God grant the letters will never be of any use. I am far from ready to die and have far too much to live for. Every letter I get from my comrade at home merely strengthens my resolve to come back from this ghastly business unscathed. It seems a long time since I endured the grim reality of witnessing young corpses lying unburied in the mud. The incessant power of artillery and the evil illuminations of flares rising and falling in no-man's-land seem a world away. I am as ready as I ever will be and yet no man is ever totally ready to enter into a duel with death and his own emotions. Time passes slowly in France.

Tuesday 30th July 1918

Things look pretty rosy over the other side. Draft day today, but writing late and we haven't left. It has been delayed and we may go tomorrow. However, I'm ready to leave now at a moment's notice and the sooner the better. I don't like the delay. I can't find anything to do tonight and I am awfully lonely. I wish we'd just go.

Thursday 1st August 1918

This morning, I was in the middle of a bonny dream about my little comrade when Sergeant Wilkins, the troublemaker with little brain and no sense, pulled off my blankets and woke me. I was angry but got my blankets and lay down again. A second time he repeated, I rose, very angry, and warned him to clear. He, like the ass that he is, again withdrew the clothes, in spite of my warning. I saw red and flew up, giving him a straight left in the mouth. I was absolutely mad and unreasonable. To my surprise he stood ground and returned my attack with interest, severely jolting my face and bringing blood to my nose and mouth. The blood, instead of infuriating, calmed me. I pressed forward now and guarded his blows, giving him several full welts in body and face. Then dealt him a knockout body punch to the ribs. He fell and remained aground. Having thus made a fool of myself, I felt inclined to kick myself. To lose my head, then allow myself to be punished by that fool and, further, for giving him the hiding. He's nowhere near my weight in the first place.

Truly, I am ashamed of myself and told the hut so. They agreed he deserved it, as he was warned and wouldn't desist. Anyhow, I went to him, apologised for hitting him and shook hands. He won't interfere again, I think. He's been woefully silent in my company since. I removed most traces of the scrap with water, though my lip was a bit thick and two fingers out of joint. Well, we leave in about thirty minutes.

Lord knows what is to happen, but I hope for the best with speedy return home and many, many pleasant days yet to come with my own beloved comrade.

Friday 2nd August 1918

Slept fitfully till we arrived at our destination, Shorecliffe, and from there we had about a mile march to No. 3 Rest Camp, Folkestone, where we were quartered in houses – 100 to a house – and given breakfast. I don't think much of the town.

We had hardly been dismissed when the 'diggers' started a two-up ring in the centre of the street. What lads we have in the AIF! Although we are only allowed out from 2 pm to 9.30 pm, three Aussies have already scaled the fence and barbed wire and got away into the town.

We are to leave early tomorrow morning. I shall now opt to sleep. Probably my last sleep in Blighty for some time.

CHAPTER 10

FIGHTING AGAIN

Saturday 3rd August 1918

Well, I'm in France again for another gamble with death and I am
hoping my luck will stand. I slept most of the way and awoke with
a stiff neck at Boulogne about 12.30 pm.

My first impressions of the town are not good. WAACS abound,
along with a sprinkling of civvies, but the place looked dirty and
uninviting. A march of a couple of miles up a long and very steep
hill brought us here to a sort of rest camp, where we have been
allotted to tents with one blanket per man. The instructions, as we
received them, were: 'It's a closed camp, but everybody must be in
by 9 o'clock.' Chinese workers are here, too, on fatigue, and their
quarters are barbed-wired like a Fritz cage.

Walsh persuaded me to walk down into the town. Here, we saw
the result of an air raid the other night, with many houses completely demolished. Apparently one bomb got headquarters, with
casualties. The populace have the wind up and many seek refuge
in the heavy concrete shelters in the streets.

Most of our lads got away to the Rue de St Pol, a street as infa-
mous as Rue de Gallions of Le Havre. From accounts I hear, the
brothels there were all crowded and queues actually formed.

Undoubtedly these places make a fortune. Walsh was telling me about how some brothels near the front have a few girls working in them for a few days. These women entertain the local battalion for a few days and can then retire for the rest of their lives on the profit. Terrible, but probably true, even though it came from Walsh! I avoided them and tried unsuccessfully to hook a couple of WAACs. One pair of fine girls gave us encouragement and then cut us dead. Mean of them, I call it. It seems they have been warned against the soldiers. Overheard one Australian ask a WAAC: 'Do they dose you up with number nines, too? And do they issue you with corsets?' Undoubtedly these Australians are incorrigible.

We've received forty-eight hours' rations and expect to get away to Le Havre tomorrow early. There's a rumour of another impending air raid tonight.

Sunday 4th August 1918

The fourth anniversary of the declaration of war! It's almost unbelievable. Had one told me it would last so long when I enlisted I'd have thought them mad.

Hope we soon get a move on. This waiting around gets me too nervous. It's almost better to be in the thick of the action. I am told the division may be stunting very shortly, so perhaps I'll get a chance to distinguish myself before many weeks.

There's no facility for posting but I may be able to send a Field Service postcard later on. I wonder how they all are at home? I've been thinking as usual of my little comrade. It does comfort me to think she's safe at home. I shouldn't like her to come over here, even as a VAD.

Wednesday 7th August 1918

Arrived in Harfleur yesterday, where comforts were distributed to the draft, consisting of cigarettes, toffees and reading matter, Australian Comforts Fund stuff. We've been issued with 120 rounds, rations and also lime juice, and move early this afternoon.

Later: I am presently waiting at Le Havre station, along with

eleven others in the 13th, to rejoin the battalion in the Somme
area. Americans troops are everywhere and have raised the morale
of everyone. They're a friendly bunch, and Walsh and I got talking
to an educated private in the AMC. I hear the private starts on $20
a month, with increases according to efficiency. An infantry lieutenant gets $100 to $150. Not bad, eh?

Thursday 8th August 1918

Reached Doullenes at about 9 am, then detrained and went on
about 2 kilometres to Bertreau-court, where the 4th Division
reinforcements are at present billeted.

We were informed of the start of a gigantic stunt here this
morning involving all the Australians and Canadians. The 13th
Battalion is in the thick of it. So far, we hear it is an immense success. There are many wounded coming by in lorries, mostly Fritz
prisoners. I feel rather unlucky to have been left out of that last
draft as I am missing a stunt which, if entirely successful, will rank
as one of our greatest successes. Rumours are rife that the enemy
is tottering. About time, too. Apparently the 4th Division was held
up for a time, but the advance has reached a depth of 7 miles and
we are still going. Hurrah!

Friday 9th August 1918

Good official news on the attack. All objectives gained, 15 000
prisoners and still counting. Of these, 7000 are Aussie captures. The
14th and 15th battalions suffered most, the latter's colonel and
adjutant being killed. Reports of Huns, guns and booty captured
are still coming in. Fourth Brigade caught it heavier than any, but
their casualties are slight.

Had a peculiar dream last night. I just remember a sensation of
travelling along at a tremendous pace and then there was a terrible crash, and then darkness. After a time I came to and my dream
went on. I wonder if it may portend anything? Now I come to
remember, I've had the same experience once or twice before, but
in each case I woke up in a sweat.

This bully and biscuits is rotten living tack. I haven't settled down to it as yet. I hear Hardiman is still at the base swinging the lead on account of his ankle. I wonder if he still pounds it with a sandbag to make it swell. By the way, my shirt may now be classed as 'talkative' – these chats are impossible to avoid. It is extraordinary that we can invent the most sophisticated weapons to kill our fellow humans but haven't yet worked out a way of killing chats!

Sunday 11th August 1918

I'm with the battalion at last, behind the village of Sailly Laurette, where I found a parcel from home, two Blighty letters and my watch. We marched up here a good 10 miles, across the ground lately in Fritz possession, and I noted the apparent lack of shell holes. Passed quite a lot of Fritz captured guns, etc. on our way to the camp. We are already harvesting the wheat crops with all speed. This village is in an awful state after our bombardment. Not a whole place standing. Either the Germans blew the bridges and destroyed the canal locks before they evacuated or else our shells had an unlucky hit.

I found the 13th just arrived in a gully and soon felt at home. The stunt was a huge success and the booty was enormous. Most of the battery are getting around with Fritz caps on and look funny. They are certainly better than the heavy tin hat. Jerry Oswald has about nine revolvers, from howitzers to the smallest, as well as watches and a bonny pair of field glasses. I believe he was magnificent in the stunt. Everybody is talking about the way he led a party of soldiers into a gap in the line and silenced several enemy machine guns which had been doing much damage. Our company casualties were eight. Sorry to hear the news about Friedman. I liked him very much.

I've just souvenired a couple of waterproofs and a couple of greatcoats from some dead Germans a quarter of a mile away. Evidently the Tommies caught it thick here. There are a lot dead and a few 2nd Division Aussies. The smell is rotten. This is the front where the Tommies were held up and the 3rd Division also struggled.

Apparently there was a rumour I'd been sent back to Australia and the boys were very surprised to see me indeed. Apparently I'm quite popular after the Polygon Wood affair. It's been a reunion tinged with sadness, though. Somehow I was half-expecting to see Paddy come bounding towards me in his usual inimitable way, but of course that was never going to happen. The regiment has somehow lost its soul when it lost him.

It's good to see everyone, though. Sad to report though that poor Lucas died of wounds last month. Edgar, who knew that I had always tried to steer him in the right direction, broke the news. The truth is that I have become hardened by death. I felt only remorse that someone who had been so keen to prove himself had fallen at the final hurdle. Should I have reported him for being underage? Perhaps. I must write to his parents. They ought to know the sheer spirit of the chap. His attempt to take on the Railway Unit champion on the *Wiltshire* said everything about him. By all accounts he ventured out into no-man's-land on no fewer than three occasions, bringing back the wounded before he himself fell victim to machine-gun fire. Edgar tells me that after the night he got windy, he never once saw him shirk any responsibility.

Hope Fritz doesn't bomb tonight. God bless all at home.

Tuesday 13th August 1918

Fritz gave a bombing display last night but fortunately none were dropped in this area. The nearest was half a mile away. I slept very badly and dreamt that I'd been hit by a German shell in no-man's-land. I couldn't move when all of a sudden Fritz made a counter-attack and began bayoneting all wounded soldiers. I woke up in a cold sweat. What is it with this dreaming?

Yesterday, while endeavouring to bomb fish in the river with a Stokes mortar bomb, Sergeant Baxter DCM and Ted Headon, who is an original, were killed, blown to pieces, and another chap was badly wounded. It's hard to think this has happened. What a waste. Everyone thought Headon was charmed. He'd been through everything from Gallipoli to Ypres.

Why people fool with things they don't understand beats me. This isn't the first time. A couple of days ago, a Stokes bomb accidentally rolled down the hill and exploded, killing six soldiers in the 16th. There's a sense that the war is in its final stages, so these incidents somehow seem even more tragic. I am sick of death. Standing at the foot of freshly dug graves of young men takes its toll after a while. Perhaps I have just been out of the war business for too long.

It has been most frightfully hot all day, but fortunately we moved off as the sun was setting. By the end of the 8-mile march, though, I was pretty knocked up. The last 5 miles were covered without a break, and the language and grumbling was shocking, I can tell you! There was no need for the forced march and the leaders should be well kicked. Bet they were on horseback.

Our humour did not improve on discovering we were to stop in an old trench, which was full of human excreta – probably the result of the occupation by the Germans a few days ago. There's also abominable effluvia emanating from two dead horses, all bloated and maggoty, just at the state of 'blowing up'. It fairly stank. Rats were freely gnawing away at the carcasses and paid not the slightest attention to our arrival. *C'est la guerre*, I suppose. One must take the good with the bad. In truth, I am far too knocked up to care.

Wednesday 14th August 1918

I believe we are 'over the bags' soon, but there are no details out as yet. It may be only rumour anyhow. The boys reckon it's time for a spell as there have been three hops in twice as many weeks. Tanks are about in any number and there is a feeling that we are about to make a big push.

Five letters came today. Mother's sixty-four, Dot's seventy-one, seventy-two, seventy-three, and one from Elsie. It's nice to get these letters here. I will drop a couple of notes this afternoon when it's cooler. This from Dot: 'Please don't smile – I wasn't to tell you that I look up to you, you stand for me as something clean and brave and straight, just like I want my son, if ever I have one, to be. I don't think two people in the world have a better understanding than you and I.'

Oh, Dorothy, that I were the chap you think me. I try, perhaps, to be straight, but I'm not brave, even though I'd like to be. No, I

fear that I'm not the chap you think I am, although I think the
world of my comrade and would endeavour anything for her. Glad
diary part seven has arrived.

I am sharing a dugout with Edgar and we have made it habitable. I don't know why we bothered as we'll probably move off in
the next day or two. Thankfully the offending smell of the horse
has been removed by the expediency of covering him with earth.
Edgar's certainly lost his innocence. When he first arrived he was
both a bit of a prude and had all the hallmarks of a teacher out of
his depth. Rarely talks about his wife. Perhaps because it hurts him
to be reminded of her.

Friday 16th August 1918

Moved yesterday and am presently in a 30-foot dugout, and can
laugh at the few shells that do happen to come over. We are pretty
safe from attack with plenty of old Fritz barbed wire and a ton of
machine guns. He'd have a bad time if he counterattacked. On
arrival, I was put on a digging fatigue to improve and carry on the
trench tonight. I'll get off to sleep now, as it's close on 1 am and
stand-to is only a couple of hours off.

Later: Slept fairly well in a bed with a tarpaulin for covering.
Plenty of water handy, too. Matches have been very scarce and we
couldn't sport one between the whole platoon last night. The
smokers were going mad!

Fritz has been far too busy, but hasn't hit us. The crashing of
shells around us is pretty disconcerting, I can tell you. Should be
safe, though. There's a big bombardment to the right. Somebody's
'pushing' some distance off. I've been chatting to Edgar about
Wollongong and thinking about home. It's a wonderful tonic for
windyness. Thank God I also have my comrade to think about in
these times.

Saturday 17th August 1918

Fritz has given us a tremendous display of concentrated artillery
fire and I have not enjoyed it.

During the afternoon, the 14th on our left pushed forward

about 700 yards and called down a Fritz barrage on them. We endeavoured to bomb out some snipers on the right and came in for some pretty violent strafing. The CSM D Company has been killed. This is a dangerous area. The problem is that the fighting seems to have opened up and hence we are not absolutely sure where the enemy is. Snipers abound but one has to take chances otherwise we'd never get out of our dugouts. There's an old Fritz hospital with the flag still flying not far away and also some very interesting remains of German positions. This evening, Edgar and myself salvaged a lamp and some candles from the latter.

All companies but us have moved forward. I was assigned to carry rations to B and D company headquarters tonight. I got my two carries over without a casualty and felt pretty knocked up after them. I found the possies all right, though Fritz gave a bit of anxiety with a machine gun playing about the track. There was no hanging around, I can tell you. My heart needs weeks, not minutes to recover. We were all shaking pathetically on making cover. Dehydration is a constant problem, there never seems to be enough water to go around. Thankfully Edgar was on hand to greet me with a dixie of tea.

There's going to be an early morning stunt by the 2nd Division tomorrow. Meanwhile, the French have been pushing away on our flank. Judging by the bombardment, it's lasted all day. It's morning now and we stand to at 3 pm. I'm very tired.

Sunday 18th August 1918

The stunt on the left was very short. Zero was about 4 pm and there was a violent barrage. Fritz got the wind up all along the line and sent up thousands of multicoloured rockets and flares. It was good to watch the Huns and their nervous attempts to see what was happening. Anyway, I've been asleep since stand-down and it's now 7 pm. Have been dreaming about home again and feel very comforted. Hope all is well with my comrade and also with Mother.

We have just been warned to be ready to move to the front line at 9.30 pm. I suppose we will be there for three days at least. A few of the boys are showing signs of nerves. Some are furiously letter-writing, others smoke constantly. Every man has his own way of coping with this impending sense that we are in for something big. Dot's pictures are my strength. It is a strange feeling that everything I have got through has been the result of the hope and sense of optimism she has given me. I have every reason to live.

Monday 19th August 1918

We've completed the changeover with a portion of B Company. I am positioned on the extreme right of our battalion front in a shell-shocked wood. Plenty of undergrowth has sprung up, affording plenty of cover for both Fritz and us. It's a lonely sort of a post and we do not talk above a whisper nor smoke at night, for though Fritz is some distance off, his patrols are quite active. We dug nearly all night and have made the possie bearable, carefully camouflaging all our working with leaves and twigs, etc. Fritz has put some close enough to be unpleasant. Few of us will sleep tonight, even if he stops his shelling. It is not clear how near he is and I, for one, have no intention to be woken by a German bayonet. The boys are ready to give him a lively ahoy if he tries to raid here. We've a ton of bombs and plenty of machine-gun support, beside the artillery barrage to depend upon. Oh yes, I forgot to mention that my 'friend', Private Munday, has been transferred to this platoon. Thank you! He's as useless as he ever was and is a chronic grumbler. I threatened to kick his seat and I swear I still will if he causes any problems.

Later: There is a rumour we may be relieved by Yanks tomorrow, but I don't fancy it myself. Fritz has been fairly active throughout the day, driving us to the 'funk holes' we've dug, but so far we've been lucky. There have been a few casualties in the battalion.

Colonel Marks was around here today and Munday couldn't show him the next post on the right. I got hit to leg, of course, and it doesn't exactly stand in my favour. Hang the man.

Wednesday 21st August 1918

Little doing. Fritz remains active with his big guns, but we've yet to see any movement ahead. Thank God! I'm not complaining.

I began a letter to Dot last night but the failing light and also a bit of strafe cut it short. Perhaps it was just as well for I got a bundle of letters with the rations this morning. Dot's seventy and seventy-five, and above all, one from Mother telling me of Elsie's engagement to Russell! Well, good luck to the pair of them and I hope they're happy enough. They'd better wait for me to come home, though, before getting married. I wonder what Father thinks, or what he will say. I got a long letter from him, also one from Elsie, Ray and Harold, as well as several others. The snap of Dot with the parsnips and cabbage is really good. It reminds me of that French expression of endearment, 'my little cabbage'. The boys are improving wonderfully in their writing, I notice. It's a bonny mail and I am really happy today over it.

We've had good news, too, of a successful stunt by the French down south. A few more successes of magnitude and the war should be over, I'm thinking.

Got a bit of sneezing gas last night, but not enough to do anything but make us uncomfortable – our artillery paid him back with interest. Nevertheless, I am taking no chances and all the boys are wearing gas masks, which is most uncomfortable. It's been very hot again today, though this morning there was a heavy mist about. Flies are dreadful, also insects which bite badly. I've two swollen wrists and a swollen knee over them. I'm pleased to say I am not yet 'chatty'. It's the rats around here that are most annoying. They are vermin of the worst kind. Images of death and rats go together in this war. They have been the winners. Bloated and ugly. I hate them. I was awoken by Edgar's cursing after feeling one of these beasts scamper over his mouth.

I wonder how much longer we will be out here, and if we will have a spell or another hop?

Thursday 22nd August 1918

Rumour came through late last night that we were hopping over in the morning. We were the pivot flank and advanced a few hundred yards to an old 1916 line, while on the left, this gradually increased to about a mile. I brought up the rear and covered the party with a couple of Jimmy Mills! The boys coped pretty well, given that Fritz put up a barrage as we were advancing. A few had the wind up but that is to be expected. Our possies were, as expected, empty. It's a very old trench, deep and in good order, with some dugouts.

Matches and cigarettes are a nil quantity here. Of the former I am the only one in the company with any (about ten) and am much in demand. One match has to do about ten men.

We move forward again at dawn.

Friday 23rd August 1918

Zero was at 4.45 am and precisely at that time our barrage opened and we got out into a sap and advanced single file. Fritz sent up his SOS at once and continued illuminating the front with flares. His artillery replied rather late and his SOS line was much too far to the rear. Some shells were falling dangerously close and there was a fair amount of mud flying around. To make our jobs even more tricky there was a load of Fritz wire around and a few got cuts and grazes in their efforts to surmount these obstacles. The Germans fought gamely and at one point there was some serious hand-to-hand fighting. The Huns were evidently determined to prevent us from reaching the Somme. Edgar was impressive and, along with Lieutenant Curtis, led the boys in with plenty of encouragement. Amazingly, we had no casualties, though one of my men got a clout on the nose with a lump of dirt. We were into our objective in five minutes, but not before I had managed to tear putties and breeches to ribbons on the loose wire. Leg bleeding but not a lot.

My section immediately got on to digging a sap across the road, which proved a fair bastard. I took a turn and worked on the hard road without a pick in order to block a communication sap with wire.

Saturday 24th August 1918

We worked till it was nearly dawn and Fritz was pretty silent. Most of the boys got down to having a sleep. Only Edgar and a couple of the young lads stayed up on sentry. I was about to call it a night when, in the distance, some 150 yards away, I distinguished some silhouettes moving in an old line. My heart began pounding as I reached for my rifle and took aim. I could feel myself breaking sweat as a figure moved into my sights. Then, flicking my safety catch, I steadied myself and pulled the trigger. A dull thud, followed by the dark figure falling, confirmed my kill. I felt little emotion, just intense excitement. If the enemy is out to get you, there is little time for regret. Edgar heard the shot and crept over to me. I pointed forward and we began to snipe in earnest. It soon became clear that there was at least a Jerry section in front of us. Lack of movement confirmed that they had their heads well down – no doubt the result of having witnessed a couple of their comrades falling, and, barely whispering, I told Edgar and the boys to cover me. This they did, firing the odd, sporadic shot around their possie while I crawled forward. It was exhausting work and I began to feel every sinew in my body straining as I made my way through the dewy, overgrown grass, armed only with a couple of 36 grenades.

My heart seemed to be beating at an abnormal pace and I questioned the sense of my action. But it was too late to turn back now. I had committed myself. Thoughts rushed through me. Gradually, though, I edged my way closer with the occasional shot from behind providing me with some comfort amid the silence. The time had come to once again assess my progress and, scarcely moving my head, I raised my eyes above the grass. There, some 30 yards off, were a few layers of sandbags surrounding a small sap. This was it. I don't which was now greater – fear of being spotted or fear of missing with my two grenades. I knew I could afford neither. I crawled on a little further and could hear the faint sound of excited whispering as I reached for one of my grenades. My left hand was shaking uncontrollably and I struggled to find the pin. Slowly, though, I pulled it away from the grenade. A faint click. Now was the moment. I raised myself and flung it towards the sap. The grenade took a few seconds to detonate and went off with a deep bang, followed by cries and excited shouts. I immediately reached for and threw the second. Further cries and then quiet, which was broken a moment later by further rifle fire behind me. It was time to break off. I had definitely struck the sap but without a rifle to protect me it would have been foolish to seek out prisoners or wounded. A flare in the distance further alerted me to the potential danger and I hurriedly crawled back. Edgar's reassuring voice on getting near the possie directed me and I slid into it, exhausted but terribly excited. Too tired to sleep, we talked until it became light, emptying his hip flask in the process.

I managed a few hours' sleep this morning and the whole thing doesn't seem real. If Edgar isn't now cursing that he's got no rum left I would probably think it a dream. I am badly in need of more sleep but Fritz seems to have woken up and has a few active machine guns and snipers. We're well hidden but it makes rest difficult. Their contact planes are also active. The boys are all deadbeat and are asleep. I'm very tired, too, so will try to get a nap. We are being relieved tonight and are going back to the supports. A party has just returned, having put a number of booby traps around the sap some 30 yards out. That should give Fritz a surprise if he thinks about counterattacking. The traps were Mills bombs with the pins almost drawn, so that any attempt to remove or surmount the obstacle would blow the person sky-high.

Sunday 25th August 1918

At about midnight our relief came along in dribs and drabs. They were Kane Fuseliers — most of them young and very windy as it was their first time in the line. The corporal wouldn't leave the trench to look at the sap we were guarding so I left him in disgust. To make matters worse, their young officer didn't know what the SOS was! We got away about 1 am. The slowest and rottenest changeover I ever hope to have. At least we did so without a casualty. Marched about 8 kilometres through Glabonniers and were deadbeat on reaching the remainder of the battalion, who had been waiting on buses for us. The company billets at Poulainville were pretty stricken, but we sergeants cleaned out a bit of a place and have made it very comfortable. Now for a long and much-needed sleep.

Monday 26th August 1918

It's cleared off fine again and this afternoon we had a bit of drill. We are pretty rusty.

The battalion is fairly ragged but they are picking up slowly. Clothes are coming in very small quantities. The Yanks left the camp in a terrible state but thankfully they didn't take all their goods. It seems they could do with a shake-up. Anyway, as a result, the boys have made up with Yank breeches and hats and are doing well. Some of the lads have complete outfits. It does look funny. Everybody seems to be full of German souvenirs too — watches, field glasses, automatic revolvers, all salvaged from the last big advance. There are plenty of the latter on sale. Pretty cheap but although I'd like to have one I'll try and salvage one of my own.

I had the most horrific dream last night and woke up in a sweat, and am still feeling quite unsettled by it. As a result I have decided to write letters to those I care about back home, to be posted back in the event of my death. I think I will also copy them into the diary in case the original should go amiss.

To Mother 26/8/1918

Dearest Mother,

I enclose a letter to Father which I think explains itself. Will you send it to him.

I have left some gear with Frances in London which will be posted to you after the war. Father, as my next of kin, will receive it and send it on to you also. If you get my diary please send it to Dorothy. I think you have understood our relationship and don't need an explanation. You may read it if you wish.

I should like Elsie and each of the boys to be given something in remembrance of me. There will be enough money for that and the remainder is, of course, for yourself. If Dorothy wants any little memento please give it to her. I am not specifying anything because well, I just can't.

I hope these arrangements are quite clear.

And now Mother, I want to express my sorrow for the occasions in which I caused you pain, but I know you will forgive me. In my duty I have fallen and perhaps it will be for the best.

Mother, tell Elsie I wish that I had been more of a brother to her and impress on the boys not to be like me. I hope both the boys will play the game and look after you and Elsie and give you comfort.

Good-bye. God Bless you all.

Eric

To Father 26/8/1918

Dear Father,

If you should receive this letter then you will know I've gone on the long trail. It is being sent to London to be posted after my death.

You, as my next of kin, will receive all my personal effects which I should like handed over to Mother. I have made a will leaving all to her. Should you receive a diary of mine, please hand it over unread to Dorothy Wright. I have, for the past twenty months, looked upon her as a comrade. Let this be sufficient justification for my request.

For what I've been to you as a son I am glad, and for where I have failed I am sorry, believe me when I say I have done my best. Thank you for your letters over the past months. I have much appreciated them.

And now, goodbye. May Elsie and the boys prove a comfort to you.

Eric

Wednesday 28th August 1918

I'm on guard over fifteen prisoners in a cage and it's not too bad a cop. I only hope no prisoner gets away.

Good news for some of the lads. Jim White and Ted Harrad got their pips today, lucky fellows, and Jerry Oswald refused RSM, silly fool. Jerry's refusing spoilt the promotion in our company. Said it would be detrimental to his Aussie leave. What a dope!

Pay tonight and everybody is celebrating. I'm glad I'm not in the billet as the sergeants have already drunk about fifteen–dozen beers (more or less). Jim White is celebrating, of course. I am half expecting to have the clink full tonight. There was a row with the 'chows'. One of our chaps was alleged to have pinched the chows' money and four of them chased the lad down the street. Was rather funny.

Thursday 29th August 1918

The guard was successful. I was relieved at 4 am and have got a few letters done and away. I expected some letters today but none came from Aussie, only one from Frances with a parcel of macaroons and cake. She's awfully anxious because I don't write more often, but I hope she appreciates it's not been very easy.

A number of the lads got drunk tonight. Edgar got well tanked. He'd been drinking Benedictine all night and became hard to handle. Another chap and I carried him out fighting, and I got a punch on the nose and severe kicks on the shins. It was the hardest half an hour's work I ever did in the AIF. Edgar of all people. Who would have believed it eighteen months ago?!

Friday 30th August 1918

Well, I've had a mail, number seventy-four from Dot, as well as letters from Mother and Raymond. Gee, but Raymond is growing. I hardly recognised that snap of him in civvies. He now looks fully grown up. I'm off to see if I can get a copy of our regimental march to send home. I'd like Dot to have it.

Sorry, I've just been called away. Word reached me that matches, a very precious article, arrived in the canteen and so I hurried away to get in early. I've been lucky and got *two* boxes. I'm in the state commonly known as 'chatty'. Damn it! It's horribly uncomfortable but one can't expect to be entirely immune when everyone else has been suffering from them.

Brass polish has been issued again; I suppose the lads will swear a treat. Better to put the Australian Army on the battlefield than on the parade ground. Anyhow, we have to appear for an inspection with polished equipment tomorrow. Mine is done.

There're trees of pretty decent apples next door, green and small but sweet, and I've been pinching them with the easily guessed result. However, they won't do any harm, I suppose.

Saturday 31st August 1918

Saw some of our Chinese labour lads on the move today with full packs – some packs – with the carrying capacity of chagg bags. They looked most peculiar with these enormous packs on their backs. Many of them carried them on poles, chow greengrocer style.

I've just seen the official number of prisoners of war of our brigade. They are as follows:

13th	244
14th	233
15th	223
16th	320
4th MG	37
TOTAL	1057

Much more than I expected.

There was a fire in the village this afternoon. All A Company's billets burnt to the ground. Had the wind not been favourable there would have been a hell of a mess.

I have seen the nearest approach to the prehistoric woman in this village today. I really must get a photo of her.

Wednesday 4th September 1918

Went to a 4th Brigade boxing tournament at Allenville. A train took us to the spot. We must be winning when transport to sports is provided.

The ring was set in the bottom of a hollow, a sort of natural amphitheatre and the boys all grouped themselves around. It was a splendid site and I suppose there were 2000 onlookers, the majority 4th Brigade, but with a fair sprinkling of Yanks, Tommies, French soldiers and civvie population, the latter being children and a few mademoiselles. The boxing was intensely amusing but I'm not going into detail. One chap, Fagan, much bolstered up with tales of ninety-nine knockouts to his credit, proved a mug. Several competitors were forced clean through the ropes, on one occasion both going the same way. The referee was rotten. Oh, by the way, the 13th Battalion won the championship.

I met a chap from the STHS, can't think of his name – short, dark, Jewish chap, quiet, just come over to the 4th Field Company. We had a chat over old times, swapped confidences and news, and he showed me a very nice 'in memorium' notice taken from a Sydney paper on Anzac Day, for old SHS, STHS and TC students who have made the supreme sacrifice.

Friday 6th September 1918

Got jersey and football boots – converted army issue– this morning and caught the GS wagon soon after dinner for Allenville Chateau grounds for a rugby match against the 15th.

It was a good game although I was somewhat groggy during the early part of the game as a result of a high tackle. The 15th backs proved too strong for us and scored a penalty and two tries in the first half. Our backs were a disappointment, mulling every chance, so in the second half we decided to play a forward game as we had the better scrum and weight.

We did so with great success but it made the game murderously rough. There was plenty of blood and hair flying but the 15th were sporty and there wasn't too much dirty work. We scored three times in the last fifteen minutes, equalising the scores. In the ruck I got a damaged left shoulderblade, several kicks and bruises in body and shins, and a nasty crack on my right hand, which was extremely painful. However, we were pleased to make it a draw and were loudly cheered by our officers, especially as we scored the last try just before the whistle blew. I foolishly played with my watch on and realised as the game ended that I had lost it. Edgar, knowing how much it meant to me, got the whole team to have a scour around the pitch. We found it and, although the glass is broken, it still goes.

War news is particularly encouraging. We are moving on Sunday, I think. Mail closes here tonight. Library books are called in, football togs taken and there is every indication of a move. I must get a few letters away.

Oh yes, there's a wild rumour about 1914 men being left out this time and being drafted home very shortly in a bunch. What a rumour! Another that the 4th Division is not fit for active service! This is a worse one. However, I think both of them are rot.

My thoughts are still wandering homewards to my little comrade and Mother. It's great to dream of the happy time to come in my reunion with them all and also our past happiness together.

Sunday 8th September 1918

We embussed at Cardonette after, in our usual battalion fashion, being marched the usual unnecessary long route on the most indirect route with full packs and blankets to the starting point. Reached a sleepy village called Bianches, a couple of kilometres behind Peronne, having passed through Dours and Villers-Bretoneux, the ground of the great Australian successes in the last two months. We are now in bivouacs at the edge of a wood. A smart downpour of rain spoilt our work halfway through but it served us well and showed us several defects in the roof of our possie. She's a good place now, holds four snugly and is 3 feet sunk in the ground. There are many French graves about, which hardly provides the most hospitable welcome.

I'm fortunate, have just got a mail of five or six letters including one from Dot and one from Mother. They're fine and Dot's remarks on Elsie's engagement are good and very interesting: 'I'm nearly as excited as Elsie – I'm glad, glad, glad! – but a wee bit wistful and envious when I think of my special happiness being such a long way off.' My darling, I shan't forget this sentiment (I think I wrote it many months ago in an early diary part): 'My wish in life is a home, a man and a baby all my very own.' Dot has that strongly developed motherly love. She sounds happy and I am glad she is keeping busy. The truth is, though, that I am missing her like mad and reading her letters brings on a spectre of emotions. I feel happy and grateful to have had the fortune to be with such a darling girl, but it is a struggle to hold back my sadness and sometimes anger that circumstances have driven us apart. I know I am doing the right thing by being over here, but how I wish I could take her in my arms again and her hold her tight to me. What a strange life this is that we should be such puppets to fate.

Father's remarks re the engagement are yet to come; Mother seems surprised at him, and saying 'pleased to hear it', but then I've so often cracked Russell up to the old man. It's not at all odd to me.

Monday 9th September 1918

Four years!

There are booby traps all over the place, bombs in the earth, wires attached to explosives and all sorts of traps for the unwary. There've been a few casualties in the 14th Battalion. I steer clear of all suspicious articles.

Good news abounds concerning the fact that Fritz is still retiring back past the Hindenburg Line and that our stunt is now not necessary. I suppose they will find another. Anyway, we are moving tomorrow, a good long march. I'll try to get some mail done.

Tuesday 10th September 1918

We moved today at 11 am. It rained all the morning and everybody got well soaked. Our packs and hats were dumped and we got bombs and ammunition served out. All blankets and greatcoats were left behind. It was pretty sloshy walking and though the distance was said to be 5 miles, I believe myself it was closer on ten the way we came. The pace was pretty hot and we were well tired when we arrived in our billets – huts which had been occupied by the 35th Flying Squadron before Fritz's disastrous advance.

Old Fritz made a good retreat, for the roads and rails were all blown up. Every bridge is completely destroyed and Peronne is in ruins. A few dud Fritzes gave the troops a scary time of it. The ground we passed over was singularly clear of shell holes. Evidently, the enemy gave very little resistance in our advance. There was an absence of graves.

We have the best possie in the brigade and we sergeants are in a hut well sunk in the ground, with a stove and all conveniences.

I've been salvaging and have a good supply of coal and am enjoying the warmth from a good fire at the present moment. It's cold and windy outside, and raining in fits and starts. I believe we are only here for the night. We've been paid and now I'll have a quiet game of poker. Money isn't much good to the troops here and there's no cigarettes available anywhere. All the boys are smoking 'bush cameos' of newspaper or love letters and issue tobacco. The troops certainly are in a bad way.

I've developed a sty on my left eye and the cold has got in. It's extremely sore. Also I have a boil on my neck. Strange to say, there seems to be an epidemic of boils in the battalion. Wonder what is causing the trouble.

Thursday 12th September 1918

Raining this morning, and we were sent on salvage fatigue around the district. We are beauts on this, I must say. We left our good positions at 4 pm to make way for the 14th Battalion in the mud and slush. I'd been to the doctor's with my eye and I found that with one eye bandaged I was falling into every puddle on the way.

Our new position is a few thousand yards away from the last base and we have had to dig in. It's hard luck, especially in this rotten weather. It is hard to know exactly where we are, but I should say it is about a mile in front of Estrees. We've yet to reach our gun lines and are approximately 7 miles from the line yet. There's a dump of Fritz flares, signal grenades, bombs and TMs a few hundred yards away, also detonators, boxes of guncotton and other explosives about. Of course I had to investigate and lost some skin from my hand firing the signal grenades. I learnt a lot about his flares, etc. and didn't know till today that his rocket contrivances were thrown from a sort of mortar. The mob started on the dump and it's a wonder we weren't blown up. We hoyed undetonated stick bombs. It was funny. Looking back, though, I think what a fool I was. I'll blow myself up one day. I'm too inquisitive with bombs.

There are big guns and troops going past up the line all the time. I can see a stunt shortly.

Friday 13th September 1918

I have been hearing news about a very successful stunt down south involving seven Yank divisions and one French division, 20 000 prisoners or so. The 13th Brigade also had a successful stunt so it is good news all around.

Aussie mail today. Dot's found a little inconsistency, she says. I wrote in one letter I wasn't flirting and in the next I said, 'One must sometimes flirt to have an outlet to one's feelings.' Perhaps it is inconsistency but if one was written in camp and another on leave perhaps it's understandable. So I'm 'a naughty boy'! How I'd love to see her. Talking of home, Jerry Oswald and Tuckey have been informed they leave tomorrow for Australia on the Christmas stunt. They are both mad with joy, Jerry's eyes sparkling and Tuckey full of talk. Bet neither sleeps tonight.

Tonight there was an issue of Aussie tobacco and cigarettes. Never was the stuff more acceptable, as smokes were unobtainable. We also got biscuits (Arnott's) and pears with extra bread rations, so we know there's a hard stunt ahead. This was confirmed tonight by being paraded and warned by Captain Turner, details of the stunt will be out later.

Monday 16th September 1918

Today we've been practising the stunt – some stunt, believe me – which I daren't describe till it's over. Sufficient that we move up tonight with our full complement of bombs, wire cutters, etc.

We are heavily loaded and will have to march a good distance. The mail is closed and I haven't written home, but I'll try and slip a note or two in to Dot and Mother. I have just volunteered for a patrol tonight and I have been warned to carry no papers and to give absolutely no information if captured. Of course I'll leave this diary in care of a friend, Sergeant Guerney, I expect. I'll write those notes now, and then have a rest until moving-off time.

Later: My patrol was aborted and we moved off across broken country at 8.30 pm with all our gear. Marched for three hours until we reached the possie to relieve 13th Brigade. There was no shelter and we were too tired to build any. Consequently, when the rain came on, and it was some downpour, we were all soaked in a moment. To make matters worse, Fritz began shelling heavily and one shell, landing near me, shellshocked poor Bradbury. It was cruel to see the poor chap. He always was nervous in the line, but it was terrible to see his muttering, shaking, wild-eyed appearance. We got him away to the doc.

Tuesday 17th September 1918

Fortunately, today broke clear and sunny so I soon got my things dry and made a fairly comfy possie. I've been up reconnoitring our ground and getting our directions. To my mind, the hop will be a grand success as the ground is good, though there's a fair amount of wire in front. We are led to expect little or no resistance and we go over in artillery formation. Some are saying that this could be one of the most decisive pushes in the war. I hope so. I can't tell you what the plan is but I don't think it is any secret to say that before breaking through the Hindenburg Line it is necessary to capture the heavily fortified trenches and belts of wire in front of it. This is what we intend to do – smash the system of outposts around here.

Well, this may be my last chance to win a decoration as a sergeant and I'll try hard, if only to be able to show it to Dot. I only hope I come through all right. I'm not at all nervous even if this could be a big one.

Thursday 19th September 1918

I'm wounded! Writing at No. 1 AGH Rouen on Thursday.

From what I can gather, the stunt was a complete success, though it took from zero at 5.20 am until 11 pm to gain all objectives – an advance of 5000 yards. Not bad, eh? Our sector of the line now overlooks the Nord Canal and Hindenburg Line. Now that it is passed I can tell you what the scheme was.

The 16th Battalion would capture and mop up Le Verguier, with the 13th (right) and 15th (left) passing on the flanks and descending down the valley to reach the Brown Line. Here, after forming up and giving Fritz the idea we had halted, we would continue to advance up to the Red Line. The 14th Battalion would then leapfrog us and advance up to the crest overlooking the canal, which was called the Blue Line.

That was the idea, but in the mist and smoke some got lost and others became casualties. I think we underrated Fritz and expected few casualties. Instead, they were heavy. Nevertheless it worked in the end. I enclose a sketch of how it was intended to work:

We got out to the tape at about 4 pm. I was on the left of our platoon connected with B Company. It's a wonder Fritz didn't act then, for it seemed like we made plenty of noise as we moved into positions. In fact, he did put a few MG bursts and flares over. He must have heard the pack of mules and the jingle of the limbers earlier in the night. The rain was torrential and we were all absolutely soaking. Smoking was forbidden, so there was little to do but sit and wait. Of course we weren't even allowed to whisper, so it was a lonely time in which I thought of Dot and home and just prayed to whomever was listening that I might survive the forthcoming hours. It seemed zero would never come. Oh Dot, what a comfort it was just reflecting on our time together.

Well, just before 5.15 am, the words 'One minute' got passed down the line, followed soon after by an enormous barrage of machine guns and artillery. The sky burst into flames. The absence of Fritz's answering flares was remarkable. MGs were good, but alas the artillery were in many places 100 yards short and, as a result, we had many casualties on the tape!

The barrage advanced 100 yards in two minutes, then 100 yards in three minutes and then 100 yards in two minutes for eleven lifts. We followed, but either fog or smoke caused us quickly to lose touch. Indeed, the smoke shelling was too much and some parties got lost while others advanced too far and walked into our own artillery fire. We really couldn't see 2 yards ahead of us at times. We walked on amid the thunderous roars of our own bombardment and the staccato rattle of machine guns. It was a sight for the gods seeing Jerry Oswald firing his Lewis gun from the hip and urging his men on. I, too, was shouting encouragement. The difference was that he was enjoying it. Wire held us up at 200 yards and I was just gathering my men on the edge of

Thiera Copse when *bang*, a shell lobbed next to me. My tin hat went spinning and I felt a blow on the neck and another in the leg. I fell and soon discovered I was bleeding profusely from a neck wound.

Another of my section was hit and he bandaged me and I him. Blood was, however, flowing freely and I was near fainting point, so was taken back to the RAP a distance of 300 yards, located in a cellar. It was just my luck to be wounded at this time and I was cursing freely, I can tell you. There is no worse a feeling than having to let your section continue its fight without you. I had shooting pains in my head and was also badly bruised in the left thigh, caused by a shell fragment, and the doc refused to let me go back. Instead, he insisted I should be taken to the 4th field ambulance.

Here I was dressed and given a feed. There were many prisoners all around and the majority were wounded. Sadly, battalion casualties seemed to be high but I have since heard the stunt was a grand success, even if it was accomplished in a mixed-up fashion. The three tanks that had been promised didn't turn up and the seven canvas dummy tanks, each propelled by a digger and a donkey, didn't materialise either.

Later that day I was taken to No. 10 CCS at Doingt, arriving there at about 10 am, where I was dressed, given something to eat and pushed off to a hospital train immediately. I slept the whole way and awoke just before reaching Rouen.

Am well, in a bed marked 'Blighty'. Wound is trivial, though painful at times. My eyes are sore and head aching. Can't write much more.

Friday 20th September 1918
Still awaiting Blighty transport.

I can't write fully as I've no more diary part to hand, unfortunately. I am being well treated. Fine nurses.

CHAPTER 11

VICTORY!

Tuesday 24th September 1918

Well, I now have my new diary part so I shall continue where I left off.

I found the hospital at Rouen great. Food was good and I was fed on chicken, etc., and I must say we Australians got many comforts that the Tommies missed. The Tommies are always sent to our hospital and us to theirs. The reason being the AIF pays 3/- per day per patient and the British only 1/10 per patient to us. There of are tons of base hospitals about, but I didn't see much of Rouen so I can't describe, if at all. It's a marvel to me that I've being given the Blighty, although I've since heard head wounds are usually sent back for fear of complications.

We got away on an American boat yesterday and struck rather bad weather from the start. Many were very sick. This boat was poor and things were pretty uncomfortable. Slept very little indeed. The treatment on this boat in the way of food and attention was awful. It was not the Yanks' fault, it's the British staff. There was but one tin of bully to eight men, a couple of biscuits, and a drink of tea. The Yank medical lads were particularly good to us but they can't stomach the Tommies. My head was re-dressed in the sick bay.

Arrived in Southampton about 2 pm and, while waiting to disembark, had the following dished up to us: 'All British wounded
this way.' Of course we Australians came forward. '*British* wounded,
I said, not Australian.' This from a Tommy officer. 'What are we
then?' I asked. 'Oh, you're Australians.' I felt like running amok. Are
we not British, then, are we spilling our blood and fighting for a
country of which we are not a part? Are we a bastard lot not to
deserve the name of British? I felt damn wild and very nearly said
things. However, let us say the insult was unintended and put it
down to ignorance. I was wild enough at the time thankfully to
think that I was an Australian, not an ill-educated, unchivalrous
Tommy such as that officer. Ungrateful, insulting ignoramus!

Food on the hospital train was cruel again – more bully beef!
But I didn't mind much. Arrived at Birmingham station where we
were warmly cheered all the way to the ambulances, which took
me to No. 1 Southern General Hospital at Monyhull, about
5 miles out of the town. It's evidently been a school, college or
asylum of some kind – tiled with red brick and very handsome,
with detached buildings all over the grounds. Here, we were given
a basin of soup and bread, a bath and a bed. Head wasn't dressed.

Attention here is pretty rotten and food is scarce. The sisters and
nurses are very free. In fact, I've never met such lack of discipline
in any military hospital before. The VADs were too incompetent
to even dress people, and the sisters, in our ward at least, didn't care
a hang. The Lord help any poor chap who is seriously wounded
who gets into this hospital. I have developed the anti-tetanus inoculation rash on my chest, down the spine and the mouth. The
latter is much swollen and uncomfortable.

Our Australian Red Cross proved a perfect blessing. We got cigarettes and chocolates, shaving soap, tooth powder, etc. given us,
and to those who smoke the gift was much appreciated, as we are
out of money. I have just written a letter to Frances to say I'm back
in England and posted it without a stamp, using the words
'wounded soldier's letter'. Also wrote home but am waiting for
stamps to post it. Just been reading about this railway strike, and
am glad the government is firm in its attitude. I can't think of

words to adequately describe the traitors. Put them in the trenches is the general cry.

I am attempting to grow a moustache; I trust it will turn out better than at last attempt.

Saturday 28th September 1918

Little to report about life in the hospital, except that I was desperate to get out. Heaven knows why I've been given a Blighty. Yesterday, I arrived in London and met up with Frances. Had a very pleasant evening and talked well into the night. She dressed my head and was surprised at the small wound and lucky escape. Then I went to bed. I showed Frances Dot's photo. She didn't pass any remark, though I was hoping to hear her praise it. I dreamt of home.

My new camp is near Weymouth. Arrived there this afternoon. Food is very fair, attention is good, and I think the boys are well satisfied. I have already had three dressings on my wound, they have a fine staff for that. At present I am in the mess, wondering if I feel like writing home now. My neck is stiff and sore from a boil which is forming. I'll get the diary posted tomorrow for Dot's perusal and she will have it before Christmas.

Met Walsh this evening. It was good to see a familiar face, although I think he must be following me. He also got wounded in the attack. I couldn't help but laugh when I saw him come pathetically hobbling up to me (with my head bandaged) with a walking stick. I am not sure which of us is more accident-prone. 'The worst is that doctors tell me the bullet entered the back of my calf so it must have come from one of our own boys,' he told me. That is as long as he wasn't running in the opposite direction! Got wounded late in the day. By all accounts a considerable number of the chaps went south in the action. What poor luck – just when the war news is getting rosy. Anyway, he's feeling rather sorry for himself so I did my best to cheer him up. Apparently he's not received a letter from his wife for two months – poor chap. 'You probably think that after what I've got up to I don't deserve one, but the truth is that I really do miss her and have written to her every week since I left Sydney.' I know that he's a fearful boaster but I am beginning to like him.

Monday 30th September 1918

In dressing my head I had a rough time, pulling hairs out of the wound one at a time with tweezers. It's rendered my head somewhat sore and a bit painful. I tried to play billiards but I couldn't do much. I have been ordered dressings and head exercises to correct the poise of my head. It's a bit skew-whiff, owing to the muscles being somewhat contracted and stiff. I'm afraid I'll feel it a bit.

Wednesday 2nd October 1918

I was half hoping for letters today but none came, it's perhaps a bit too early to expect them. The war news is simply splendid. With Bulgaria out, Turkey breaking up and Fritz retiring on the Western Front, things are looking particularly rosy. How nice it would be to get home to my own little comrade and all the attendant joys of Manly.

Walsh and I were assessing how we've changed, both physically and mentally over the past year and a half. He tells me I've filled out more – not fat, although he went on to say that my effort to grow a moustache was hilarious and thinks I should lose it 'if the wind doesn't do so before then'. I objected and am determined to keep it growing. Anyway, he's bet me that the war will be over before I have anything resembling the real thing. Went on to say I am more outspoken and a bit of a devil – certainly less shy than I used to be. Says that I am the same thinker I ever was and always have something to say. That great god 'ego' which I have almost always hoped to shun stares me in the face. Am I, after all, an egoist, a systematically selfish, self-opinionated fellow? Anyhow, I've set out to say less. I pointed out that perhaps I'd spent too long having Jack Walsh before me!

Friday 4th October 1918

I went into Weymouth to buy a few odds and ends, walked in over the swamp, which cuts off a mile or two. The khaki element has spoilt the place as a seaside resort for all. It was never high-class, but now is full of prostitutes and loose women. Walking back along the promenade I couldn't but notice it. Girls, giggling girls, showing every encouragement. All seats, plots of grass and dark spots down on the beach were occupied by couples in loving embrace – khaki and women everywhere. Perhaps I do an injustice to some honest lovers, but I speak of the majority here. The sight disgusts me.

I'm very seldom in the mood for a 'hook' under such doubtful conditions as those found here. I remember but for a provident accident in 1915, I would have even now been counted as one of the fallen, or perhaps only misled. Anyhow, it's revolting to me to think our lads are making such complete fools of themselves to the detriment of a true love they have once borne or are to bear for some little comrade, even as I have found for myself. Oh Dorothy, there are many times when you have influenced me thus; who can deny the words: 'There is nothing like the fine love of an innocent woman to keep a man straight.'

Tuesday 8th October 1918

So Germany is suing for peace, or at least an armistice to discuss peace. The note to President Wilson is probably just another sub-terfuge of old Fritz to give him time to prepare a line of defence on which to fall back. If we grant that, then the advantage we have so lately won will have been wasted. Now is the time to hit hard and crumble his last and weakest resistance to secure our terms and a lasting peace.

I've been finishing off an album today for Dot and it looks real-ly good. The colours in the rising sun look good and I've copied a purely Australian design for the title page and put 'Greetings to Dorothy' in the battalion colours. I am eminently satisfied.

Got a letter from Edgar giving the battalion news. So they are out for a long spell. My name was taken today as one of the 1914 men. I don't expect anything from it, but I didn't mention that I'd already been home once. If I get another trip, well and good, but I'm not holding out any hope on that score at all.

Sunday 13th October 1918

Today a most unexpected thing has happened. I was warned I was to proceed to Parkhouse on this 1914 stunt tomorrow morning at 6.15 am! All those who joined up in 1914 are getting the first tickets home and it seems I will be included, in spite of having already once returned. Oh joy, if I could only spend 10th January in Manly. But that is hoping too much altogether, though the rumour is that there are five transports waiting to be filled up and to go via America. I may come a thud, but I'll take my good fortune and say naught. I'd obviously willingly give up furlough in return for getting back to Australia. Walsh was terribly jealous but wished me well. Oh, how I hope I get away all right and don't come a thud.

Monday 14th October 1918

Us 1914 boys got away at 6.15 am with forty-eight hours' rations, and struck Fidworth six hours later. Our numbers increased on the journey to about thirty and we marched up together to No. 2 Camp Parkhouse, a distance of about 3 miles. First impressions of the camp have been very good. There are many of the old 13th, and most of them were surprised and happy to see me. The boys seem to have come from everywhere.

There are very few parades here and every consideration is given to the men. Extra rations, plenty of blankets, sports with big prize money, free tea and biscuits at the YMCA hut, all concerts reserved for the 1914 lads, free entertainment at the Fidworth Garrison Theatre as guests of the officers, etc. We are tin gods on our own and I for one much appreciate it, even though I feel myself not entitled to it like some of the boys.

Some of the men have come the big 'G' here already, I mean those who have already been back once, so I don't think my chance a good one. Still, I may scrape through anyway. I've sent word through to all my friends in case I do get away in a hurry. There are all sorts of rumours floating, none dependable, but we won't be here very long.

Thursday 17th October 1918

Today I had a positively fine letter from Dot. I think it's easily the finest letter I have ever got from her. How she does trust me, the little darling! I'm glad her choice of photo is my choice, and I am glad she likes them so. I'm happy to know she is satisfied with me.

The latest news is that a man may have his leave in Blighty, the USA, Canada, New Zealand, South Africa or any part of Australia, seventy-five clear days, 3/- per day subsistence, seventy-five days' pay at the beginning of leave, all accumulated pay and 25 per cent of deferred pay is allowed for the men. Arrangements may be made for the Anzacs' brides to go out, also. Surely, we are the men of the moment. So far I haven't come the 'G', though fifteen artillerymen have been pulled out so far.

Most of the boys have been paid today and the camp is pretty rowdy. There are all sorts of rumours still around, one that a boat of 1914 men has been torpedoed with 700 casualties. I hope it isn't correct. However, I really think that we will be moving in a few days. I wanted to meet some WAACs tonight, as I felt like some female company. However, nothing doing, I walked back early with a friend and am now feeling tired after the chilly 6-mile walk.

Oh yes, there was a parade today with presentation of medals, etc., and an Aussie flag had been prepared. On being unfurled it became clear that it only had four stars on. The officer went sore but wound up with 'Never mind, it's only Tassy, she's slipped off.' Roars from the Aussies, all except the boys from Van Diemen's Land!

Monday 21st October 1918

Gutzers are right! Oh, aren't I stiff. Here I am, nearly right through with the business, and now I'm upended. I was warned for orderly room at 9 am and all unsuspecting, I waltzed along to find myself one of a crowd of fifteen and they were more or less agitated. Enquiring, I discovered that with few exceptions all these boys had been home once – then I knew! Oh, fool that I have been to build up such hopes, such castles in the air. Why, it was only last night I wrote my comrade to tell her that I was all set. And now a gutzer! A list had come up to Fidworth and my name was there, branded as ineligible for the 1914 trip home.

We were told to put our case in writing and it would be submitted to Fidworth for consideration, but were warned there was but little hope. I put in mine and the staff officer read it. I told him straight

I didn't expect any result but while there was life, I hoped. He said: 'You had all that time in Australia and you put in for this trip! Well, I wish you luck and admire your cheek!' He was very decent.

Anyway I've gutzed and there's an end to my scheming. I'll have to unpack, rewrite my letters and grin and bear it. After all, I mustn't grumble, for I've had a good spin. I do hate to hear all these other men openly grousing and cussing and raving over their bad luck. Why don't they accept the decree – they've had their spin, fate has been kind to them with one trip home already. Well, I'm getting used to disappointments. I'll send a message home to Dot via Private Hughes, he's a Manly boy, and Toohey, an old 13th lad as well. I know Dot will fall on his neck and otherwise embarrass him. Perhaps she will even play the piano for him. They leave at 3 am tomorrow and all their kits are stacked. I won't be up to see them off, so I have said goodbye to them all and wished them *bon voyage*.

Now I'll go to bed and reconstruct my dreams of a reunion with Dot before New Year, and I hope for a speedy return after all.

Wednesday 23rd October 1918

The boys have gone, leaving an empty atmosphere about the camp. Parting with the boys stirred many regrets. I felt my disappointment at not joining them very keenly, indeed, as I shook their hands. 'Don't worry, Evans. Won't be long before the war's over and you'll be back in Oz,' etc. I hope they are right. We all feel horribly jealous.

I promised a WAAC girl last night that I'd meet her in Tidworth this evening and, although I didn't feel like it – partly due to the pain in my right eye from a large sty – I decided I couldn't let her down. The little devil didn't turn up. It doesn't do much toward inspiring confidence in the opposite sex. I reckon I have reason to be annoyed.

Forgive me, my comrade, but I simply couldn't write you tonight. The spirit is there but the mood is not. I want some music to awaken me. I am a bit despondent, too, but my never-failing remedy – writing to Dot – is failing me now.

Saturday 26th October 1918

On parade this morning, news was read out. The boys are

becoming rowdy as a result. I feel very lazy and pretty rotten. I'll probably return to Weymouth tomorrow. We hear the draft that left on Wednesday had a rough time of it and spent two nights in the train. They go aboard today. No sign of a movement for the remainder of us.

Met George Woodbridge, an old 'Techite' today, and had a fine afternoon with him. He's off to France on Monday with the machine-gunner. He's a fine-looking lad indeed. In looking for his hut this afternoon I wandered up to the wrong camp and enquired for him in the syphilitic treatment camp, all unknown to me. I went in one hut and asked for him, when I noticed an unpleasant 'chemist's shop' smell.

They asked what unit and I replied 'the Machine Gun School'. 'Oh,' they said. 'This the pox joint!' I beat a hasty retreat. These men undergoing a 606 course are allowed about the camp and wear red or blue bands only to denote their condition. I have noticed them daily at the hospital just below, lined up for their injections. I pity some of the younger lads, scarcely more than boys, the unlucky ones, but the majority are evil-looking, drink-sodden creatures! They seem to revel in their misfortune, too. Some men are past understanding.

One thing I will never be able to understand in this army is how some of our men can so persistently bum cigarettes from passers-by? Anybody. And if they are refused they are indignant and often run to a choice string of foul language. Don't we have some beauts with our AIF?!

Well, my comrade, I'm afraid of late I haven't been thinking as constantly of you as I should, though I certainly did consider our early meeting quite a lot. Why, I haven't even written a decent letter for some time and I don't feel in the mood, even now. However, please be assured that my thoughts about you haven't changed.

This flu is raging and causing ever so many deaths. Many of our boys are suffering. Well, tomorrow I leave with a party of eight men, all gutzers, and return to the camp at Weymouth.

Two days later it is my birthday. I hope I am more cheerful.

Tuesday 29th October 1918

My dearest own
Dearest, I dream of the distant hills,
Smiling clear as the morning skies,
Burning with love divine.
Ever it seems a voice is near,
Speaking to me in accents clear,
Whispering the words I long to hear,
My own, my dearest own
(Brown is more poetic than green)!
Dearest, when warring days are over,
I will return anew,
Dream what the summer holds in store
When I come back to you.
Two brown eyes with love will shine,
Two little hands be clasped in mine.
My heart, my lips will answer thine
My own, my dearest own.

Here is my little birthday thought with apologies to the writer, T. Hutchinson, for the alterations to suit my fancies.

It's hard to think of this as my birthday, I don't feel any older today. I've so far celebrated it with a dental inspection and classification of B1A2 with a TAB inoculation and a two-day no-duty chit. Now it's up to me to write to my comrade. I am thinking she'll be hurt at being left in the lurch so much. I'm getting intolerably lazy and good for nothing.

This influenza epidemic is terrible. The number of deaths are alarming. I don't want another attack myself.

Thursday 31st October 1918

I've been scanning my correspondence chart and I can't help remarking on my falling off. It seems strange that I, a very fond writer, can't keep up my correspondence. All the girls have practically dropped out. They are lucky to get one a month, but Dot stands away out above them all. I've ceased to have such an interest in girls. Dot gets it all. Mother still gets her letters, Father has suffered, and Flip and Russell likewise. It's a peculiar state of affairs, anyhow. Dot is the only one to whom I stick. Surely 'tis a sure sign of my affection in this direction.

Peace, I wonder if it is any nearer? Will Germany fight on? I sincerely hope not but the news seems to indicate that peace before Christmas is still a pretty distant hope.

Saturday 2nd November 1918

A rough night – firstly because it's raining and blowing a hurricane and secondly because some sergeants were 'celebrating'. So I must try to get some sleep early. The drunks awakened me by breaking windows, electric globes, overturning tables, etc. but it didn't last long, thank goodness.

Received a letter from Eyles in France. Edgar's got VD! I can scarcely believe it. Can this be the same person I took to the drum area in Durban? Walsh unkindly collapsed laughing on hearing the news!

Spent the evening in the music room as per usual, and gave the usual items. I'm getting quite a dabster at monologues now and am feeling much more at home with them. I even sang a song in order to get another chap to follow suit.

Monday 4th November 1918

Last night I went to the mess late, only to discover about six sergeants in the mess from our hut indulging in a whisky-drinking competition. They were sinking double and triple headers as fast as they could. I sensed some trouble ahead and hurried home to get to bed. Nor was I mistaken.

It must have been 11.30 pm when I was awakened by a tremendous crash. I sat up in bed and there in the hut was a regular mix-up. I couldn't believe my eyes. A chap alongside my bed limp and motionless, his face all cut and bloody, lying in a pool of blood. Stools and tables were overturned, and there in the middle of the muck were half-a-dozen maniacs cursing, shouting and swearing, fighting each other, punching anybody they could reach. I thought I was dreaming, but it was no dream. 'Who's on my side? Are you on my side?' a man was screaming when – wallop – a fist caught him between the eyes and he bit dust with an 'ugh'. They hit each other for no reason whatever.

Walsh, in a surprising bid to be a peacemaker, tried to calm the situation down when – smash! He fell to the ground and didn't move. After lying there a while he cautiously raised his head, surveyed the scene, and then crawled to bed – the best thing he could do. One chap made a swing, missed, spun around, caught his leg in the debris and stumbled over, striking his face against the stove, where he lay bleeding.

It was time to interfere and a couple of us commenced to pick up the fallen ones, put them to bed and make them as comfy as possible. One 15th Battalion QMS, Montgomery, while acting as a stretcher-bearer, caught a blow on the shoulder, not being quick enough to dodge it completely. Anyhow, everybody was at last put to bed, and all went quiet save for the gurgling and spluttering of one chap, whom I honestly feared would die before the night was out.

This morning revealed the hut in a terrible condition. Men had spewed all over the place, blood was everywhere and all our gear was overturned and all over the floor – a hell of a mess. The men's faces were pictures, all bloody, eyes closed up, black as ink, one man with his thumb out of joint, another with a sprained wrist and none of them was aware of how they received their injuries.

They treated it as a tremendous joke, all except one chap who was very bitter. 'Who started it? ... Who hit me? ... Did I knock you? ... Tell us all about it,' they were asking one another and us spectators. What I knew is just what I saw, but I gathered that the row started outside when one of them knocked another out. Then commenced the rough and tumble. And their eyes! Oh my hat, what pictures! It's laughable, on reflection, though it was damn serious last night when I feared there'd be murder.

And now I come to think of it, fancy such a thing occurring – for men to soak themselves in whisky until they were mad enough to nearly kill each other. No wonder I have such an aversion to drunks. I don't think I shall ever drink after this little occurrence. It's engraved on my mind.

Well, so much for that. Tonight I've written a couple of letters; very unsatisfactory letters, too, I simply couldn't write, though I tried very hard indeed to get the mood.

I fear my head is due to break out soon, it's getting swollen and soft. Hope it keeps off until I am on furlough, then I can report at some nice hospital and have a really good time.

Early this morning my wound started bleeding and bled without check for about half an hour. I went on sick parade and the doctor examined it and told me the reason was that it had healed too quickly. Said it was nothing to be frightened about as the wound was quite superficial, and it was just some foreign matter coming to the surface. I now have my head bandaged up again and everybody is either asking me if I have boils or connecting my trouble with the drunken brawl of Saturday. Anyhow, I look quite the wounded here again.

Well, this book is very nearly finished and I hope it gets home to my own little comrade all correct. If everything goes well, it should be with her soon after peace is declared. What with Germany alone, and Austria, Turkey and Bulgaria out of it, it can only be a matter of months at the most. Why, I might even be on my way home! How bonny that would be. My diary would then be complete in twelve parts and how I would enjoy going through them right from the beginning with my sweetheart, explaining and enlarging as I went on.

Oh, Dorothy, soon you'll be reading this and I don't think it's necessary to tell you that I love you stronger and better than ever. I want you so very much indeed. Good night, beloved. God keep you well and happy till I can once more get home to you and then oh, what a celebration we will have.

My latest communiqué read as follows: 'Am quite well, head is better. My moustache is doing fine. Don't laugh.'

Thursday 7th November 1918

Germany accepts armistice terms! Such is the news, but I for one am sceptical as yet, as are most of the sergeants. Anyway, it's an excuse for the boys to celebrate. There's a hell of a noise in the canteen. They're making a night of it, anyway.

The news came to us as we sat in the music room. In the middle of a song, there was a great outbreak of cheering in the lobby which interrupted the singer. A chap burst in upon us, paper in hand, breathless and red in the face, yelling, 'War is over!'

He was too excited to explain for some minutes but, on regaining his composure, he informed us that armistice terms had been accepted. Most of the boys immediately thought it was the end of the war and there was a loud burst of clapping, cheering and stamping for ten minutes. The boys then sang patriotic songs until they were hoarse and made a great noise. Most were too excited to keep still and rushed around like madmen.

I am excited, but sceptical. Anyway, the news certainly cut our concert short. One of our officers came along to tell us the news was true and that Germany was clearing out 'hell for leather' from the occupied territory. True to Australian humour, a digger yelled out, 'Is there to be a parade tomorrow?' Laughter and cheers. Then came the eternal feminine touch. Mrs Rutham, who has been helping behind the bar, spoke and told the boys that she would treasure the memory of this day forever. Said she'd rather have been with the boys on this day than anywhere else. How they cheered her warmly expressed sentiment and she blushed!

Commenting later, I cannot help noting the effect the news has had upon the boys generally. We sergeants, with few exceptions, are not inclined to optimism. However, the news is certainly in the papers and it's even been put on the noticeboard of one of the orderly rooms. I, with the majority, am not convinced, but I must admit having reflected very seriously upon the effect on me if the news is dinkum.

How fine it would be to get peace for Christmas and to be on the way home. Oh, it's too good to dwell upon. If tomorrow the news is confirmed, perhaps I shall indulge in further dreams.

Friday 8th November 1918

So it was rumour after all. Well perhaps it's just as well that I hadn't put too much confidence in the news. But I am afraid it has shattered many hopes.

I hear that the boys, celebrating in No. 10 canteen, refused to let the place close, and further, broke the place down, stole the till and declared beer free. The girls in the bar were molested in a manner which reflects no credit upon the Aussies. A lecture by the wing commander warned us against paper rumours. He stated that he did not believe war would be over this year. I hope he is wrong. Let us hope at least hostilities will have ceased by this time and then we will have a right joyful Christmas. I think those responsible for printing that rumour should be brought to book. It's disgraceful to think that in a time such as this people should be allowed to publish such false statements merely to line their pockets.

Saturday 9th November 1918

The boys are beginning to gig me about my moustache, it's rather straggly as yet and is almost ginger. If it were dark it wouldn't be so bad. Anyhow, I'll keep it for a few weeks longer and give it a fair chance.

Sunday 10th November 1918

I hear Frances has been down with the flu. It's terrible.

News is very good. I am hoping for the best but I cannot be too optimistic. It seems that the whole country is just seething with excitement. Chaps down from London reckon the place is simply crowded with people awaiting the news. Special Sunday editions of the *News of the World* publish glaring headlines of 'THE WAR IS WON'. Still, there's no news of the armistice being signed. Riots in Berlin seem to be serious and will probably hasten the end.

It's now up to me to write my home mail. I feel more in the mood for it today, even though the absence of home mail doesn't tempt me to start.

Monday 11th November 1918

The Great War is over after 1561 days. Fighting continues right up to the ceasefire deadline at 11 o'clock in the morning. The guns outside Westminster signal the news. Queen Mary declares it is 'the greatest day in the world's history'.

I am writing at 3 pm and the news of the signing of the armistice is in the air. I haven't seen any authentic news yet, though. I am hoping that this time it is quite true.

An hour later:

SPECIAL ORDER
Armistice information has been received from HQAH Depots in UK that an armistice with Germany was signed this morning. The band will play round the Depot at 17.00 in honour of the occasion.

So ran an order published at 4 pm. It further asks us to remain calm and to do nothing to bring discredit upon ourselves.

The fighting is finished. Hurrah! Hostilities ceased at 11.00 am on the eleventh day of the eleventh month! Celebrations have already begun. The camp is very excited. I have been put on special piquet for tonight to quell disturbances. I can see some rough times. The boys know they are destined to return home.

Later: The whole place is agog with excitement, there's already been some window smashing by the drunks and a raid on our canteen. When that closed, the boys came up in force to our mess. I arrived there just in time to see them retreat with their tails between their legs.

The band has been playing around the camp all evening and there's cheering all over the place. Everybody seems perfectly wildly happy and excited, and well may they be so. Peace! And after four years of war and bloodshed. Within myself I am a tumult of joy and even though I don't expect to get home until some months, I am already planning for the future. Oh, my comrade, how dear you are to me!

My letters which I wrote to be posted after my death will now be of no use. Thank God. The war is finished and we have won. Hurrah!

Wednesday 13th November 1918

Of course, there is still much excitement today, the conditions of armistice are giving satisfaction to all and everybody is rejoicing. The boys are rather hard to manage and are having much their own way. Many are AWOL, as is to be expected, and many were caught endeavouring to get to London. Rumour has it that Little Willie is assassinated. What is certain is that he has cleared out. There was the usual parade today, but tomorrow is to be a general holiday. I hear there is a rugby team to be picked for a tour around the country and I should like to be picked. A good dose of training should make me really fit and well, which is just the way I want to feel.

There's a hell of a lot of piquets since the news came in, perhaps necessary, but it seems the heads have the wind up. The men don't like it and usually we get about half of them, the rest clear out and avoid doing any duties at all. It's useless to do anything at this stage, for they are uncontrollable. I hear London is still going mad, too.

I'm still hoping for my mail, I can't understand my rotten luck. I'm just dying for news of home.

Friday 15th November 1918

A general holiday was granted to the troops yesterday – victory leave. It was a fine and sunny morning, so I went for a bit of a walk down through the village and strolled through the church cemetery. The place was full of Australians' graves, the influenza epidemic being responsible. There was also the grave of the matron of Sutton Veny Hospital who died a few days ago. It was rather a despondent place to be at in such a time so I continued my walk. Later, went out to Warminster with a few of the boys but nothing report-worthy occurred.

What a nice surprise this morning. Four letters from Mother, two from Dot and another from Raymond, but for some reason I was disappointed. Dot's letter wasn't satisfying at all, somehow, I was hoping for a more natural one. She was evidently very tired when she wrote. I had to cackle at Mother's 'You must be growing (or have grown) into a very naughty boy!' I am afraid poor Mother won't understand me.

Well, I'm glad Dot is having a happy time, I only wish I were there to take her about. I am very envious of her closer friends at this time. I received a letter from one of her friends, Yolande, this morning she talks about the end of the war. 'Won't she be pleased?' is her P.S., presumably talking about Dot.

Detailed today for canteen sergeant, a job I don't take kindly to. The canteen girls are giggling fools. I started at 6 pm in the beer bar. I have control of both wet and dry canteen. In these times of peace and celebration it's a precarious job. I don't mind that part of it, I'll risk the chance of my head being split open with a pint pot during a brawl, but I do object to the atmosphere of filthy language and drunken men. I won't stop in this job for long. At least it exempts me from parades.

Saturday 16th November 1918

For some reason, ever since the end of the fighting I have been inflicted by horrible dreams. Even when I wake up I can't seem to get them out of my head. The one that is most recurring is about Paddy Nolan. I hear his cries out in no-man's-land, but flares and machine-gun fire prevent me from risking everything to go out to search for him. At first his shouts are audible and clear, but gradually they fade away until there is silence all around. Even the guns stop. I wake up in a cold sweat.

If that is not bad enough, I also have developed a bad cold, not flu though. There's frost every morning and I have seven blankets! Received a note from Frances today. She seems to have recovered after a nasty bout. Many haven't been so lucky. Poor old Corporal Briggs, for instance, survived every bullet and shell that Jerry could throw at him for three years, only to get this damn influenza. It took just three days before it killed him. What a tragedy. No doubt, after the armistice he had written home to his girl telling her to expect him back soon. Now he is resting forever in England.

Monday 18th November 1918

The boys here are always commenting on the fact that I don't drink, smoke, swear or talk detrimentally of women – strange to say, I'm not an object of jeers for it, though at times I do think they are inclined to 'gig' at me. What do I care? My comrade is the reason I don't indulge, in the latter at any rate, and I am everlastingly grateful for her influence on me.

Montgomery has just received a telegram to say he is the father of twins, and how my inside revolts to hear the suggestive talk and the suggestive treatment of so sacred a thing. 'Are they yours, Monty? ... Don't get snared,' etc. Well, well, it's the army all over.

My throat is still troubling me and I have influenza pains. However, I took a hot bath and have gone to bed early. The boys advised some hot rum. I have just accepted and it is having a remarkable effect.

Thursday 21st November 1918

Throat worse this morning. It's intensely cold and I have been lying around the fire all day. I shall be glad to get out of this country and back to my own little comrade, whom I know is waiting anxiously for me. I can hardly swallow, but as I have no temperature I am fit, according to army standards.

Had a batch of delayed Aussie mail tonight – August's – Dot's eighty-two, Mother's seventy-two, one from Raymond and Harold, and three from Father, etc., all excellent reading. I am much bucked up. Dear little girl, to write to me so often, I'll never lose my love for you! As I guessed, the old man had been wishing I had a rise in rank, and so do I. It looks far too much like incompetence, though I am satisfied myself it isn't. It's up to me to make good in civil life now to prove it.

In the mess is a poster, which just reads: 'PEACE – the people of Sutton Veny salute you for your bravery and courage.' It's a fine gesture and one that the boys appreciate. Walsh has a dose of VD which he is having secretly treated. Silly fool. He's still the same self-opinionated little fool, with a tremendous swagger over his conquests, etc., but still, it was good to have him to talk to.

CHAPTER 12

WAITING FOR AN 'AUSSIE'

Tuesday 26th November 1918

Today I was called to the orderly room about my application for furlough, and I have reason to believe that I am to get it as from Thursday week, though I shall endeavour to put it off for one week.

There are tons of jobs to be had. They are permanent jobs lately held by low-category men who are now to be returned to Australia. A3 men are now being taken on. I won't have one, although I've been offered several, including catering and bookkeeping, as I fear if I do I will be kept longer on this side.

Have been inclined to arguments lately, the boys say I'm always out for one, but we dozen occupants of our hut are good-natured and nobody loses their block when sarcastic or nasty things are said to one another. We spend most of the time gambling. There's nothing better to do. I'm glad I'm not a smoker as I am able to use the cigarettes as gambling chips. They are a terrific price in England and the scheme whereby they are sold duty-free, if ordered and paid for a week in advance, is a great saving to the men. This week I've put in for some De Reskes for furlough. I always believe in carrying them on leave as so many girls smoke nowadays and expect a cigarette.

Tonight, in search of pleasure, I went with another sergeant down to the village pictures – Charlie Chaplin – but the projector went bung. Even though women were present, the diggers still used filthy language to express their displeasure. I often wonder if they ever reflect for an instant that their mother was a woman.

Dot will begin to think I am forgetting her. That is not so, I dream nightly of my comrade and the time, not far distant I hope, we are to have together.

Got a parcel from Frances today, throat lozenges, sweets and some cake, etc.

Tuesday 3rd December 1918

I've managed to get my furlough put off until the 12th. That will bring me back on Boxing Day! Came home to find a parcel from my own little girl. It is worth everything to me, especially her enclosed letter number eighty-one. The smallest thing from her is more valuable to me than the best and biggest from anybody else.

All men I hear are to be marked A3, ready for France, or else C class for early shipment back to Australia. I suppose I will have to get A3, though I badly want to get home early, I'd certainly forego my furlough to get an early boat. I may as well try to put in an application to be returned early, as all men who enlisted up to June 1915 are to be sent back in the first batch. Hopefully they'll not discover I've already been back! It's worth a go, anyway.

Wednesday 4th December 1918

I went to bed at midnight and at about 1.30 am was rudely awakened to be told that someone, or some crowd rather, had raided our bar, and they wanted some help to chase the mob. I dressed quickly and went up, but the mob had dispersed when I arrived. They'd cleared out all our stock, about £10 worth, I should think. Some of the earlier-comers chased three of the mob and caught them, so we put them in the clink. They protested violently but they were shut in the cooler. Several of their cobbers came along afterwards, but slunk away when they saw the crowd of sergeants there.

I went back to bed but no sleep came at all. I tossed till dawn. The cowardly mob that led the raid should be shot. I'd have much pleasure in catching a few of them at their game. They're not men, they are curs! That's that.

I now hear that B1A3 are going home, too; I hope so, in case I put in an application to be considered for early return to Aussie. I mentioned that I was a 1914 man and – I must be an awful liar by nature – that I had considerable interest in the Japanese merchandise trade and wished to get home to develop it! Perhaps something will come of it.

So Mother got the photos safely. I have two of her letters and Dot's taken the one with the hat on. I am rather surprised. I thought Mother would like that one best. Certainly the one she picked is my fancy too, though. Elsie and Ray's letters are very cheery too, and Flip writes with news of his enlistment. October 1 is the latest mail date – not bad, eh? Also got a telegram from Miss Pringle asking if I'd like to bring a friend. She's evidently looking forward to my visit. I've telegrammed her to say that I would be arriving on the 12th, and gave her the train time.

Tuesday 10th December 1918

Intended going to the movies but slipped a bit and got there too late. Instead I went with another sergeant to the manor house for a while. The sergeant became quite confidential and told me of his troubles. He got a girl into trouble and married her before the baby was born. They are unfortunately very unhappily married. I'm sorry for both the girl and him. He's only young, with all his life before him, but I really admire him for doing the right thing by the girl.

The hut is quite empty now, as the last of the first batch of the early returnees to Australia go tonight. I don't expect to get much sleep tonight. They are going straight to the boat, lucky devils. One chap masquerading as a sergeant major was clinked. Later, Sergeant Woodburn came in to say goodbye. He was drunk and very, very funny with his 'Thank you very, very much for your kindness and friendship, my old China plate.'

Later: I have just come from the mess, where there was an argument that got out of hand – loaded revolvers were brandished. I couldn't leave for about an hour as it would have looked as if I had the wind up, though I was dying to get to bed.

Thursday 12th December 1918

I left camp in time to catch the 10.58 am train. Changed at Bristol, where I had three hours to wait for a connection, so I got rid of my bag and went to the town centre. From there I took a tram to see the wonderful suspension bridge at Clifton, the largest suspension bridge in the world, started in 1834 and finished in the '60s. It is 234 yards long in the span and is held by three separate steel cables in gridiron formation. Also had a glimpse of a German submarine, the U96, which had just come up to Bristol. It was moored alongside the docks there and I tried to get aboard, but it wasn't to be open for inspection until 11 am tomorrow. There was a great crowd looking on. It was a big submarine, quite a late one, and was in a pretty rusty condition, but our navy men were getting it ship-shape.

Got into a carriage with some repatriated prisoners of war who had been in Germany for twelve months. They looked well, but told awful tales of starvation and being whipped to do their work. They were up by Mons and complained they rarely received Red Cross parcels. Some got cards notifying them that bread was being sent to them, but they never got it. They were simply abandoned by their German captors when the armistice was signed. Apparently, the German guards who had been in the line treated them far better than any others and they were greatly satisfied at the cessation of hostilities. The boys, there were three of them, were off to their various homes in Devon on a month's furlough.

Miss Pringle and her mother were awaiting me at Teignmouth. Mrs Pringle was elderly, and awfully kind and motherly looking. Her daughter, about thirty, is not attractive, has funny eyes, a rice-pudding face, horrid protruding teeth and an impediment in her speech, but she is very nice mannered. We had a really fine evening. They all insisted that I should sing so I had to submit to the weight of positive argument. They live about five minutes from the station and I was made to feel at home as soon as I stepped inside the house. It's a three-storey semi-detached building and I have a nice bedroom with a double bed looking out over the sea. I am bound to be happy, and I feel quite at home. Mrs Pringle is the daughter of a clergyman and a bit religious, but very broad-minded. Said she thought I was thirty at first sight but has since decided I am much younger now.

Friday 13th December 1918

After breakfast I went out down to the town to have a look around. It's rather quiet at this time of the year. Saw a most curious notice in a baker's window: 'Save your coal and gas. Dinners cooked here for you. Price 1d each!' That tickled me. Went around the wharves and docks, watched men fishing with no small luck. The esplanade is nice but somewhat neglected since the war. There were not too many people about and I take it an Aussie is a bit of a curio, judging by the stares I got.

Hooked a girl on my walk, aged about twenty-six, well built, about 5 foot 6 inches with awfully pretty red hair. She's Cornish, she said, but hasn't the broad dialect and is well educated. The hook was all mine, although she's an awful flirt. I was with her until about 12.30 pm, walking and talking throughout. The little devil then revealed she is expecting her man sometime soon, but I strongly suspect she doesn't love him. I told her I'd probably see her in the morning and came home in time for dinner.

I am very well fed here in spite of the shortage, but the Devonshire cream and butter is missing, owing to rations. Mrs Pringle urges me to eat and eat more. Oh yes, I'm quite happy!

This place is awfully pretty, red and green; the red earth and cliffs are beautiful. It's hilly country, but oh, so pretty. I've got a lot to explore. I really do want my little comrade to come walking with me – this place would be even bonnier then. Well, it won't be long now I expect, so I won't start grumbling.

I am writing in the living room and the diary is exciting lots of comment. They desperately want to read it. I wonder why?!

Sunday 15th December 1918

Met my red-haired friend yesterday morning. I learnt her name is

Betty. It was raining, but we went for a walk. Sheltered under an old building and flirted most abominably. Went out over the river in the penny ferry to Shoreham, quite a quaint place where there are still a number of Belgian refugees. Saw a most quaint old church.

Yesterday was election day and one naturally expected some excitement. The women, voting for the first time, were all smiles. Outside the polling booth I noticed three of them hobnailing their friend as she came out with 'How did you get on?', etc. There were very few political views expressed by anyone, and one comment takes some beating. In a loud voice, one chap said: 'I think the least we can do is vote for Colonel Mildmay, seeing he's out at the front. Never mind what party he is, it's the least we can do!' Fancy that as a reason for voting. No wonder this country is ill governed when men so ignorant are allowed to vote. The educational system here needs some drastic reforms.

The Pringles also have the impression that I am engaged to Dorothy. I showed them a photo of her and they all jumped to conclusions. Mrs Pringle particularly praised the knitted socks she has made me, especially my comrade's birthday pair. Says she's never seen an example of nicer knitting. Dear little girl, with her labour of love. I've much to be thankful to her for, I know.

The Pringles had a discharged soldier to tea tonight, on crutches, quite a decent old chap. We had a bit of music, etc. I think the Pringles very decent and kindhearted. There was a mothers' meeting tonight so I did a bunk and went to the pictures with the soldier. The picture of the surrender of the German fleet was particularly good. There is a great number of nurses about and they ogle one at every opportunity, but I don't fancy them. They're not my sort at all.

Thursday 19th December 1918

Met red-haired again this afternoon and very nearly forgot myself. It's her fault, she leads me on and I am only human, after all. I really and honestly want to be good and wholesome, too, for my comrade's sake. I won't go for another walk with her. I suppose I shouldn't blame her – it's not chivalrous. Somehow I've felt quite mean. I love my little girl oh so much and I really don't want to do anything I'd be ashamed to tell her.

Mrs Pringle thinks I mistrust every woman but Mother and my girl. She says she thinks I'll marry happily and take a great delight in my home.

Wednesday 25th December 1918

Christmas Day! Bells have been chiming all day long. Yet to me it doesn't seem at all like Christmas, more like a Sunday. It's been a glorious day – the sun shining and not a cloud. Still, somehow it isn't my idea of an English Christmas, after all. I look for piles of snow and big log fires, mistletoe and crackers, etc. Such romantic notions have been rather quashed, but there has been a war on so I shouldn't be surprised. Went for a walk. Arrived home in time for dinner but I wasn't very hungry. In any case, there wasn't exactly a feast in the usual acceptance. There was no poultry, but we had a joint of beef. I thought it was delicious but it didn't meet with Mrs Pringle's approval.

I placed the gifts on the plates at breakfast and there were cries of delight. Mrs Pringle gave me a silver matchbox, quite a bonny affair, old, probably one of her husband's. I much appreciated the sentiment. It must have meant a real wrench to give that for I know she was very happy and loved her husband very much. She told me as much herself. For example, she never goes to church on Christmas Day anymore because she always used to go with her husband and it now makes her feel very unhappy. He's been dead ten years.

She's a decent old sport but, oh, I do wish I could have spent this Christmas at home with Dorothy, but it will be all the sweeter next time.

Friday 27th December 1918

Back at camp after a very successful fourteen days of furlough.

Now to review my letters. There were two numbered eighty-eight, also eighty-nine, ninety and ninety-one from my dear comrade, eighty-two and eighty-three from Mother, one each from

Elsie, Ray, Harold and Father. That's the lot; there was also a local one, from Frances.

Well, it's a really satisfying mail from my dear chum. But, oh, how I envy Ray Foulkes taking Dot to the national park. I was really jealous on reading about it as Ray always had a bit of a reputation as a one with the girls, but now I have had time to consider it all, it's not half as much as I am doing over this side. So poor Dot sympathises with my fourth wound. I sometimes worry that mother would be terribly upset if she knew how much more I tell Dot. Perhaps she understands the situation even though I've never told her. Oh, I'm jealous again. What right has Major Burrett to take my little comrade to a dinner and theatre, I'd like to punch his nose.

Dot wants me to pull up on the gambling stakes, though she doesn't say so. I'm interested about Elsie looking forward to being married. I guess Dot is just a wee bit jealous, too: 'The right man I know loves me, but he has never asked me to marry him, yet I am content to wait until he does - if it is ten years.' What a wealth of love and affection lies beneath those words, oh, however, was it that I should be the lucky man? Oh, Dorothy, some day – perhaps I can offer you more than I do at present.

Yes, that mail has bucked me up so. It was by far the best of my Christmas presents, I think.

Sunday 29th December 1918

The doc made an exam and I was marked 'Fit – Home Service'. I hope to be on the boat by about Saturday. I am told I will be boarded on Monday and in all probability I'll be on a boat and away by 15 January. What a joy to get home around the end of February! I must get all my gear clean and ready to move. The sooner on the boat, the better.

Got a letter from Frances today. She enclosed a slip about Anzac brides. She's a laugh. Sometimes I think that, although she teases me a lot and is rather harsh about some of my traits, I may secretly have a place in her heart. She's never been overt about it at all quite the opposite! But it is just an inkling. Foolish perhaps! Anyway, I have written to Dot again today and couldn't help myself from filling the letter with a lot of sentimental piffle. I badly want to see her.

Wednesday 1st January 1919

New Year's resolutions should, of course, be my first consideration, and in days such as these, are necessarily very glad and joyful ones.

Summing up last year, I know I have failed in a lamentable manner, but my love for Dorothy has not diminished one iota and I still think of her as the one and only. My own dearest comrade. Still, I know I have failed in some respects and I haven't been as good as I wanted to be, and I have many little sins, none of which, I must confess, have caused me very much in the way of sleepless nights. Still, the war is over and many of my shortcomings go with it, I hope.

Well, now for the peace resolutions. No more of the army, hard work now for me and I'll be successful for my little girl. I will earn money and provide a home for my true mate. I'll endeavour to prove that my love is true and good and honest and consistent. Harder than ever will I try to prove worthy of her. Oh, give me the strength, and should I fail, may it be then that my comrade will forgive.

There it is, written on the first of January and, oh, how I pray to be able to fulfil its conditions in full.

Yesterday I was marched over to No. 6 camp, an embarkation company, and saw in the papers that I am set for the *City of Exeter*, sailing on the 9th. She's a fast passenger steamer of some 9300-odd tonnes, travelling via Suez and carrying passengers to Colombo. I am hoping for a good and quick passage. This afternoon I sent a cable reading, 'Sailing Ninth, "City of Exeter", Happy New Year. Love, Eric', so I feel much easier in my mind. Bade farewell to Walsh before I left. Strange to say, but I will miss him. He was as sick as a dog that I am returning before him but isn't sure whether he will have a wife to return to, anyway. He probably won't if his VD doesn't clear up. She still hasn't been in touch with him. It's been many months now. Most peculiar, to say the least.

Demobilisation forms have been supplied to us, all asking a lot of unnecessary and personal questions about age, place of residence, occupation, etc. It's altogether unnecessary, I think. Fancy asking a man in any case if he wants to be an early returnee to Aussie. Some of the answers to the questions are quite funny. A typical one in answer to 'Do you desire to return early to Australia and why?' is, 'Yes, I've seen enough of this one' or 'Yes – family reasons', the latter in many cases from single men.

My moustache has had a tough time of it. They all suggest that I should start the New Year without 'encumbrances'! I've started the New Year well anyhow and am told I am to become the acting sergeant major for the *City of Exeter* crowd. Some dog!

Friday 3rd January 1919

I am presently running the camp without an officer. It's snowing very heavily and my feet are freezing. To leave the hut is to invite an ambush of snowballs. Gosh, but it is cold – hurrah, here is a batch of Aussie mail, what grand luck. It will be my last, I suppose. There's one from Dot, Mother and Lillian, and three from Father, latest one dated 4 November 1918. I am very lucky. I can't understand just why I've been marked severely wounded. It's too bad to do that and make them so anxious.

Anyhow, I'm feeling ever so pleased and happy about it all. It's great to have such a fine lot of people to write to me. Oh, what a fine little comrade I have in Dot!

By the way, my wound has discharged a bit today, but it hasn't been very bad.

Saturday 4th January 1919

There was a foot of snow piled around our door this morning and it was crisp but fine. Everything looked very pretty, a typical English winter scene as I used to be given to expect, but it was too cold and so, as we are soldiers, the prettiness was overlooked and the men cursed it because they had to parade. There was a little snowballing and the snow hung around most of the day, but it is raining now so it will soon clear.

On the face of the fact that I have been asked to take the job as ship's sergeant major as a WO class 1, carrying extra duty pay over the heads of a dinkum RSM and a CSM, is a sign, I think, that I am satisfactory. The extra duty pay of 4/6 per day would be quite acceptable and I know that a recommendation has already been forwarded to headquarters about it and if I'm lucky, I'll 'click'. I've got a bonny orderly room and a good bunk, and the work is extremely interesting, so I don't mind it a bit. It will make the time pass quite pleasantly.

Sunday 5th January 1919

I've got things much more ship-shape (literally too!) and feel easier in my mind. My recommendation for ship's sergeant major has gone through and I've been told to put up the coat of arms and to get a 'Sam Browne'. I am also entitled to a batman – ho, ho, I'll have a swelled head, yet. I expect to be on the boat soon as there is much to be done before the men board. That will suit me nicely.

I got Dot's latest photo and don't exactly like it. It seems too posed, though it's a bonny likeness and I am ever so pleased to have it.

Wednesday 8th January 1919

There were two unnumbered letters from Dot, and one each from Mother and Father, the latter's running to sixteen pages. I suppose these will be the last letters I'll receive this side of the world. Poor Dot's been offending some of our narrow-minded gentry. I'm glad Dot doesn't mind that I'm still only a sergeant and have no decorations, though I know she'd think much more of me if I had some. It is a shame but nothing can been done about it now and I fully believe, and feel that the men I served with would agree, that I have given a good account of myself. Her letter ended with the words: 'Brace yourself for the most fantastic welcoming. I will be waiting at the wharf, I can promise, and am longing to embrace my hero soldier.'

Yes, I guess there'll be some big celebrations when I lob back home. I've found that when I've been writing the daily occurrences in this book, I've been framing my note for Dot to read, too much so, in fact. I think it's more like a personal letter from myself to my own darling comrade. Rumour has it that the boat doesn't now leave until the 14th of this month. Hang the damn thing. I'm pins and needles now to get home.

Friday 10th January 1919

It seems strange that I, having written my daily note, have actually finished it off without a word of 'our' day. I came to my senses just as I finished writing. I have not written to my comrade, deeming it useless. I really have been thinking of our great day, though the pressure of work drove it from me when I started at 9 am and it's only just come back again at 10.30 pm.

Sunday 12th January 1919

I got word at 11 am that I was to leave this afternoon and proceed to Manchester, as the boat is coaling in the ship canal. I have everything ready now and am waiting for my car to take me to the station.

Well, goodbye Sutton Veny, I hope never to see this place again. I have really not a good word to say for the place. I've got rigged out with a new hat and tunic on the strength of my new appointment and if I can get a pair of slacks, I'm all set. I've even got a batman now, some style!

I can hardly believe that I am about to go home. It seems so long ago that I first met my comrade. I seem to have known her for a lifetime instead of a mere three years. Well, well – I hope to always think of her as I do now, as my own true little comrade. Yes, I think when I first fell in love with Dorothy it was the biggest surprise I have ever experienced. What a thud!

We eventually arrived in London at 8.15 pm and had to wait again until 11.45 pm for the next train. Found ourselves still travelling way after midnight. I am absolutely exhausted.

Monday 13th January 1919

The train was slow and dirty, but the carriage was well heated and I slept fairly well. We arrived at the central station and entrained for Islam. On the journey down, the guide explained the ship was coaling and we would have to carry our kits for three-quarters of a mile as no transport was available.

There was heavy fog when we arrived and one couldn't see 5 yards in front when we got off the train. We eventually found the boat and got on board. Everything was dirty, etc., but first impressions were good. The steward gave us an excellent breakfast and if that is a sample for the rest of the trip, we are set. I have a nice two-berth cabin for myself. The rest of the sergeants will have to sling hammocks.

We were due to leave at 10 pm but owing to the fog it was impossible and departure deferred to 2 pm. I went back to Manchester and had a feed. Rang Frances to say a final goodbye. She was rather tearful and that in turn got my emotions to rise. She has looked after me so well and has been such a good friend. Thought about ringing Alice, but thought better of it. Best to leave with happy memories rather than to open up old wounds. I eventually boarded the boat again at 9.50 pm to find out that the ship now sails in the morning. I'm dead-tired so I'll get to bed at once. Wonder what my little girl is doing tonight? It's great to know that soon I'll be with her again.

CHAPTER 13

HOMEWARD BOUND

Wednesday 15th January 1919

We're off! Troops began to arrive about 1 pm yesterday and were stowed away with few hitches. Passengers arrived at the same time and I got well in with some nurses by getting them a fatigue party to carry their luggage. I was very busy running around all day. Our officers were all pretty drunk, especially the adjutant, and people seemed to think I was an enquiry bureau, a fatigue party and a runner, all together. I allotted twenty-three berths to sergeants and the remainder swing in hammocks. The deck space for the troops is poor, but below on the troop decks there's no crowding at all. One of the chaps found three rats in a state of decomposition down there and you should have heard the language!

There's a big wind and a fairly rough sea today. Most people are well sick, but I am lucky and don't really expect to be sick. There were very few at dinner tonight.

Friday 17th January 1919

Most of the boys are still frightfully sick and they were lying about all over the decks. I felt very much like vomiting myself after seeing them all about, but managed to get over the feeling successfully. Had a great deal of trouble issuing fatigues today and feel jolly tired. The boys got obstreperous and refused to keep to their allotted decks. Unfortunately the provost sergeant wasn't tactful and nearly provoked a fight. It is going to be quite tricky getting them to follow any orders as they are beginning to feel the first taste of freedom. Anyway, I had a talk to them and most listened. A few made obscene remarks and I 'hopped them out' but the curs wouldn't come out and say it to my face.

A little kiddie, 18 months old died of seasickness last night and was burnt at 4 pm. I didn't attend the service. I am told this is the first death this captain has had on his ship in 25 years.

Monday 20th January 1919

A truly beautiful day. We passed Gibraltar at around 9 am and in spite of the heat later in the day, the mountains on our port side, presumably Spain, were snowcapped. My jurisdiction, which extends over all on the boat except the officers, makes me quite, the man and I take orders from no officer except the CO troops or his adjutant.

Somebody instituted a love letter competition and I entered two articles. One, the letter of an ill-educated Aussie, and another a dinkum. I wonder if my little girl will think it foolish and think I oughtn't? Later, at tonight's concert, they read out the two winning love letters. I am now more than glad I didn't win, for a love letter read under such conditions becomes such utter piffle. It wasn't natural, the winning one, more a composition.

The highlight of my day was when I received a letter from the King. This is it:

The days are getting hotter, but we managed a very successful afternoon with a decent boxing display followed by a pillow fight. I entered and was successful in beating my opponent.

Friday 24th January 1919

Passed Malta on the port yesterday afternoon.

Payday for all (I drew £2) and as a result nearly everybody is below gambling. There's been a bit of discontent among the sergeants about accommodation in cabins. This boat is now like a miniature Monte Carlo. All sorts of gambling games are on board and it's quite an abject lesson to go below and see them at work.

The passengers' concert and fancy-dress ball was, however, the outstanding feature of today. As to the first, it was absolutely putrid and that is praising it up. It is extraordinary the diggers were polite enough not to count them out.

The fancy dress, however, was very good indeed. Noteworthy were a monkey, a dervisher (eastern devil), a digger (Sister King in shorts with her knees darkened with permanganate of potash), a pierrot, several 'male' ladies, a ghost, the moon, a wounded Aussie in a tin hat, gas mask and bloody bandage around his head, etc., and thousands of others. I enjoyed watching the dancing for a while, but it made me want my little girl ever so badly, so I came away to write this. A number of yarns are circulating about the lady passengers and officers!

Sunday 26th January 1919

We were all warned to wear life belts from 10.15 am until in port, as we were passing through a minefield. On entering Port Said, four steamers sunk with just their masts above water illustrated just how dangerous this area is.

Port Said is just the same as when I last saw it. A fine place, but alive with disease. No-one was allowed ashore, not even passengers. Lots of Lighthorse came along the banks to greet us and our lads stripped, hopped over the side and swam to them. If I'd have been a private I'd have done likewise. Police boats kept the natives from around us. I actually felt sorry for the redcaps as they were stoned or rather 'potatoed' at every opportunity by our lads. At our bows is a small sunken steamer, which was purposely torpedoed nine months ago as she was carrying dynamite and a fire burst out.

Have been talking to the embarkation staff officer, who tells me the Port is full of influenza and that those troops who slipped boats here would be put in a compound and find themselves last home.

Monday 27th January 1919

When I awoke we were passing through the Ismalian Lakes, so I missed the sights of the old fight at El Kantara. A couple of Aussie Flying Corps planes later came around to wave at us and performed a flying exhibition.

The day has been hot, and the everlasting sand, sand, sand on both sides! It's very monotonous and brings back many memories of those days of training in Egypt before going to Gallipoli. It all feels such a long time ago. We passed many signs of our old fortifications, Ferry's Post being recognised by many. Our trench systems still stand – but are beginning to cave in.

Just after the Bitter Lakes we tied up to allow the *Wyrema* to pass amid much cheering. The whole canal is a wonderful piece of work, 87 miles and undoubtedly a highway of the world. It takes thirteen hours to pass through.

We anchored midstream to await some troops and just mooned about. Picked up sixty-five in all – mostly C class men with great tales to tell of the Allenby victory. They are all very anxious to get home. Cleared Suez by 8 pm.

Wednesday 29th January 1919

The Red Sea, notorious for its heat, is playing its part. I'm half-dead. There's sports this afternoon and I am too done up to watch them. I had to put a chap in the clink for direct disobedience, a thing I was very reluctant to do on a return voyage, but it was very necessary.

Thank goodness I'm popular or I'm afraid I'd have been hurt today, as the diggers were in a fine state of ferment. This was because we had decided to give a concert to the passengers and to let the men come in only after the passengers were seated. They felt that they were being excluded and, of course, started talking big. I had to quell the hostility and gradually all, except a few curs who considered the passengers were entitled to no consideration, quietened. The concert was excellent. I gave by request 'The Hat' and was well received.

Saturday 1st February 1919

Felt bad yesterday so went to see the SMO. He examined me and said there was nothing much wrong except a high pulse and gave

me a tonic. He agrees it's the gas and then the reaction caused by
the heat. Anyway, I feel much better today.

We are out of the Red Sea now. I didn't see Hell's Gate or
Babel-Mandeb, as I was down below. There's rumour of cholera at
Colombo, so goodbye to our hopes of leave now if that is true.

Have just burnt out a couple of warts on my right hand. I have
discovered ever so many tiny ones in infant stage, too, and as I found
the burning stage too painful I took to using caustic soda. It's made
my hand look horrid and black, but that is far better than leaving
them till I get home.

A musical competition came off tonight. In the comic song I
got second with 'Swim Sam Swim', and I think a fair decision. I
said 'Gunga Din' for the third competition and was told that they
had never heard it said better or with more telling effect. Some of
the boys got quite a shock when they saw me take the platform.

Have bet 7/6 we do not reach Colombo harbour by 12 noon
on Friday.

Friday 7th February 1919

I am writing in port. We arrived about 3 pm. Incidentally, I won
7/6 in the bet. Catamarans and fishing boats provided us with the
first signs we were near land.

Apparently, the Australians' name stinks in Colombo. The captain showed me a cutting taken from a daily paper about our
behaviour. Among other things, we have been accused of rape,
theft and molestation of the Cingalese and coolies, etc. Oh, it
makes me ashamed of the AIF sometimes, even given that they
were in all probability horribly drunk. There is no excuse!

There are innumerable bumboats selling bananas, oranges,
pineapples and coconuts. As is usual, the men are foolish enough
to pay about 1200 dinar more than their value. Everybody is eating fruit. Of course, we have the usual tribe kicking about, selling
postcards, silk and jewellery, changing 6d of coppers for 2/6, etc.
There are, among others, a boy contortionist and a juggler. I tested a few of the 'jewels', rubies, sapphires, etc., and found their
colour and quality suspect even if they were dinkum stones. They

marked glass and didn't crush or splinter when put between two coins and jumped on. As a matter of fact, I badly knocked about a half crown and a florin, testing them.

A crowd of diggers got a lot of amusement by making the young locals box one another. My, but they do hit, but they couldn't knock each other out with sledgehammers. Very funny to watch – far more amusing than any of our own bouts.

I was due to appear at a concert tonight – our concert party is really quite classy now – but I have been feeling very unwell, my legs refuse to act and everything I do is an effort. I do hope I can pick up and look myself when I land. At present everybody is remarking that I look really unwell. The heat is also really dreadful and I have developed a rash from it.

Saturday 8th February 1919

I felt bad again this morning so I went to see the SMO once more, but I have improved throughout the day and was determined not to miss out on the fun.

Four of us hired an 'overland' for two hours at 10 rupees an hour (15/-) and we went on a bonny 40-mile trip around the place. Saw Mount Lavinia, about 10 miles out, and visited the famous Cinnamon Gardens. We then went down to the native fruit bazaar (which, incidentally, is meant to be out of bounds!), and tasted a number of weird fruits. Here, I saw the awful sight of a syphilitic, crippled girl about 2 feet high, with big running sores on her back. It made me sick. There was also kiddie minus one leg at the knee and the other near the ankle, who made considerable pace on all fours alongside my rickshaw.

System of bargaining is asking four or as much as ten times the value of the things. Had much amusement watching the boys trying to make bargains and then buying some utterly worthless trinket at an outrageous price. It was laughable. I bought a set of the usual ebony elephants, or at least I believe they are ebony. Also purchased two blouse-lengths of what I think is really good-quality silk crepe-de-chine, in my favourite colours of grey and blue. I wonder which one Dot will prefer? I've had a bellyful of bananas, oranges and cool drinks and if I'm not sick I deserve to be.

The locals were generally very friendly, although I hear there was one small row with our chaps. Most of the boys were exceptionally well behaved. Several came home paralytic, having drunk crook or doped whisky, but that is no surprise. I was glad to get free of the town at 4 pm and came aboard in a launch. Most of the mob arrived by early evening, and the piquet boat with the stragglers by about 6.30 pm. We got away before 7 pm.

A rotten thing happened as the boat was departing. A digger, well drunk, threw bottles, sticks and life belts at the coolies and shouted dirty, filthy language at them. It's only a cur who'd do such a thing to chaps who'd been so friendly to him.

It seems strange that I entirely missed the anniversary of my sailing from Australia – the 7th – I was too busy thinking of Colombo. Anyhow, we're on our homeward run, next stop Aussie and I am oh, so happy. It's bonny to think that in such a little while I'll be with my dearest little comrade again. It seems almost too good to be true – not three weeks now!

And my diary, too, is nearing completion. I will probably miss it, but a diary while at home is hardly worth keeping. I'll write 'Finis' very soon and I shan't forget that, first and foremost, it was for Dot that I have written it. I hope she's been satisfied.

Tuesday 11th February 1919

The boat is not making a good trip and is doing less than 300 miles a day; 280, 281, 284 are fair samples. It's cruel. I hear we are burning 100 tons of coal, as against 80 previously. The coal must be awful. Was medically inspected today and classed 'disability nil', I hardly think that's fair, as I am far from well.

To take a trip aft to the black crew's quarters is an eye-opener. They are good chaps and possess an excellent sense of humour, but it is some sight watching them preparing their food and grinding their curry powder from chillies and spices. Their main diet seems to be curried, stinking, dried fish and rice. There are two distinct galleys divided by iron bars, one for Christians and the other for Mohammedans. They eat out of the common dish or platter, three or four at a dish, squatting on their haunches. Each one puts in his hand, mixes up his curry and his rice and then, after paddling his hand in it, conveys it by the handful to his mouth. Occasionally he washes it down with a drink of water. It does look very funny, but they think the way we eat is equally amusing too!

Today we discovered an RAMC sergeant who deserted and stealthily crept aboard at Colombo in a bid to get home quickly. The adjutant caught him and hauled him along to me. I can't help but feel sorry for him. He's quite a decent chap, but now, unless he's very lucky, he will be put ashore at Fremantle and sent back to Colombo to be court-martialled. I expect he'll be stripped and get a couple of years. The adjutant was very decent to him. I have him down in the mess now under open arrest.

Went around collecting mascots in the shape of monkeys. We had to destroy all to be able to declare a clear ship. They chloroformed the only monkey found, much to his owner's disappointment, and threw him into the ship's furnace. The ship is clear now.

Saturday 15th February 1919

Have decided I'd better start a course of sunbaking to get up a colour. I want to look real well when I get home. Oh, I'm rather pleased with how my moustache is coming on. It has come in for some abuse, though! I do hope Dot likes it.

The voyage is dragging frightfully these last days and our daily mileage is still about 280. Wish she'd get a move on! A very hot day today. The most exciting events were the finals of all classes of the boxing tournament and we witnessed some very good bouts. There was very heavy punishment given and taken.

Press news shows influenza is bad in Victoria so, getting a touch of 'vertical breeze', I went down to get another inoculation. I would never forgive myself if I introduced the complaint at home.

Discovered a case of mumps among the native crew. He's been isolated aft and I am hoping we won't be quarantined. Troops are allowed to send Marconigrams, but I have no money so am sitting tight. I have been musing on what will happen today-fortnight – it seems too good to think that Sunday-week I'll be back again

with my own little comrade. This journey seems to be taking forever. I can hardly contain myself. Oh, how wonderful it is to think
I'm nearly home!

Monday 17th February 1919

Had a long chat with Corporal Smith while lying in the sun yesterday and now find my skin very tender.

We have paid the Western Australians their disembarkation pay.
There are less than a hundred who are getting off. We held a
farewell smoke concert tonight to wish those of our comrades
who are leaving us at Fremantle good luck. It was quite a success
and we had a pleasant musical evening. A turn which much
amused us all was a skit on 'my moustache'. The verse was something like this:

> If I were WO Evans
> I would, I would
> I'd buy a pretty joey
> I would, I would
> And I'd get him to nest
> In that funny little mow-ee
> If I were WO Evans.

It brought down the house.

Orders have been flashing via wireless all night. Evidently they
want us to go on to Albany and not touch Fremantle. It seems
they've the wind up about influenza, they have asked for a guar-
antee there has been no 'dog's disease'.

Wednesday 19th February 1919

We are much elated at the prospect of getting a sniff of Aussie. The
boys all declare they can smell the gum leaves, notwithstanding
that the breeze is from our starboard quarter. All the Western
Australians are ready to disembark.

Well, tomorrow we'll see Aussie after a long absence. It's almost
too good to be true. Some of the lads say they can see the flash of

a lighthouse but I haven't picked it up so far.

Thursday 20th February 1919

When I awoke at 6.30 am we were stationary and taking on fruit and provisions from a launch some 1½ miles from land. Some funny tales are flying about concerning the port health authorities. Apparently we are an infected ship. A nice reception for men who've been away fighting. It appears they won't allow us to land our troops here and must proceed to Albany. They're properly scared. Everybody is swearing, but it's no use. The skipper is very annoyed, and says they're wasting his company's money and time unnecessarily.

Have seen an Aussie paper and this flu seems fairly serious, but it seems ridiculous to talk of Sydney-folk wearing masks! Fancy your people to meet you in masks! Suppose I am quarantined for three weeks? Good Lord, that would be unbearable. Still, we'll have to put up with it, though it's a rotten homecoming for us all, I think.

I followed my batman in a three-round fight today against a chap named Callaghan, winner of the welterweight boxing tournament. I staked all I had on my man. Everybody thought me foolish but I proved otherwise as he fought a draw and I had my stakes returned. Oh, I must say, there was a wonderful trot of heads at the two-up ring today. A man did sixteen heads and thus made his original stake of 2/6 into £144. Simply marvellous!

Friday 21st February 1919

Arrived Albany at about 2 pm. Saw two solitary women on the wharf to wave to us. What a disgrace! These men have risked their lives over the past few years and the homefolk aren't even prepared to give them a welcome home. We all feel disgusted at such a dreary homecoming for the WAs. They got off at about 5 pm and went over to quarantine. Are we lepers? I feel thoroughly ashamed of Australians at present. I wonder what they'd say if they had the flu as bad as Blighty. Our boys are talking of writing to the WA papers thanking them for the grand reception. If we were unclean, I could understand it. Anyway, we gave the WAs cheers as they were being ferried over to quarantine. Next stop, Adelaide.

Tuesday 25th February 1919

Well, the Adelaide doctors (port health officers, I suppose) came aboard and proceeded to 'inspect' all hands. A regular farce. Anyhow, after it was all finished I heard them remark that, 'The men will have a three-day quarantine and you will continue in strict isolation.' This is fine news, really, as it is not the three weeks that some on board were reckoning.

At least we were treated much more decently at this port than the last. The Red Cross had sent fruit – apples, pears and watermelons, and I must say I did enjoy the latter. We had plenty of papers sent aboard, too. Thankfully, we didn't linger very long after the South Australians disembarked. In fact, we were almost away before the last one was clear of the gangway. They had the usual farewell from the boys – cheers, singing, shouts and hurrahs. We should be in Melbourne in less than forty-eight hours.

Friday 28th February 1919

Well, we've dropped some more boys off in Victoria. Hurrah! Some of our boys have written letters to the Melbourne papers about our welcome, which once again was terrible. A further disappointment is that it looks like we are pretty certain now to go to Hobart, after all. It just means more time on this boat before home. What an enormous expense for twenty-six men! It's simply scandalous to think of wasting at least £6000 to take them across.

Since nightfall I've been gazing across the lights of St Kilda. I forgot to mention that our old Red Cross sergeant disembarked at Victoria even though he lives near Sydney. He didn't want his wife to find out he had VD.

Later: We had just moved into our old anchorage this evening when the news was brought by a navy man in a launch thus: 'Have you enough water and coal to take you to Sydney?' 'Yes.' 'Then proceed straightaway and drop the Tasmanians at quarantine as you go out!' There was an uproar of cheers from the boys and ever since then everybody has been smiling and looking quite pleased. I shan't forget that cheer the boys gave.

Well, we are on our way to Sydney. I do hope we won't be kept on ship. All I want is to slip off and see my beloved.

Sunday 2nd March 1919

Conjectures are rife as to what time we will arrive in Sydney. The boat seems dreadfully slow. We had 291 miles to do from noon today and I do not think we will get in till 2 pm or 3 pm. The troops are happy and hope that at New South Wales there will be no quarantine.

Some fine Red Cross goods of fruitcake, chocolates and cigarettes have just been issued. The boys are in good heart. Well, my dreams will be pleasant tonight, anyhow. I'm tired.

CHAPTER 14

DOT

Monday 3rd March 1919

I've seen Dot! She was on the *Belubera* and waved a brown hat. At least then, she is not ill. Oh, I feel so glad to have seen her. I wanted to jump in the sea and swim over to her. I also think I saw the family on the *Kuring-gai*, waving the '2 blue flag'.

But let me go to the beginning of the day. I was too busy straightening up ship to notice much until we reached the Heads and anchored in quarantine for half an hour. The *Cook* came alongside and hailed, 'Do you want to stop here?' 'No!' everyone shouted in unison. 'Then weigh anchor and follow us, sir.' There were loud cheers and at once everybody wore an euphoric look. The general conversation was: 'Ah, this is more like we expected … Wish some of the other states would take a jerry', etc.

All boats gave us a cock-a-doodle-doo as we went up the harbour. The Customs launch came aboard and delivered two letters of welcome, one from Mother and one from Minnie. I was disappointed in not getting a note from Dot, but since I've seen her I'm feeling better, thank you. Then the health officer came aboard with a mark around his neck and got it pretty thick from the lads. 'Is that an issue?' etc. Unperturbed, he went straight to the captain and said, 'You're quarantined – don't tell the troops till I get ashore!' This only came out afterwards for as he left the ship, he simply said to the boys. 'We don't know what's to be done yet, boys.' The hog, the hypocrite, he deserves to be knocked.

As the troops won't go ashore till tomorrow, we have had to reissue messing and sleeping gear. There was some cursing, I can tell you. A mob of lads tried a getaway on one of the ship's lifeboats but were caught in the act. I, too, feel inclined to break ship and chance the result. I'm fed up, disgusted and if ever I fight again for a bastard country and set of people like Australians again, I deserve hanging. Here we are, now stuck up, no sickness, all because some silly asses have the wind up. Once I'm out of here, I'm finished with the army, with its petty rules, and the discipline, for good. Well, I'll cool off now. Perhaps I'll get a few letters in the morning. I want some money badly, too.

I must be patient and wait, I suppose. I kiss you goodnight, Dorothy.

Tuesday 4th March 1919

So, after all, the attempts of the boys have borne fruit. Carmichael's answer came back this morning: 'Have made urgent representations on your behalf. Quarantine lifts tomorrow. Sit tight.' This is a win, decidedly.

We are likely to be put into No. 1 wharf Woolloomooloo at 10.15 am Thursday. Have been looking out all day for a sight of the Manly ferries and anyone I know. But I've been out of luck. I'm ever so tired of this army stunt and I'll be so glad to get back again to my real friends. Oh, I wish I could get ashore.

Wednesday 5th March 1919

Letters! Thank goodness! First, four telegrams from Father, Russell and Elsie, and even one from Mrs Wright – fancy one from Dot's mother! Then a letter from Mother and a note from Dot, to look out for her on the 3.15 pm boat from Manly today. 'Oh Eric, it is going to be the happiest day of my life when you get off that ship. I'm so excited and got no sleep last night. I knew that our love could survive whatever the war threw at us and it has.' No-one can describe how happy I am to read those words. In times of trouble the thought of my darling comrade have kept me going and I am at last to see her again. Oh, to get off this ship.

I saw Dot on the *Barrenjoey* this afternoon and waved madly, but the dirty dog of a captain didn't come close enough, though, for me to shout a welcome. Never mind, I've seen her again, which is the main thing.

Evidently shore authorities are much concerned at the troops' plight. We got a message on board signed by a full colonel: 'Please tell the troops the quarantine was caused by the federal authorities and not the military.'

I think I'll send diary part thirteen off to Dot in the morning via Corporal Smith. That will soften her disappointment a little, perhaps.

Thursday 6th March 1919

What a day this has been! But I'll start from the beginning. The doctor came aboard early this morning and told us we could go ashore after lunch. On hearing the news, I immediately sent a wire to Dot and to Mother. The waiting was unbearable.

Went ashore about 2.30 pm and saw Mother running towards me with arms outstretched and looking oh, so excited. On reaching me, she at first couldn't say a word, but, on regaining her composure, kept saying, 'Isn't it lovely!' and couldn't seem to get anything further out.

Further along the wharf stood the beautiful figure of Dot, with a huge smile, etched on her face. She hadn't changed a bit. On approaching her, I noticed tears rolling down her cheeks. Inwardly I was bubbling over, but I was afraid if I let myself go I'd make a frightful ass of myself, so I walked towards my dear little girl, feeling as if my legs would buckle at any moment, and gave her a hug and a kiss. Not the kiss I had intended to give her either, but I'll save that for afterwards. A soldier standing by said to the crowd, 'Give him a chance', and they gave me plenty of room. After our embrace, we looked at each other but at times such as those, there was little one could say. Our expressions said it all. I was home at last and the war was over. Mrs Wright was there, too, as were the boys and Elsie, and we all danced along the wharf. Harold and Raymond called a taxi and the lot of us got aboard. Mrs Wright didn't want to come, but I insisted. I did want my little girl very much.

As we neared home all the little nippers – Lord only knows where the mob of about fifty came from – lined up, cheered and waved flags. The dope of a chauffeur tooted his horn to bring all the neighbourhood out, and got his desired result. It was almost too much for me, but I kept my composure and couldn't take the smile off my face.

We went inside and I did feel so strange. I couldn't eat anything but was oh, so full of happiness and excitement. All say the same, 'You have grown' and 'You are looking well.' Dot played the piano and I mooned around or talked. It was so bonny, I can't describe my feelings. I unpacked my elephants and put them on the table. Everybody went mad over them. Father arrived a little later on and was overjoyed. He surprised me by conversing with Mother as with an ordinary acquaintance. I am very happy as this really does make things easier.

Well, we had a bonny time and I had Dot for a couple of minutes all to myself, but I could only say, 'Oh Dot dear, I do love you', and she replied, 'I am still the same Dot, Eric dear.' Oh, how I loved those words. How I wanted to take her in my arms and never let her go. My dear little comrade hasn't altered one little scrap and I love her more than I ever did before. I still have lots to tell her. It only comes out in little bits, but I have plenty of time. I find I didn't enter up in the diary about that Codford girl. I am really annoyed, because it looks as though I didn't want to say anything about it to her. But I told Dot a lot she knew nothing about. I'm so glad she understands me so well. I can tell her anything and do not feel the least bit uncomfortable.

The night simply flew by and I wouldn't let Mrs Wright and Dot go till about midnight. Mrs Wright would only let me accompany them down as far as the hill. But I simply had to go a little way with Dot. She put up her face for me to kiss when I said goodnight and I gave her a proper kiss. Mrs Wright looked shocked and said 'Dot!'

'Oh, Mummy, it's Eric,' Dot replied, and we all laughed.

My homecoming has been absolutely splendid and I am so happy. I don't think I'll find any difficulty in starting graft. Anyhow, I have a very great incentive to work now. I want money and a home for Dot. I must tell her exactly the position. I'm sure she'll understand. Well, I'm to be a good civvy. When I sum it all up, I'm glad. No more 'bosses', no more harsh discipline, no more rotten treatment and hardships. That is all in the past. I hope never to have to wear khaki again.

Oh, yes. I think I'll be very successful and happy in the future. Everybody is so very good to me and Father thinks I'm a tin god. I hope that he realises his expectations in me. And now *Finis*. Somehow it's hard to stop and I guess I'll miss it a bit, sometimes, but then I've Dot to tell all to now.

EPILOGUE

ERIC EVANS AND DOROTHY WRIGHT spent many days and hours talking and making up for the time they had been apart. Eric, disappointed at not having received his commission, was all the more determined to make a success of civilian life and provide the life for himself and Dorothy he had dreamt of in the trenches. They never married, however. The ravages of war had taken their toll on both of them and as time passed they realised that they had both changed as a result of the experience. The relationship ended in the early 1920s.

Some two decades after his homecoming, Eric travelled to South Africa, a country he had always held dear. He decided to settle there. Soon afterward, the world was once again engulfed in war and Eric immediately enlisted, not as an Anzac, but as a member of the South African forces. This provided him with another opportunity to achieve his ambition to be a commissioned officer in the Imperial Forces, and World War II would see him rise to the rank of major. He was later honoured with an MBE for his services during those years.

After World War II, Eric met and married his first wife, Elizabeth, and they settled on a farm north of Johannesburg. When Elizabeth suffered a premature death from cancer, he decided to sell the farm and purchase a family hotel in Port Alfred, a sleepy coastal village on the east coast. In later years, Eric met and married Margot Peel-Yates, an elegant British woman who was a trained classical pianist; they lived a quiet and happy existence together. Eric was, plagued throughout his life, however, by the injuries received during the wars. In particular, he increasingly suffered from respiratory problems, the result of the mustard-gas poisoning he incurred at Passchendaele.

Eric Evans passed away in 1985 of natural causes. His wife Margot died eleven years later. He is survived by a daughter, Stephanie, and her children, Fraser and Alison.

GLOSSARY

Afrikander a South African–speaking Afrikaan, of Dutch descent

AGH Rouen Army General Hospital

AMC Army Medical Corps

Aussie, an to be sent back to Australia

AWOL absent without leave

Bar DSO Distinguished Service Order (awarded twice) for gallantry and dinstinguished conduct. The DSO was only awarded to officers

Bar MC Military Cross (awarded twice) for gallantry

Bar MM MSM Military Medal for other ranks who showed gallantry (awarded twice); Meritorious Service Medal for efficiency and length of service

batman an officer's servant

Boche slang for German soldier or German; from the French *bosche*, meaning 'cabbage head' or 'hard skull'

bumboat a slang term for any small craft used by vendors selling goods

CB confined to barracks

chats lice

chows Chinese labourers

CMG Companion of the Order of St Michael and St George

coolies Indian labourers or peasants

CSM colour sergeant major

dabster dab hand, expert

DCM Distinguished Conduct Medal

dixie a small round shallow metal container/dish/bowl used as a plate for food

draft group to be selected to go to France

drum Australian slang for brothel

DSO Distinguished Service Order

enfilade fire firing of guns so as to sweep the length of target

fatigue task

funk holes sleeping dugouts cut into the face of the trench

gazump shell

GHQ general head quarters

GOC general officer commanding

gormandising eating well and heartily

GS wagon general serice wagon used by the Royal Army Corps for supplies

gutsed stems from 'gutser' meaning a sharp rebuff or disappointment

gutser/ big G those that had already been drafted to the front but were turned down

HE high explosives

Home Service birds a term for troops who stayed at home performing Home Sevice, while the Australian Imperial Force went overseas

hopover going over the top

howitzers type of heavy artillery

Jimmy Mills grenades

Marconigrams message sent by Marconi's system of wireless telegraphy

MC Military Cross

men-o-war large war ship

MG machine gun

miners conscripts or volunteers involved in digging the trenches

MM Military Medal

MQ military quarters

Neptune's Day celebration of crossing the Equator

OC officer in command

OMS orderley mess sergeant

on the tape on the front line

OTC Officer Training Corps

pips metal decorative 'stars' which commissioned officers wear on their shoulders to designate rank

piquet a patrol

piqueted comes from the word 'pike', meaning wooden pole with sharp-pointed head; carried by sentry guards to keep control of troops, to guard them and keep them in order

provost soldier on detail in Military Police

putties rectangular canvas leggings used for protection

RAMC Royal Army Medical Corps

ranker an officer

RAP regimental aid post used for troops requiring medical attention

redcaps military policemen

reveille military wake-up call

RSM regimental sergeant major

rubber–heels type of shell

sap trench

Sam Browne an army officer's belt and straps

Shut in the cooler jailed

STHS Sydney Technical High School

Shanghai Australian slang for shirker/absentee

SHS Sydney High School

singlestick also called 'backsword'; one-handed fencing stick fitted with a hand guard; a form of fencing

SMO senior medical officer

sock to leg punish

swinging the lead shirking responsibility/loafing

Tassy Tasmania

TC Technical College

36 grenades a type of hand grenade, No. 36 Mark 1

Tommy regiment regiment of British soldiers

TMs trench mortar

VAD voluntary aid detachment

VC Victoria Cross

WAAC Women's Auxiliary Army Corps

Wilson's Promontary A bulge of land on south-eastern coast
of Australia

whizz-bangs small calibre, high-speed shells, fired in a flat
trajectory and only heard on impact

WO Class 1 warrant officer class 1

zero the time to attack

ABOUT THE EDITOR

PATRICK WILSON was educated at Marlborough College, Wiltshire, England. He studied history at Manchester University and currently teaches modern history at Bradfield College, Reading.

Wilson's published books include *Dunkirk: From Disaster to Deliverance*, commemorating the sixtieth anniversary of the famous evacuation, and *The War Behind the Wire*, which accompanied a major BBC documentary series on prisoners of war. He recently completed a series of seven books for children on the elite forces.

.